EVIDENCE
Fifth Edition

By

Steven Goode
W. James Kronzer Chair in Trial and Appellate Advocacy
University Distinguished Teaching Professor
University of Texas School of Law

THOMSON
™
WEST

Mat #40679130

© West, a Thomson business, 2003

© 2008 Thomson/West
    610 Opperman Drive
    St. Paul, MN 55123
    1–800–313–9378

Printed in the United States of America

ISBN: 978–0–314–18813–7

TEXT IS PRINTED ON 10% POST CONSUMER RECYCLED PAPER

I.   Analytical and Exam Approach

A.   What's Evidence All About? [§1]

A typical trial involves questions about both law and facts. Before the relevant substantive law can be applied, a factfinder (the jury or, in a bench trial, the judge) must determine what happened. Once the factfinder decides what happened (that is, decides what the facts are), the factfinder applies the law to the facts and arrives at a verdict. The law of evidence is concerned with **the factfinding part of a trial**. It tells us what is and what is not admissible evidence. Looked at one way, it tells the lawyers what information they will be able to present to the jury in their effort to establish that their respective version of the facts is the correct one. Looked at another way, it tells us what information we will allow jurors to consider as they perform their factfinding function.

B.   Evidence as an Obstacle Course [§2]

There are numerous grounds upon which a court may exclude a particular piece of evidence.   In thinking about the admissibility of any piece of evidence, picture an obstacle course. At the starting line stands the piece of evidence that a party is seeking to introduce. At the finish line is the jury box. That piece of evidence must be able to hurdle any number of a series of obstacles that its opponent puts up (by way of objections) in its path to the jury box.   For example, the opponent may object that this piece of evidence is inadmissible because it is (a) irrelevant, (b) hearsay, (c) presented through an incompetent witness, (d) privileged, (e) impermissible opinion, and (f) in violation of the best evidence rule.   Each of these is an independent obstacle (objection). **Each one will have to be hurdled before the evidence can be deemed admissible and be heard by the jury.**

C.   Approaching Evidence Problems: "Hear Pa Brown" [§3]

This book divides the law of evidence into ten subject areas. (This corresponds with the way the Federal Rules of Evidence, many casebooks, and evidence courses divide up the law.) When you approach an evidence problem you need to think about all the obstacles (objections) that can possibly be raised to its admission. The mnemonic HEAR PA

BROWN will clue you in to the various grounds for objection.

HEAR — Hearsay

P — Privileges
A — Authentication

B — Best evidence rule
R — Relevance
O — Opinion testimony
W — Witnesses
N — Notice (judicial notice)

1. Answering an Exam Question [§4]

Almost every evidence problem you get will fall into one or more of these areas. On an essay question, you are typically asked to discuss all the plausible grounds for exclusion. Run through HEAR PA BROWN in your mind. Relevance is usually addressed first in an essay question. If there is a hearsay problem, discuss it. If the evidence raises a privilege problem, discuss that. Don't stop simply because you conclude the evidence is inadmissible hearsay. Within the time constraints, discuss all plausible issues. The idea, after all, is to show off all you know that is pertinent to the question.

2. State the Objection, Then State the Response [§5]

With respect to a particular piece of evidence, state the objection that is most likely to be raised; if it is not obvious, state why the objection is appropriate. Then discuss the arguments for admission that can plausibly be raised in response to the objection and reach a conclusion as to the validity of the objection. Be sure to discuss both sides of the argument. Next, if there is another ground for objecting to the piece of evidence, discuss it in the same way. If not, go to the next piece of evidence that might be objectionable and discuss it in the same manner.

3. Discuss Each Objection Separately and Completely [§6]

Do not address all the objections at once. Take them one at a time and fully resolve each one before moving on to the next. This will make your answer clearer and more effective.

NOTE: WHAT'S MISSING FROM HEAR PA BROWN
You may have noticed that although this book contains ten subject matter areas, HEAR PA BROWN covers only eight. Don't worry. One of the omitted subject areas is "General Provisions," which deals mostly with procedural matters. The other is "Presumptions." You don't have to keep a look-out for presumption issues. They are red-flagged in the question. If there is a presumption issue, you will see it.

D. The Federal Rules and the Common Law [§7]

Until the latter part of the 20th century, the vast majority of states (with California as an important exception) followed the common law in dealing with questions of evidence. Despite differences in detail from state to state, a majority common-law rule could be discerned in most areas of evidence law. The enactment of the Federal Rules of Evidence in 1975 sparked a dramatic change. Although the federal rules embraced many common-law rules, they also departed from the common law in many respects. Since their enactment, 42 states (plus Puerto Rico and the military) have adopted codes of evidence based on the federal rules. Due to the dominant position they have assumed, this book focuses on the federal rules. However, it also pays attention to the common law for two reasons. First, sometimes it is necessary to understand the common law in order to understand a federal rule. Second, some professors like to test on the common law. So throughout the book you will find references both to the law under the federal rules (FRE) and the common law.

II. General Provisions

A. Limited Admissibility [§8]

One of the most important general principles in the law of evidence is that **a piece of evidence may be admissible for one purpose but not another, or admissible against one party but not another.** Such evidence may be admitted under the doctrine of limited admissibility.

EXAMPLE: LIMITED PURPOSE
Evidence that Tenant told Landlord, "The carpeting in the hall is loose," is hearsay and not admissible if offered to prove the

carpeting was loose. However, it is not hearsay and is admissible if offered to prove Landlord had notice of the defect.

EXAMPLE: LIMITED TO PARTY
Defendant and Co-Defendant are on trial for bank robbery. Prosecution offers Co-Defendant's confession. It is admissible against Co-Defendant but not against Defendant.

B. Limiting Instructions [§9]

When evidence is admissible only for a limited purpose, the judge must, upon request, instruct the jury to consider the evidence only for its admissible purpose. For instance, in the example above, the court would tell the jury that it may consider Tenant's statement as proof that Landlord was put on notice but not as proof that the carpeting actually was loose. Similarly, when evidence is admissible against only one of multiple parties, the judge must, upon request, so instruct the jury.

1. When Courts May Exclude [§10]

The trial court may exclude evidence with limited admissibility if it believes that the limiting instruction is inadequate to protect the objecting party against unfair prejudice. The court may feel that the danger that the jury will consider the evidence for the forbidden purpose far outweighs its probative value as to the permissible purpose. For instance, in the second example above, the court might conclude that even with a limiting instruction, the jury would consider Co-Defendant's confession as evidence against Defendant as well. In such a case the court might (a) **exclude** the statement entirely; (b) order references to Defendant be **excised** from the statement; or (c) order **separate trials** for Defendant and Co-Defendant.

C. Preserving Error for Appeal [§11]

Litigants must be sure to take all required steps in order to preserve for appeal erroneous rulings by the trial judge regarding the admission or exclusion of evidence.

1. **General Principle: The Deck Is Stacked in Favor of the Trial Judge [§12]**

   The system is designed to affirm the trial judge's ruling whenever possible. **Whichever party complains on appeal that the judge erred must have done everything necessary to inform the judge of the evidence rule in question and its application to the evidence in question.** If you remember this basic rule, you will be able to handle all questions regarding whether a party acted properly to preserve an evidentiary ruling for appeal.

2. **Erroneous Admission of Evidence [§13]**

   If a party complains on appeal that the trial judge erroneously admitted evidence, it must show that (a) it **specifically objected** to the evidence; (b) it did so in a **timely fashion;** (c) the evidence was inadmissible **on the stated grounds**; and (d) admission of the evidence affected a **substantial right** of the appellant. [FRE 103(a)(1).]

   a. **Specific Objection [§14]**

      The objection must be stated with enough specificity to put the judge on notice as to its legal basis and give the proponent of the evidence an opportunity to respond. Thus, merely stating "Objection, your honor" is insufficient. The objecting party must explicitly identify the particular basis for claiming the evidence is inadmissible (e.g., hearsay, impermissible character evidence, probative value is substantially outweighed by danger of unfair prejudice).

   b. **Timely Fashion [§15]**

      The objection must be made at the first reasonable opportunity. Failure to do so constitutes waiver of the objection.

   EXAMPLE

   During trial, counsel for Defendant elicits from a witness an answer that includes inadmissible hearsay. About thirty seconds later, counsel for Plaintiff realizes what has happened and objects. The witness is already answering the next question. The judge will overrule the objection.

Counsel for Plaintiff failed to object to the hearsay in a timely fashion.

(1) Motions in Limine [§16]

A motion **in limine** ("at the threshold") is a motion made prior to trial seeking a ruling on some evidentiary issue that is likely to arise. Traditionally, the effect of the court's ruling on a motion in limine has been a point of some controversy. Some courts view the motion in limine ruling merely as a **preliminary ruling**: the party that lost the motion must still raise the question again at trial (out of the presence of the jury) in order to preserve the issue for appeal. Other courts view the motion in limine ruling as sufficiently **final** that the issue need not be raised again at trial. Still other courts look at the **facts of the particular case,** with special emphasis on the nature of the issue, the degree to which the issue was fully presented, and the extent to which the court's ruling was equivocal. Federal Rule 103(a) takes the latter approach. A **definitive pre-trial ruling** frees the party from the need to object again at trial.

c. Erroneously Admitted Evidence: Affirm Unless Inadmissible on Stated Grounds [§17]

If the objection failed to state a proper legal basis for excluding the evidence, the trial judge's decision to admit the evidence will be upheld **even if the evidence should have been excluded for some other reason**. In other words, it is the responsibility of the party, not the trial judge, to find the right ground for exclusion.

EXAMPLE

Prosecutor calls Witness to testify against Defendant. In response to one of Witness's answers, defense counsel states, "I object, Your Honor. The testimony is irrelevant." The court overrules the objection. Defendant is convicted. While working on the appeal, defense counsel realizes that although the answer was relevant, it contained inadmissible character evidence. Defense counsel argues on appeal that the evidence should have been excluded. The appellate court will uphold the trial court's decision. The court made a correct ruling on the stated objection. Although defense counsel could have made a valid objection, he failed to state the proper ground for exclusion.

3. **Erroneous Exclusion of Evidence [§18]**
   If a party complains on appeal that the trial judge erroneously excluded evidence, it must show that (a) it made **an offer of proof** at trial; (b) the evidence could not have been excluded **on any ground**; and (c) exclusion of the evidence affected a **substantial right** of the appellant. [FRE 103(a)(2).]

   a. **Offer of Proof [§19]** ·
      If the court excludes proffered evidence, the proponent must make an **offer of proof** to insure that the trial and appellate courts are aware of the substance of the proffered evidence.

      (1) Excluded Evidence is Witness Testimony [§20]
          If the court excluded a witness's testimony, the offer of proof may be made by (a) having counsel relate to the court the substance of the witness's testimony; or (b) taking the witness's testimony (outside the presence of the jury) in question and answer form.

      (2) Excluded Evidence is Exhibit [§21]
          If the excluded evidence is a document, chart, or some other form of tangible exhibit, it should be marked for identification and made part of the record.

   b. **Erroneously Excluded Evidence: Affirm If Inadmissible on Any Ground [§22]**
      Even if the judge excluded the evidence in response to an objection that raised an invalid ground for exclusion, the judge's ruling will be affirmed if there exists any valid reason for excluding the evidence. The reason for this is simple. It would make little sense for the appellate court to remand the case for a

new trial so that the evidence could once again be excluded, this time on the proper ground.

EXAMPLE

The trial judge excludes evidence upon a hearsay objection. Even if the evidence was not objectionable as hearsay, the decision to exclude will be upheld if the evidence could have been excluded under some other rule of evidence.

4. **Limited Admissibility Revisited: More Deck-Stacking [§23]**

Suppose Tenant offers his statement to Landlord, "The carpeting in the hall is loose." As we will see later, this statement is inadmissible hearsay if offered to prove the carpeting was loose, but is not hearsay if offered to prove that Landlord had notice of the defect. Landlord objects on hearsay grounds. If the judge overrules the objection, the ruling will be affirmed. The appellate court will tell the complaining party (Landlord) that it was his responsibility to narrow his objection to the hearsay use of this evidence. Further, Landlord should have requested a limiting instruction that the statement could be used only as proof of notice. If, however, the court sustains the objection, the trial court's ruling **will still be affirmed.** In this instance the appellate court will tell the complaining party (now Tenant) that it was his responsibility to narrow his offer of the evidence to its nonhearsay use (i.e., to have stated at trial, "I'm only offering this to prove notice"). This is just another example of the basic principle that the party complaining on appeal must have taken the appropriate steps at trial to object (Landlord) or respond to a valid objection and explain why the evidence was admissible (Tenant).

D. **Preliminary Fact Questions for the Court [§24]**

The admissibility or inadmissibility of a piece of evidence sometimes turns on the existence or non-existence of some preliminary fact. In some instances, before ruling on admissibility the court must be satisfied that the preliminary fact does or does not exist. In other instances, the court will leave it to the jury to decide whether the preliminary fact exists.

1. **General Rule: Court Decides Whether Preliminary Fact Proved [§25]**

    The trial judge decides any factual issues related to questions such as whether:
    - a witness is qualified as an expert;
    - an expert's testimony is reliable and relevant;
    - a statement is hearsay;
    - a hearsay statement falls within an exception; or
    - a statement is privileged.

    The judge must resolve such factual issues under a **preponderance of the evidence** standard. In resolving these issues, the judge may consider evidence (other than privileged matter) that is not itself admissible under the rules of evidence. [FRE 104(a).]

    EXAMPLE

    Defendant objects to certain testimony on the ground that it is a privileged communication he made to his wife during their marriage. The proponent argues the statement is not privileged because (a) it was not made in confidence, and (b) Defendant was not legally married to "wife" at the time the statement was made. The trial court should uphold the privilege claim only if it is satisfied by a preponderance of the evidence that (a) the statement was made in confidence, and (b) that Defendant was legally married to "wife" at the time. In deciding these issues, the court may consider evidence that would not be admissible under the rules of evidence (such as inadmissible hearsay).

2. **Jury Gets to Decide A Few: "BARK" [§26]**

    Four preliminary fact issues are left largely to the jury. These can be remembered by the mnemonic BARK: **B**est Evidence Rule; **A**uthenticity; **R**elevance; **K**nowledge.

    a. Best Evidence Rule [§27]

    Most "best evidence" issues are decided by the judge. See § 615. However, if there is an issue as to (a) whether the writing ever existed; (b) which of two or more writings is the original; or (c) whether some secondary evidence accurately reflects the contents of the original (e.g., a claim that the original was altered, as in the movie, *The Verdict*), the jury, not the judge, decides.

    b. **Authenticity [§28]**

The jury decides whether a writing or document has been authenticated. See §576.

    c. **Relevance [§29]**

The jury decides issues of conditional relevancy. See §40.

    d. **Knowledge [§30]**

The jury decides whether or not a witness has personal knowledge. See §423.

III. Relevancy

A. **Basic Principles of Relevancy [§31]**

Evidence must be relevant to be admissible. However, not all relevant evidence is admissible. In fact, most of the rules of evidence address the question of when relevant evidence is and is not admissible.

1. **Definition of Relevancy [§32]**

A piece of evidence is relevant if it has any tendency to make the existence of any fact of consequence to the case more probable or less probable than it would be without that piece of evidence. [FRE 401.]

2. **Two Aspects of Relevancy: [§33]**

This definition of relevancy has two components. First, the proffered piece of evidence must **logically** tend to prove the fact that it is offered to prove. Second, the evidence must be offered to prove a fact that is **material** to the case. That is, the fact that the party is attempting to establish must relate to an issue that the substantive law deems of consequence to the outcome of the case.

EXAMPLE

Defendant is charged with rape. He seeks to testify that Complainant invited him to her bedroom. This evidence is relevant. The testimony logically may tend to prove that Complainant consented, and her consent is an issue that the substantive criminal law deems of consequence to the case. But if Defendant were charged with statutory rape, the testimony would be irrelevant. Although it still might tend to prove consent, the substantive law says that consent is not a defense to a statutory rape charge.

3. Relevancy vs. Sufficiency [§34]

A common error in relevancy analysis is to confuse the question of whether evidence is **relevant** with the question of whether the evidence, taken alone, is **sufficient to justify a verdict.** A piece of evidence may be relevant even though it does not, by itself, prove its proponent's case. Indeed, most pieces of evidence are, by themselves, inadequate to sustain a verdict. A piece of evidence is relevant so long as it tends to make the existence of a material fact more (or less) probable than it would be without the evidence.

EXAMPLE

In the rape example immediately above, Defendant's testimony is relevant, although it does not by itself prove consent. Complainant may have invited Defendant to her room to show him something, without the slightest intention of having sexual relations with him, or Defendant may be lying. In either case, if the jury believes the testimony, it may logically think it more likely that Complainant consented than it did before it heard the evidence. That is all the test of relevance demands.

4. More or Less Probable [§35]

A piece of evidence must have a tendency to make the existence of a material fact more or less probable **than it would be without the evidence**. The focus is on the marginal effect the evidence would have on the case. Suppose, for example, that at a particular point in the case the evidence would point to about a 30% likelihood that Defendant Pharmaceutical Company's drug caused Plaintiff's illness. Plaintiff then offers a piece of evidence that would raise that likelihood to 35%. The evidence is relevant: The existence of a material fact (causation) is **more probable than it was without that piece of evidence**. The fact that the evidence fails to establish that it is more likely than not that the drug caused the illness does not render the evidence irrelevant. Of course, Plaintiff will lose if, by the end of the case, she fails to prove causation by a preponderance of the evidence. But that is a question of the sufficiency of the evidence rather than its admissibility.

5. Direct vs. Circumstantial Evidence [§36]

a. Direct Evidence [§37]
Direct evidence proves a consequential fact directly. No inference has to be drawn from the evidence to the consequential fact.

b. Circumstantial Evidence [§38]
Circumstantial evidence requires the factfinder to draw inferences from the evidence in order to conclude that some consequential fact exists.

EXAMPLE

Eyewitness testimony that the defendant shot the victim is "direct evidence" of defendant's assault. If the jury believes the witness's testimony, it will conclude that the defendant shot the victim. Testimony establishing that the defendant had a motive to shoot the victim and that the defendant was seen leaving the victim's apartment with a smoking gun is "circumstantial evidence" of the defendant's assault. Jurors might certainly conclude from such evidence that the defendant shot the victim, but they would have to draw a series of inferences to get from the evidence to the conclusion.

c. Relative Strength of Direct and Circumstantial Evidence [§39]
Direct evidence is not inherently stronger than circumstantial evidence. Direct evidence may be strong or weak. The eyewitness who testifies that she saw the defendant shoot the victim might be biased against the defendant or have bad eyesight. Likewise, circumstantial evidence may be strong or weak. Evidence that the defendant had a strong motive to harm the victim, was seen leaving the victim's apartment with a smoking gun, and had blood stains on his clothes that matched the victim's blood type is all circumstantial, but would weigh heavily against the defendant.

6. **Conditional Relevancy [§40]**

Sometimes the relevancy of a proffered piece of evidence depends on the existence of another fact that has not yet been proved. Such evidence is said to be **conditionally relevant**. A court should admit such evidence either (a) upon the introduction of evidence sufficient to support a finding of the existence of the other fact or (b) subject to the introduction of such evidence. [FRE 104(b).]

EXAMPLE

Defendant is on trial for extortion. The prosecution calls Victim to testify that Bruiser visited him in his office and said, "You better give that contract to the right person, if you know what's good for you." This testimony is conditionally relevant because it tends to prove Defendant's guilt only if Bruiser can be linked to Defendant. The court can (a) refuse to admit it until the prosecution introduces evidence sufficient to support a finding of a link between Defendant and Bruiser, or (b) admit it subject to evidence of a link between Defendant and Bruiser being introduced later in the trial. If the court chooses the latter option and the prosecution subsequently fails to offer evidence linking Defendant and Bruiser, the trial judge will strike from the record the evidence of Bruiser's visit and order the jury to disregard it.

B. **Reasons For Excluding Relevant Evidence [§41]**

There are **two basic reasons** for excluding relevant evidence. First, evidence may be excluded because of **extrinsic social policies**, even though exclusion will hinder the factfinder's efforts to determine what happened. Second, even though it is relevant, the evidence may be excluded because admitting it would lead to **less accurate factfinding**.

1. **Extrinsic Social Policies [§42]**

In some instances, accurate factfinding is subordinated to the goal of promoting some other social concern. For example, evidence may be excluded because it is privileged, or is evidence of a subsequent remedial measure. See §81.

2. **Accuracy in Factfinding [§43]**

Although relevant, evidence may lead to less accurate factfinding because its probative value is outweighed by the danger that it will confuse or prejudice the jury. It may also be excluded because its probative value simply is not worth the time it would take to present the evidence.

a. Discretionary Exclusion [§44]
FRE 403 requires the court to exclude relevant evidence when its **probative value is substantially outweighed** by countervailing concerns such as the **danger of unfair prejudice, confusion of issues, or misleading the jury**, or by considerations of **judicial efficiency** (such as undue delay or presentation of cumulative evidence).

b. Specific Evidence Rules [§45]
Some evidence rules deal with specific categories of evidence, setting forth when such evidence is admissible and when it is not. For example, specific rules deal with the admissibility of character and habit evidence, evidence of liability insurance, and proof of prior sexual conduct. These rules are discussed below, beginning at §80.

NOTE: LEGAL VS. LOGICAL RELEVANCE
Some courts and professors still speak of logical and legal relevance. By **logical relevance**, they mean evidence that meets the definition of relevance set forth in §32. By **legal relevance**, they mean relevant evidence whose probative value is not outweighed by the countervailing concerns mentioned above.

C. Discretionary Exclusion: General Principles [§46]
Courts have broad discretion to balance the probative value against the danger of unfair prejudice, confusion, etc. Appellate courts are generally deferential to trial court rulings under FRE 403 and will reverse a ruling only upon a determination that the trial court abused its discretion.

1. Measuring Probative Value [§47]

a. Probative Value Must Be Determined in Context [§48]
When balancing probative value against the danger of unfair prejudice, confusion, etc., the trial court must consider the probative value of a piece of evidence in

the context of the case. For this purpose, probative value is not an absolute; it is the incremental probative value that counts. Thus, a piece of evidence may be highly probative of a particular point if it is the first piece of evidence offered to prove that point. But if a lot of other evidence has already been adduced on that point, the incremental probative value of that same piece of evidence may be substantially diminished. (This is why cumulative evidence is excludable under FRE 403.) Similarly, a court may consider the existence of alternative, less prejudicial means of proof when balancing probative value against prejudicial effect. See Important Case, *Old Chief v. United States*, following § 54.

b. Trial Court Does Not Discount Based on Credibility Determination [§49]

The probative value of a piece of evidence is the probative value it would have if the factfinder believed the witness. The trial court may not discount the probative value because it believes the witness lacks credibility. For purposes of FRE 403 balancing, the testimony of a witness the trial court believes to be lying has the same probative value as the identical testimony of a witness the trial court believes to be telling the truth.

2. Unfair Prejudice, Confusion of Issues, Etc. [§50]

a. Unfair Prejudice [§51]

Most evidence that a party presents is designed to help its own, and harm its opponent's case. In that sense, almost all evidence is prejudicial to the opponent's case. But FRE 403 balances probative value against the danger of **unfair** prejudice. Evidence is **unfairly** prejudicial if it tends to appeal to the jury's sympathies or otherwise lead it to decide the case on an emotional basis. Evidence that is logically powerful (e.g., testimony that the driver who allegedly caused the accident drank six scotches in the hour preceding the accident) is not unfairly prejudicial. Evidence also poses the danger of unfair prejudice when it is admissible for one purpose, but not another. The danger stems from the possibility that the jury will consider the evidence for the impermissible purpose.

b. Confusion of the Issues [§52]

Evidence presents the danger of confusion of the issues when it would tend to distract the jury from the issue before it. For example, in a slip-and-fall case, evidence of another slip-and-fall that allegedly occurred nearby, two years before the slip-and-fall in issue, might tend to confuse the issues. The jury's attention might be diverted by having to listen to a good deal of evidence about whether the slip-and-fall two years ago really occurred and, if so, under what conditions. See §57.

c. Misleading the Jury [§53]

Concerns about the danger of misleading the jury tend to focus on the possibility that the jury will give undue weight to the evidence. For example, for any one of a number of reasons a jury might overvalue evidence that a witness passed a "lie detector" test. The jury might believe that "lie detector" tests are more accurate than they actually are. Alternatively, the jury might fail to recognize that, even if accurate, a "lie detector" test reveals only whether the witness believes that he or she is telling the truth, and cannot discern whether the witness is mistaken in that belief.

d. Limiting Instructions [§54]

Trial courts may use limiting instructions to diminish the danger of possible unfair prejudice, confusion, etc. posed by a piece of evidence.

IMPORTANT CASE: *OLD CHIEF V. UNITED STATES,* 519 U.S. 172 (1997).

Old Chief was tried for assault and for being a convicted felon in possession of a handgun. To convict him of the latter charge, the government had to prove that he was a convicted felon. In an effort to keep the jury from learning that he had been previously been convicted of felony assault, Old Chief offered to stipulate that he had been convicted of a felony. But the government insisted on proving the conviction, including what the prior conviction was for. Old Chief appealed his conviction, claiming that the probative value of the conviction was substantially outweighed by the unfair prejudice to him.

The Court first held that whether the evidence meets the definition of relevance under FRE 401 is unaffected by the availability of alternative means of proof, including the defendant's offer to stipulate to the fact of a prior conviction. But the existence of alternative means of proof may affect the probative value a court should assign to a piece of evidence when balancing its probative value against the danger of unfair prejudice. Even so, ordinarily a defendant may not render relevant evidence inadmissible by stipulating to the element of the crime to which the evidence is directed. A party is generally entitled to prove its case by evidence of its own choice. The introduction of evidence is a party's means of telling its story, and a piece of evidence often has probative value that extends beyond any linear scheme of reasoning. Under the peculiar circumstances of this case, however, the court erred in admitting the evidence. The existence of a prior conviction was a self-contained element of the crime; all the jury needed to know was defendant's status as a convicted felon, and defendant was willing to stipulate to that. The fact that his felony was for assault could add nothing to the prosecution's story. It did, however, present the risk of unfair prejudice, particularly since he was on trial here for assault.

D. Discretionary Exclusion: Similar Happenings Evidence ("SHE") [§55]

Because courts exercise their power of discretionary exclusion on a case-by-case (indeed, issue-by-issue) basis, it is hard to draw bright-line rules about how courts will rule when a party objects that relevant evidence should be excluded because its probative value is substantially outweighed by the danger of unfair prejudice, confusion, etc. But certain types of issues occur with some frequency and courts tend to approach them in the same way. One area in which courts are frequently called upon to rule is the admissibility of **similar happenings evidence ("SHE")**.

1. "SHE": In General [§56]

Sometimes, as proof of the occurrence in issue, a party wishes to use evidence of **other events or transactions** between the parties now engaged in litigation or involving another party or parties similarly situated. For example, in a slip-and-fall case, a party might want to offer evidence that other people slipped and fell on defendant's premises. **Generally, courts are reluctant to admit such evidence.** Often the probative value of such evidence is suspect and substantially outweighed by the danger of confusing the jury or wasting time. **Nevertheless, under certain conditions courts are likely to admit similar happenings evidence.**

2. **"SHE": Prior or Subsequent Accidents [§57]**

    Evidence of other accidents or injuries offered to prove the negligence of a party or the dangerousness of a condition may be admissible if its proponent shows that the other accidents or injuries **occurred under circumstances substantially similar to those surrounding the event in issue**. Without such a threshold showing, the probative value of the other accident or injury evidence will clearly be insufficient to outweigh the danger that it will confuse the jury or waste the court's time. Even when such a showing is made, the court may still determine that the probative value is substantially outweighed by the danger of confusion or waste of time, and exclude the evidence.

    EXAMPLE

    To prove that a particular stairway in a theater was dangerous because the carpeting was loose, Plaintiff may attempt to offer evidence that two other persons tripped and fell at the theater. Normally, the court will require a showing that the other falls occurred at the same or a similar place, were relatively proximate in time, and that the conditions surrounding the other falls were substantially similar in nature. If the crowd conditions, the lighting, the way the carpet was tacked, or any other material fact was different, the court may exclude the evidence. If, however, substantial similarity is shown, the court may admit the evidence as tending to prove the dangerous nature of the stairway. In addition, if the other falls occurred sufficiently **prior** to Plaintiff's, they may be used to prove that Defendant was on notice that the stairway was dangerous.

3.   "SHE": Other Contracts or Dealings to Prove Terms [§58]

Where the plaintiff and the defendant have a contract but there is a dispute as to the terms of that contract, evidence of other similar contracts **between them** is generally **admissible**.   On the other hand, evidence of similar contracts with **other persons** is ordinarily **inadmissible**. Remember, however, that the court has broad discretion in this area.

EXAMPLE

Plaintiff, a furniture manufacturer, contracts with Defendant, a retailer, to sell various items of furniture on July 1. The furniture is delivered and Defendant is billed $500 for freight charges. Defendant claims that the freight charges were to be included in the price and offers evidence that freight charges were included in a previous order from Plaintiff in May. Plaintiff claims that its freight policies have changed and offers evidence that since July 1 it has charged freight to all its other customers. Defendant's evidence of prior dealings with Plaintiff is admissible to prove the terms of the July 1 transactions unless there were some substantial differences in material conditions (e.g., the May purchase was a special "close-out" deal). Plaintiff's evidence of subsequent dealings with other customers probably would be excluded since the parties were not the same. But remember, the court has broad discretion on such relevancy issues and could admit the evidence, especially if it admitted evidence of the May deal.

4.   "SHE": Other Contracts or Dealings to Prove Agency [§59]

When the authority of an agent to make a contract is disputed, evidence of similar contracts entered into by the purported agent ordinarily is admissible even if the parties are different.

EXAMPLE

Plaintiff enters into a contract with Agee, a salesman for Defendant, to purchase 5,000 cartons of bunting for $20,000, which is 30% off Defendant's regular price. Defendant refuses to deliver, claiming that Agee had no authority to reduce the regular price. Plaintiff sues Defendant. Plaintiff may offer evidence that Agee had entered into contracts with Tribble and McGee in which he gave a 30% discount, and that Defendant honored those discounts.

5. "SHE": Non-Observations and Non-Occurrences [§60]

Using evidence that an event or condition was not observed or that other injuries did not occur to prove the non-existence of the event, condition, or injury raises relevance problems similar to those just discussed.

a. Non-Observation to Prove Non-Occurrence in General [§61]

The probative value of such negative evidence is ordinarily deemed to be so slight as to render the evidence inadmissible. If, however, the proponent shows that the event **probably would have been observed had it occurred**, evidence of its non-observation will be admissible.

EXAMPLE

Plaintiff slips on a broken ketchup bottle in Defendant Market. Defendant Market contends that the bottle must have fallen within five minutes of Plaintiff's injury and that it was not negligent in failing to discover and eliminate the danger. In response, Plaintiff seeks to testify that she was in the store for at least 30 minutes and that she did not hear the bottle fall. The court should admit the evidence if Plaintiff shows that she probably would have heard the bottle if it had fallen while she was in the store. If, on the other hand, the store was too large, too noisy, or too crowded to justify the conclusion that Plaintiff probably would have heard the bottle fall, the testimony is inadmissible.

b. Absence of Business Record to Prove Non-Occurrence [§62]

Most states and the FRE permit a party to prove that an event or transaction did not occur by evidence that there is no business record of such an event or transaction. However, the proponent must show that it is the practice of the business to regularly record all events or transactions of the type in issue. [FRE 803(7).] See §314.

EXAMPLE

Plaintiff may prove that Defendant did not pay an outstanding debt by proving that Plaintiff's regular business records did not reflect any payment, and that Plaintiff regularly records all such payments.

    c.   **Absence of Similar Accidents [§63]**

Evidence that a place, a particular product, or a similar product has been used over a period of time without any accident occurring similar to the one in issue is relevant to prove that the place or product is not dangerous. Before such evidence of safety history is admissible, however, its proponent must establish that (1) the place or product involved was used a significant number of times under **conditions or circumstances substantially similar** to those involved in the accident in question, and (2) the **witness would have heard** of any previous accidents.

EXAMPLE: NO SIMILAR PRODUCT ACCIDENTS

Plaintiff is injured when a stone is thrown from Plaintiff's lawn mower into his eye. Plaintiff sues Defendant, the manufacturer of the mower, contending it was defectively designed because it provides no protection against such accidents. Defendant claims that the design is proper and that Plaintiff's injury was a freak accident. Defendant offers evidence that over 50,000 mowers of the same model used by Plaintiff have been sold over the last three years and that not one single complaint similar to Plaintiff's has been received. This evidence can be admitted if Defendant establishes that: (1) other customers used the mower under substantially similar conditions; and (2) Defendant probably would have received complaints if stones were thrown from the mower and injured the user.

6.   **"SHE": Sales of Similar Property to Prove Value [§64]**

Evidence of the selling price of a particular piece of property ordinarily may be used to prove the value of similar property. For example, a party may prove the value of a destroyed car through evidence of the recent selling price of a substantially similar car. Also, evidence of the selling price of a particular parcel of real property is admissible to prove the value of a similar tract of land. The proponent of such evidence must, however, satisfy the court that the properties are **substantially similar in nature** and that the other property was sold **under substantially similar market conditions**.

a.   Unaccepted Offers [§65]

Prior sale prices used to establish value must be genuine, and the price must actually have been paid. Unaccepted offers are generally inadmissible to prove value. A party may, however, introduce evidence of an unaccepted offer made by his opponent.

7.   "SHE": Previous Claims or Lawsuits to Impeach Present Claim [§66]

In an effort to discredit a plaintiff's or complainant's charge, a defendant may seek to offer evidence of prior similar charges made by the plaintiff or complainant.

a.   Chronic Litigant [§67]

Evidence that tends to show only that the plaintiff or complainant is a chronic litigant (i.e., has been involved in numerous other suits) is inadmissible.

b.   Prior Fraudulent Claims [§68]

If the plaintiff or complainant has previously made similar fraudulent claims, such evidence is often admitted to prove the falsity of the present claim.

8.   "SHE": Causation [§69]

When causation issues are complex, evidence of what happened to other persons similarly situated may be admitted to establish causation.

EXAMPLE

A plaintiff trying to establish that defendant caused his cancerous condition by dumping toxic wastes in a local river may introduce evidence of an unusually high cancer rate among persons living near the river.

9. "SHE": Business Custom to Prove Conduct [§70]

Evidence of an established business practice may be used to show that the practice was followed in a particular case.

EXAMPLE

Evidence that letters put in the "out basket" by 9:30 a.m. are routinely taken out and mailed by an employee before noon that day is admissible to prove that a particular letter put in the "out basket" before 8:00 a.m. was mailed before noon that day.

E. Discretionary Exclusion: Other Common Examples [§71]

Apart from evidence of similar happenings, there are other categories of evidence for which courts have developed certain basic approaches.

1. Reenactments, Demonstrations, and Experiments [§72]

When a party seeks to prove a fact by **reenactment** (e.g., Plaintiff seeks to show the condition of Defendant's brakes by testimony of a police officer that he tried the brakes right after the accident and found them in good condition), **demonstration** (e.g., to prove Defendant could not have turned off a dishwasher while on the telephone, Plaintiff demonstrates the impossibility of trying to repeat the act), or **experiment** (e.g., a scientific test of a boiler's capacity to hold pressure), the evidence is admissible only if its proponent shows that the reenactment, demonstration, or experiment was conducted under conditions or circumstances **substantially similar** to those surrounding the event being replicated.

2. Industry Standard to Prove Or Disprove Negligence [§73]

A party may offer evidence of the standard in the industry as evidence of what reasonable conduct would be. Thus, evidence that a defendant's conduct fell short of the standard of care in the industry would tend to show negligence. Conversely, evidence that a defendant did comply with the industry standard would tend to show it did not act negligently. For example, evidence that all other manufacturers of batteries use a particular ventilation technique not used by defendant would be admissible as tending to show defendant's negligence in failing to ventilate its facilities properly.

a. Relevant, But Not Conclusive [§74]

The industry standard, however, is not conclusive evidence of what constitutes reasonable conduct. Everyone in the industry may be negligent.

b. Medical Malpractice Cases [§75]

In medical malpractice cases, however, the usual standard of care is that of doctors practicing in the defendant's local community. When specialists are involved, a national standard of care and knowledge will be applied.

3. Statistical Evidence [§76]

Statistical evidence, **if improperly used**, presents a danger of unfair prejudice. Therefore, it is sometimes excluded, especially if the proponent of the statistical evidence is unable to prove the accuracy of the data underlying the statistical calculations. Another common pitfall is where the proponent inaccurately represents what the statistic stands for. For example, evidence that a defendant's blood-type matched the blood found at a crime scene and that only one percent of the population has that blood-type does not mean that the likelihood of defendant's guilt is ninety-nine percent. (It just means that there is one chance in a hundred that a randomly-selected person would have that blood-type. In a city of 100,000 people, there will be 1,000 people with that blood-type.) When, however, the proponent is able to demonstrate the accuracy of the underlying data and uses the statistical data properly, courts typically admit the statistical evidence. In race and sex discrimination cases, for example, statistical evidence frequently forms a major part of the plaintiff's case.

IMPORTANT CASE: *PEOPLE V. COLLINS*, 68 Cal.2d 319, 66 Cal.Rptr. 497, 438 P.2d 33 (1968).

This case exemplifies misuse of statistical evidence. Defendants were tried for robbery and assault. Although the victim was unable to positively identify the defendants, they matched the description she gave of her assailants. One defendant was a black male with a beard and mustache; the other was a white female with blond hair and a ponytail. They drove a partially yellow convertible. The prosecution called a mathematics professor who testified about a law of probability: that the probability of the joint occurrence of a number of mutually independent events is equal to the product of the individual probability of each event (e.g., the odds of a coin landing heads up three times in a row are $1/2$ x $1/2$ x $1/2$, or $1/8$). Then, based on an assumed probability for each described characteristic of the assailants (e.g., partly yellow car: $1/10$; man with mustache: $1/4$; blond woman: $1/3$; interracial couple: $1/1000$; etc.), the prosecutor used the law of probability to calculate that there was but one chance in 12 million that any couple possessed the characteristics of the defendants. Therefore, he argued, there was only a one in 12 million chance that the defendants were innocent.

The Supreme Court of California reversed, holding that such evidence was too confusing, misleading and prejudicial. Among other things, the court pointed out that the prosecution failed to establish the accuracy of the probability factors upon which the 1/12,000,000 calculation was based. To the contrary, the prosecutor had made them up. In addition, the prosecution failed to prove that the various probability factors were mutually independent, as is required by probability theory in order to make the calculation. In addition, even if the individual probabilities were both accurate and independent, the 1/12,000,000 would only represent the odds that a randomly selected couple would share the described characteristics. It would not represent a likelihood of guilt or innocence. Therefore, the California Supreme Court ruled that any probative value of the statistical evidence was far outweighed by its tendency to mislead and confuse the jury.

4. **Photographs and Repulsive Objects [§77]**

    Photographs, frequently in color and often gruesome, and repulsive objects (e.g., a piece of skull, a glass eye, or a blood-splattered pair of panties), are often objected to on the ground that their prejudicial impact substantially outweighs their probative value. Courts must decide each objection on its own merits, so no hard-and-fast rule can be stated. More often than not, however, these objections are overruled.

5. Jury views [§78]

The court has very broad discretion with respect to allowing in-court exhibitions (including demonstrations) and out-of-court jury views of matters and places in controversy.

a. View of Scene [§79]

A view of the scene may be helpful to the jurors, but it may expose them to information that is not evidence, such as a post-accident remedial measure (e.g., installation of a safety device). Thus, such views will be permitted only under strict safeguards and only where counsel and the parties are present.

F. Specific Relevance Rules: General [§80]

The preceding sections discuss the court's general power under FRE 403 to exclude relevant evidence. In addition, the Federal Rules (codifying common-law practice) contain **specific rules** that govern the admissibility of certain classes of relevant evidence. Some of these rules are based on **extrinsic social policies** (see §42), some are based on concerns about **accuracy in factfinding** (see §43), and some on a **combination** of these two concerns.

G. Subsequent Remedial Measures ("SRM") [§81]

FRE 407 codifies the traditional common-law rule that excluded evidence of a party's subsequent remedial measures when offered to prove the party's negligence. The rule, however, does not exclude all evidence of subsequent remedial measures. Careful attention must be paid to the various textual elements of the rule. In addition, courts sometimes accept arguments based on the underlying rationale for the rule and admit evidence that the text of the rule seems to exclude.

1. Elements of the Rule [§82]

The original version of the federal rule (and the version of the rule adopted by most states) applies only when a party seeks to offer evidence of a (1) **remedial measure** (2) taken **subsequent** to the accident or injury that is the subject of the suit (3) for the purpose of proving **negligence or culpable conduct**. The rule's applicability in products liability actions provoked a substantial amount of controversy, both in the federal courts and the states. The federal rule was amended in 1997 to resolve this controversy (see §87), but most states have not amended their rules to conform to the federal change.

2. **Rationale for the Rule [§83]**

The rule excluding SRM evidence is based both on **public policy** and **relevance** concerns. Public policy concerns tend to predominate. The law wants to **encourage parties to take safety measures** and believes that parties will be less likely to do so if they fear that such actions will be used as evidence against them in subsequent litigation. Thus, the rule is designed to exclude relevant evidence for the sake of promoting the extrinsic social policy of safety. But the rule is also based in part on the notion that SRM evidence, although relevant, is often **not highly probative** of a party's negligence or culpable conduct.

3. **Remedial Measure Defined [§84]**

Any measure that **would have made an injury or harm caused by an event less likely to occur** if it had been in place before the occurrence of the injury or harm qualifies as a subsequent remedial measure. An SRM can take many forms, such as a **repair or improvement** (e.g., addition of handrails to a stairway), a **design change**, (e.g., a change in gas-tank placement), a **change in procedure** (e.g., a change in schedule for waxing floors), or a **policy change** (limiting the number of drinks that can be served to patrons of a bar).

4. **Subsequent [§85]**

The remedial measure must be taken **after the occurrence of the injury or harm allegedly caused by an event**. A remedial measure taken after a product was purchased, but before the occurrence of an injury or harm allegedly caused by an event, is not a subsequent remedial measure.

EXAMPLE

Plaintiff purchases a 2004 Honda. In 2005, Honda changes the design and installation of its seat belts. In 2007, Plaintiff is severely injured while driving her 2004 Honda. She sues Honda, claiming the seat belts in her car were negligently designed and installed. When she offers evidence of the change Honda made in its 2005 models, Honda objects, arguing that this is an inadmissible subsequent remedial measure. It is not. The change was made before, not after, Plaintiff's injury, so it is not a subsequent measure.

5. **Inadmissible to Prove Negligence or Culpable Conduct [§86]**

The original version of federal rule (and the rule in many states) renders evidence of an SRM inadmissible only when offered to prove that the party that took the measure was negligent or guilty of culpable conduct. This limitation gives rise to two sets of issues. Is evidence of an SRM admissible in a products liability action? Second, even in an ordinarily negligence case, what types of things other than negligence or culpable conduct may an SRM be used to prove?

6. **Applicability in Products Liability Case: Federal Rules [§87]**

Because the text of FRE 407 originally excluded SRM evidence only when it was offered to prove negligence or culpable conduct, plaintiffs in products liability cases brought on a strict liability theory claimed that they should be allowed to introduce such evidence. One argument for admissibility was **textual**. Since such cases do not involve claims of either negligence or culpable conduct, the evidence is not being offered for the forbidden purpose of proving negligence or culpable conduct. A second argument related to the **public policy** rationale for the rule. Economic incentives for manufacturers to make their products safer are so strong that they will take remedial actions even if the law of evidence allows such evidence later to be used against them. A third argument related to the **relevance** rationale for the rule. Evidence of a subsequent remedial measure is more probative of a product's defectiveness than it is of a party's negligence. Federal courts interpreting the original version of FRE 407 almost unanimously **rejected** these arguments. FRE 407 was then amended in 1997 to codify these decisions. The rule now provides that, in addition to negligence or culpable conduct, SRM evidence is not admissible to prove a **product defect**, a **design defect**, or the **need for a warning or instruction**.

7. **Applicability in Products Liability Case: State Rules [§88]**

Many states' rules are based on the original version of FRE 407 and so textually prohibit SRM evidence only when offered to prove negligence or culpable conduct. States differ on how to interpret their rules. Some state courts follow the federal courts' approach and exclude SRM evidence in products liability cases as well negligence case. Others, however, accept the argument that products liability cases should be treated differently from negligence cases and admit SRM evidence in products liability cases.

8. **Admissible for Other Purposes [§89]**

The rule excludes SRM evidence only when it is offered to prove negligence or culpable conduct (and in the federal courts and some states, that a product or design was defective or the need for a warning). If the SRM evidence is **offered for some other purpose**, it may be admitted. These other purposes are sometimes referred to as exceptions to the general rule. But they are not really exceptions. Since the general rule excludes SRM evidence only when it is offered for a particular purpose, these other purposes for which the evidence is offered simply fall outside the general rule of exclusion.

a. **Ownership or Control [§90]**

Evidence of an SRM may be used to prove ownership or control of the instrumentality if it is in dispute.

EXAMPLE

Plaintiff sues Defendant, a general contractor, for injuries suffered at a construction site. Defendant denies liability, claiming that the sub-contractor was responsible for safety measures at the site. Plaintiff offers evidence that after his accident, the general contractor erected a fence around the site. This is admissible to prove safety measures were a matter in Defendant's control, although the evidence is not admissible to prove Defendant was negligent.

b. Feasibility of Precautionary Measures [§91]

If a party claims that the product, policy, site, etc. at issue could not have been manufactured or operated in a safer way, evidence of an SRM by that party will be admissible to show such a change was feasible.

EXAMPLE

Plaintiff is injured when a wood chip hit him in the eye as he was operating a power saw. He sues Defendant, the manufacturer of the saw, claiming that the saw was defectively designed. Defendant claims the saw could not feasibly be made safer. Plaintiff offers evidence that after his injury Defendant changed the design of its saws to shield users from flying wood chips. The evidence will be admissible to rebut Defendant's claim that such a change was not feasible.

c. Impeachment [§92]

Evidence of an SRM may be used to impeach a party's testimony at trial.

EXAMPLE

Plaintiff, who was accidentally shot when a shotgun was being unloaded, sues Gun Manufacturer. The president of Gun Manufacturer testifies that the gun was "perfectly safe and we wouldn't want to make it any different." Plaintiff may impeach this witness by demonstrating that Gun Manufacturer changed the design of the gun to allow its safety to be in the "on" position when the gun is being unloaded.

9. Third-party Remedial Measures [§93]

Several courts hold that FRE 407 does not bar the admission of an SRM made by someone who is not a party to the litigation. They reason that a **third party will not be deterred** from taking a remedial step by the fear that its action will later be used as proof in a case to which it is not a party. Therefore, allowing the use of such evidence does not conflict with the policy concerns that underlie the rule. Note, however, that even if FRE 407 does not render such evidence inadmissible, a court may still exclude the evidence if it determines that the SRM's probative value is substantially outweighed by the danger of unfair prejudice, confusion of the issues, etc.

EXAMPLE
Plaintiff, an Army officer, was severely injured in a helicopter crash. She sues the manufacturer of a helicopter, claiming that it was defectively designed. The manufacturer claims that the crash was caused by the Army's faulty maintenance. It seeks to introduce evidence that, after the accident, the Army (a non-party) changed its maintenance procedures. Despite the language of FRE 407, a court might admit this evidence because it is evidence of a third-party remedial measure.

10. Compelled Remedial Measures [§94]
Just as some courts allow evidence of third-party SRM's, some courts have admitted evidence of remedial measures that the **government compelled** a party to make. The compulsory nature of the SRM negates the danger that the party would be deterred from taking it by the fear that it may be used as evidence against the party.

H. Compromises and Offers to Compromise [§95]
FRE 408 codifies the traditional rule that evidence that someone offered to compromise a disputed claim or actually did compromise a disputed claim is not admissible to prove liability for or the invalidity of the claim or the amount of damages.

1. Elements of the Rule [§96]
The rule excludes evidence of (a) a **compromise or** an **offer** to compromise (b) a **disputed claim** (c) when offered to prove **liability for** the claim, the **invalidity of** the claim, or the **amount of damages**. The rule applies in three basic situations:

• when a plaintiff wants to offer evidence that the **defendant offered to settle** a claim as a means of proving the defendant's liability or the proper amount of damages;

- when a defendant wants to offer evidence that the **plaintiff offered to settle** a claim as a means of proving the invalidity of the plaintiff's claim or the proper amount of damages; and

- when a plaintiff wants to offer evidence that the **defendant settled with a similarly-situated party** as a means of proving the defendant's liability or the proper amount of damages.

EXAMPLE: DEFENDANT'S OFFER TO SETTLE

Plaintiff sues Driver for injuries suffered when Driver's car struck Plaintiff's car. Driver offers to settle for $75,000. Plaintiff may not introduce evidence of Driver's offer to settle as evidence either of Driver's liability or the amount of damages suffered.

EXAMPLE: PLAINTIFF'S OFFER TO SETTLE

Plaintiff brings a slip and fall action against Store, seeking $2 million in damages. Plaintiff offers to settle for $50,000. Store rejects the offer. Store may not introduce evidence of Plaintiff's offer as proof of the invalidity of Plaintiff's claim or the amount of damages.

EXAMPLE: DEFENDANT'S SETTLEMENT WITH ANOTHER PARTY

After an airplane crash, Plaintiff 1 sues Airline for $1 million. Airline settles the case for $900,000. Plaintiff 2, another injured passenger, sues Airline and seeks to offer evidence of Airline's settlement with Plaintiff 1 to prove Airline's liability. The evidence is inadmissible.

2. **Rationale for the Rule [§97]**

   Exclusion of settlement evidence is based primarily on the **extrinsic social policy** of encouraging out-of-court settlements. At common law, there was also some feeling that such evidence was irrelevant because an offer to compromise a claim might result from the desire to avoid a lawsuit as much as from a belief that one was not liable. Under modern notions of relevance, however, such evidence categorically cannot be said to be irrelevant. Nevertheless, concern still exists that the jurors will fail to appreciate the many reasons why a party might choose to compromise and so place undue weight on such evidence. Thus, the rule is also grounded in some part on concerns about **accurate factfinding**.

3. **Disputed Claim Requirement [§98]**
    This rule protects settlement evidence only if the offer, settlement, or statement **relates to a claim that is disputed** either as to liability or amount of damages.

EXAMPLE: NO DISPUTE AS TO LIABILITY OR DAMAGES
Plaintiff sues Defendant on a $500 note. Defendant tells Plaintiff, "I know I owe you the $500, but it will cost you that much to litigate it. I'll give you $250 to settle." This statement is admissible since Defendant disputes neither the validity of Plaintiff's claim nor the amount of damages involved.

EXAMPLE: BUSINESS NEGOTIATION
Statements made during the course of a negotiation for a business deal or a licensing agreement are not protected.

4. **Compromise Requirement [§99]**
    The rule covers only statements that constitute a compromise or that are made in an attempt to compromise a claim. This means that some element of quid pro quo must be present.

EXAMPLE
A letter written to a wrongdoer laying out the injured party's version of the facts and demanding payment in full of all damages is not a protected offer to settle.

5. **Express Admissions During Negotiations [§100]**
    Evidence of conduct or statements made **during compromise negotiations** is also **inadmissible** under this rule. Thus, even express admissions made during negotiations (e.g., "I ran the red light. I'll pay you $500 to settle.") are inadmissible.

    a. **Exception: Limited Use in Criminal Cases [§101]**
        For many years, federal courts disagreed as to whether FRE 408 precluded the admission in a criminal case of evidence that the accused had settled or offered to settle a related civil claim. FRE 408 was amended in 2006 to answer this question. The

amendment was a compromise. FRE 408 continues to **exclude** in a criminal case evidence that the accused **settled or offered to settle** a related civil claim. But amended FRE 408 **permits evidence of statements or conduct** during compromise negotiations regarding a **civil claim made by a government regulatory, investigative, or enforcement agency** to be introduced in a subsequent criminal case.

EXAMPLE

The Securities Exchange Commission brings a civil suit against Defendant Company. During the course of settlement discussions, Defendant admits that it overstated its profits and destroyed various documents. Defendant and the SEC settle, with Defendant paying a civil fine. The Department of Justice then files a criminal action against Defendant for obstruction of justice. Evidence that Defendant settled the civil suit is not admissible against Defendant in the criminal action; evidence that Defendant admitted that it destroyed documents, however, is admissible.

EXAMPLE

A shareholder brings a civil suit against Defendant Company. During the course of settlement discussions, Defendant admits that it overstated its profits and destroyed various documents. Defendant and Shareholder settle. The Department of Justice then files a criminal action against Defendant for obstruction of justice. Evidence that Defendant settled the civil suit is not admissible against Defendant in the criminal action. Nor is the evidence that Defendant admitted that it destroyed documents; such evidence is allowed in a criminal case only when the civil case in which the statement was made was brought by a government regulatory, investigative, or enforcement agency.

6. **Proper Uses of Compromise Evidence [§102]**

FRE 408 makes compromise evidence inadmissible only when it is offered to prove the validity or invalidity of a claim or the amount of damages. It, may, however, be admissible when offered for another purpose.

a. **Bias or Prejudice [§103]**

    Compromise evidence may be used to prove the bias or prejudice of a witness. For example, a plaintiff may ask a witness, "Didn't defendant just pay you $10,000 [a generous amount] to settle your claim against her?" This question is being asked to show that the witness may be biased in favor of defendant as the result of defendant's generosity toward her.

b. **Undue Delay [§104]**

    Compromise evidence may be used to rebut a contention of undue delay. For example, if Defendant asserts that Plaintiff delayed unduly in filing suit, Plaintiff may establish that he did not file sooner because he was negotiating a settlement with Defendant.

c. **Suit on the Compromise Agreement [§105]**

    When a plaintiff brings an action to enforce the terms of a settlement agreement, evidence of the agreement will, of course, be admissible.

d. **Limits on Impeachment [§106]**

    Although compromise evidence may be used to impeach a witness by showing bias or prejudice, statements made during compromise negotiations may not be for impeachment either as a means of contradicting the substance of the witness's testimony or showing that the witness made a prior inconsistent statement.

I. **Offers to Pay Medical or Similar Expenses [§107]**

    FRE 409 excludes offers to pay or actual payment of medical, hospital, or similar expenses occasioned by an injury. This is sometimes referred to (somewhat inaptly) as the Good Samaritan rule. However, while the federal rule bans use of the offer or fact of payment itself, it does not ban other statements made in connection with the offer. This rule applies to unilateral offers, i.e., offers that are not made in an effort to compromise a claim. If the offer to pay (or payment of) medical or similar expenses is made as part of settlement discussions (or a settlement), the rule on compromise offers (see §95) governs, and the statement of liability would be inadmissible.

EXAMPLE
Plaintiff and Driver are involved in an auto accident. Driver rushes up to Plaintiff and says, "It was all my fault; I'll pay all your medical bills." The offer to pay the medical bills is not admissible; the statement of liability ("it was all my fault") is admissible.

J. Offers to Plead [§108]

To facilitate the plea bargaining process, certain pleas are inadmissible in either a civil or criminal proceeding against the defendant who made the plea. [FRE 410.] Neither a **guilty plea that is withdrawn** nor a **nolo contendere** (no contest) plea, **whether or not withdrawn**, may be used against the defendant. Evidence of a guilty plea that is not withdrawn is not excluded by this rule.

EXAMPLE
Plaintiff sues Defendant for injuries suffered in an auto accident. She attempts to prove that Defendant entered a nolo contendere plea in response to criminal reckless driving charges arising out of the accident. The evidence is inadmissible. If, however, Defendant had entered a guilty plea to the charges and the plea had not been withdrawn, the evidence would be admissible.

1. Statements Made During the Plea Process [§109]

In addition to pleas, FRE 410 excludes evidence of certain statements made in the plea process. **Statements made during plea discussions** are protected (e.g., offers to plead guilty or statements of liability), as are **statements made during the actual plea proceeding** (where the defendant may have to acknowledge his guilt).

2. Statements Not Protected [§110]

Statements that are made **outside the context of plea discussions or the plea proceeding** are not protected. Therefore, FRE 410 does not cover statements made either to law enforcement officials (e.g., police officers), without an intent to negotiate a plea, or after a plea agreement has been finalized. In addition, since FRE 410 does not protect a guilty plea that is not withdrawn, statements made during negotiations that result in an unwithdrawn guilty plea are likewise unprotected.

3. **Only Defendant Who Made Plea or Statement is Protected [§111]**

    The rule provides only that a covered plea or statement is inadmissible **against the defendant** who made the plea or statement. The rule does not forbid its use against another party, although some other rule (e.g., hearsay) may be grounds for excluding such evidence.

4. **Waiver [§112]**

    A defendant's **knowing and voluntary agreement to waive** the protections of FRE 410 is valid. Thus, if a defendant agrees to waive the protections of the rule, the government may later use statements made by the defendant during unsuccessful plea negotiations. *United States v. Mezzanatto*, 513 U.S. 196 (1995).

5. **Exceptions [§113]**

    FRE 410 creates **two exceptions**. First, an otherwise protected statement made by the defendant is admissible when another statement made during the course of plea discussions or proceedings has been introduced and **fairness dictates** that the otherwise protected statement **ought to be considered contemporaneously** with the already-introduced statement. Second, if a defendant is tried for **perjury or false statement**, FRE 410 does not prohibit the prosecution from introducing a false statement made by a defendant under oath, on the record, and in the presence of counsel (for example, in a plea proceeding).

6. **Rule Covers Pleas and Statements, Not Judgments [§114]**

    FRE 410 bars the use of certain pleas and statements made in connection with the plea process. It does not govern the evidentiary or procedural effect of a **judgment** that is entered based upon a plea. Other evidence or procedural rules, however, may prevent the use of such a judgment.

EXAMPLE

Defendant enters a plea of nolo contendere to a criminal charge of driving while intoxicated. The court finds Defendant guilty and enters a judgment of conviction. Soon thereafter, Plaintiff, who was a passenger in Defendant's car and was injured as a result of Defendant's drunken driving, sues Defendant. FRE 410 precludes Plaintiff from introducing Defendant's no contest plea, but does not prevent Plaintiff from proving that Defendant was convicted of drunken driving. The judgment of conviction, however, is hearsay—it is the judge's statement that Defendant was driving while intoxicated—and is not admissible because there is no applicable hearsay exception. See §403.

K. Liability Insurance [§115]

Evidence that a person was or was not insured against liability is not admissible to prove that the person acted negligently or wrongfully. It is admissible, however, to prove other things, such as agency, ownership, control, or the bias or prejudice of a witness. [FRE 411.]

1. Reason for Exclusion [§116]

Liability insurance evidence is excluded in an effort to promote **accuracy in factfinding**. If offered to prove negligence, it has little or no probative value, but may be quite prejudicial. When offered to prove something other than negligence, it may, however, have substantial probative value, as shown below.

2. Disputed Ownership or Control [§117]

If the existence of an insurance policy is relevant to prove ownership or control of a vehicle or premises and ownership or control is in dispute, evidence regarding liability insurance is admissible because it is not being used to prove negligence. Thus, if Defendant claims he does not own a car, the fact that an insurance policy was taken out in his name is admissible to prove his ownership.

3. Showing Bias [§118]

On cross-examination, counsel may show bias by eliciting the fact that a witness is employed by an insurance company that has a financial interest in the outcome.

4. Inseparable Reference to Insurance [§119]

If a party makes a statement directly bearing upon liability or fault, the statement will be admissible notwithstanding a reference to insurance coverage (e.g., "I was driving too fast but my insurance will cover all your damages"). If it is possible to sever the insurance reference from the admission without lessening its evidentiary value, the court should strike the reference to insurance.

5. Evidence of No Insurance [§120]

A defendant may not introduce evidence that she is not insured unless a plaintiff has falsely suggested that she is insured.

L. Character Evidence [§121]

One of the trickiest areas of the law of evidence concerns the admissibility of evidence of a person's character or of a person's character trait. The common law developed a fairly complicated (some might say bizarre) set of rules to govern this question, which have for the most part been incorporated into the Federal Rules. Character evidence is always a favorite topic for exam questions. If you break down the question and follow the rules carefully, reaching the correct result is not that difficult.

1. The Three-Step Process [§122]

Always analyze character evidence problems by asking the three following questions. (What-May-How?).

- **What** is the evidence being offered to prove?
- **May** character evidence be used to prove this? If so, ask the third question.
- **How** may character be proved?

2. Possible Uses of Character Evidence [§123]

There are several purposes for which character evidence might potentially be offered, and it is crucial to distinguish among them.

a. First Possible Use: Character as an Element of a Claim or Defense [§124]

A person's **character might itself be an element of a crime, claim, or defense**. That is, the substantive law may require that a person's character or character trait be proved before a claim or a defense can be established. In such cases, the person's character is not being used as circumstantial evidence to prove something else. The person's character is itself what must be proved. Not surprisingly, when character is itself an element of a claim or defense, character evidence is admissible. [FRE 404.] The following are examples of cases in which the substantive law makes character an element of a claim or defense and, therefore, admissible.

EXAMPLE: NEGLIGENT ENTRUSTMENT OR HIRING.
Where Plaintiff claims that Defendant negligently entrusted his car to Driver, Plaintiff must establish as one of the elements of his cause of action that Driver was not the type of person to whom a car should be loaned (because, for example, he was a terrible driver). Thus, Driver's character trait of being a terrible driver is something that Plaintiff must prove to make out his claim. (Plaintiff will also have to establish that Defendant knew or should have known about this character triat, but that is a separate element of his claim.)

EXAMPLE: DEFAMATION—TRUTH AS A DEFENSE.
In a libel or slander case, a defendant may assert the defense of "truth." If, for example, Defendant called Plaintiff a "liar and a thief," Plaintiff's character as a liar and a thief will be an element of Defendant's defense of truth.

EXAMPLE: ENTRAPMENT.
Some versions of the entrapment defense to a criminal charge focus on the defendant's predisposition to commit the crime. Thus, Defendant's character may be an element of the entrapment defense.

EXAMPLE: MENTAL CONDITION OR COMPETENCY.
In cases raising issues such as the sanity of the defendant, the competency of a testator to make a will, or the mental condition of the respondent to a civil commitment proceeding, character is an element of the claim or defense.

b. **Proving Character When It is an Element of a Claim or Defense [§125]**
When character is an element of a claim or defense, it may be proved through the use of **reputation** or

opinion testimony [FRE 405(a)] or **specific instances** of conduct. [FRE 405(b).] See §135.

c. **Second Possible Use: Character Evidence to Prove Conduct [§126]**
A party might want to introduce evidence of someone's character or character trait **to prove how that person acted on a particular occasion**. That is, the character evidence will be offered as circumstantial evidence: the jury is to infer from the evidence of a person's character that the person **acted in conformity with his character** on the occasion in question.

(1) **General Rule: Inadmissible to Prove Conduct [§127]**
The general rule is that character evidence is not admissible as circumstantial evidence that a person acted in conformity with his character on a particular occasion. [FRE 404(a).]

EXAMPLE
To prove Defendant murdered Victim, the prosecution seeks to prove that Defendant has a violent character. This is inadmissible.

EXAMPLE
Plaintiff sues Defendant for fraud. Plaintiff offers evidence that Defendant has committed numerous acts of dishonesty in the past to prove he committed fraud on this particular occasion. This is inadmissible.

(2) **Rationale [§128]**
The reason for this is that character evidence is **not** considered **highly probative** on the issue of how a person acted on a particular occasion. On the other hand, such evidence may be **highly prejudicial**. The jury is likely to rule against Defendant because it has decided Defendant is a bad person.

(3) Exceptions to General Rule vs. Nonapplicability of General Rule [§129]

Several exceptions exist to the general rule forbidding the use of a person's character evidence to prove how he or she acted on a particular occasion. These are discussed in §§145 through 181. Be sure to distinguish these exceptions to the general rule from those situations in which the general rule simply does not apply because the evidence is being used to prove something other than how the person behaved on a particular occasion. These are discussed in §124 above and §§130-134 immediately below.

d. Third Possible Use: Character Evidence to Prove Something Other Than Conduct [§130]

Character evidence is sometimes used as circumstantial evidence, but for the purpose of proving something other than that the person acted in conformity with his character on a particular occasion.

EXAMPLE: CUSTODY ACTION.
In child custody proceeding, the court may consider a party's character in deciding who should have custody of a child. The party's character is not itself an element of the claim or a defense. Nor is it being used to prove how the party acted on a particular occasion. But it is circumstantial evidence that bears on which party should be awarded custody of the child.

EXAMPLE: DAMAGES.
In a wrongful death action, the deceased's character is relevant to the issue of the proper amount of damages for loss of consortium. The deceased's character is not itself an issue that must be proved and it is not being offered to prove how the deceased behaved on any particular occasion. Nevertheless, the deceased's character is circumstantial evidence that can be considered in deciding the value of the plaintiff's claim for lost consortium.

(1) Character Evidence Admissible for This Purpose [§131]

FRE 404 excludes character evidence only when it is being offered to prove how the person acted on a particular occasion. Therefore, FRE 404 does not bar the use of character evidence when it is offered as circumstantial evidence of something other than conduct. The real issue is how character may be proved when it is being offered for this purpose. See §136.

e. Sounds Like Character Evidence But is Not [§132]

Sometimes evidence is offered that looks and sounds a lot like character evidence, but is really not.

(1) Self Defense — Pre-Emptive Strike Theory [§133]

One theory of self defense is that the defendant reasonably feared that the victim was about to inflict severe bodily harm on him and so struck the first blow to victim. In such a case, the victim's character is not the issue. Instead, the issue is **what the defendant reasonably believed about the victim**. For example, a defendant might have reasonably (but incorrectly) believed that the victim was a violent person who was about to kill him. The defendant's reasonable perception might justify his striking the first blow even though it turns out that his perception of the victim's character did not correspond to the victim's actual character. Be sure to distinguish this theory of self-defense from a second theory of self-defense in which evidence of the victim's violent character is used to prove that the victim acted violently and struck the first blow himself. See §158.

(2) Injury to Reputation [§134]

In defamation cases, damages are measured according to injury to the plaintiff's reputation. Thus it is the plaintiff's reputation, before and after the tort, not his character, that constitutes the measure of damages. As we all know too well, a person's reputation can vary dramatically from his true character.

3. **Methods of Proving Character [§135]**
    In theory at least, there are three types of evidence that might be used to prove a person's character: (a) reputation; (b) opinion; and (c) specific instances of conduct.

4. **When Different Methods May Be Used—Overview [§136]**
    Reputation and **opinion** testimony may be used to prove character **whenever character evidence is allowed**. The rule governing use of evidence of specific instances is more complicated. **Specific instance** evidence is admissible to prove character **when character is itself an element of a claim or defense**. Specific instance evidence ordinarily may not be used to prove character when (under one of the exceptions to the general rule) character is being offered to prove that a person acted in conformity with his or her character on a particular occasion. But specific instance evidence may be admissible in cases involving charges of sexual misconduct or child molestation. See the discussion in §§165-181 below. Finally, the law is ambiguous about how character may be proved when it is being used as circumstantial evidence to prove something other than conduct (e.g., in a child custody case). Although the rules are not clear, most courts allow specific instance evidence, as well as reputation and opinion evidence, in such cases.

5. **Methods of Proving Character: Reputation [§137]**
    Evidence of a person's reputation in the community might be offered to prove the person's character. For example, evidence that a person is known in the community as a violent person tends to prove that he is a violent person.

    a. **Foundation Required for Reputation Testimony [§138]**
        A witness called to testify as to another person's reputation in the community must first demonstrate that she has knowledge of the person's reputation in

the community, although she need not actually know the person herself.

b.   Relevant Community [§139]
Traditionally, reputation evidence was limited to the person's reputation in the community in which he or she lived. Courts now accept testimony relating to the person's reputation in other significant "communities," such as the place where the person works.

c.   Substance of Reputation Testimony [§140]
When a witness gives reputation testimony, she is allowed to state only that the person's reputation in the community for the relevant trait is "good," "bad," "excellent," "terrible," etc., and **may not give reasons** why that reputation exists.

d.   Hearsay [§141]
Reputation testimony calls for the recitation of hearsay, but an exception to the hearsay rule exists for such testimony. [FRE 803(21).]

6.   Methods of Proving Character: Opinion [§142]
A witness may testify as to her opinion of another person's character. For example, a witness might testify in a defamation action that she knows the plaintiff and that in her opinion, the plaintiff is a liar and a thief. This method of proof is not permitted at common law, but is allowed under the federal rules [FRE 405] and in many states.

a.   Substance of Opinion Testimony [§143]
As is the case with reputation testimony, an opinion witness may state only her opinion of the person's character. She **may not give reasons** as to why she holds that opinion.

7.   Methods of Proving Character: Specific Instances of Conduct [§144]
Evidence that a person has engaged in specific acts might tend to establish the person's character. For example, the fact that someone has committed four thefts tends to establish that he is the type of person who steals. This method of proof presents the greatest danger of unfair prejudice and so its use is limited. See §136.

8. **Character to Prove Conduct: Exceptions to General Rule. [§145]**

   Recall that the general rule is that evidence of a person's character is not admissible as proof that the person acted in conformity with that character on a particular occasion. [FRE 404(a).] This **general rule applies both in criminal and civil cases**. There are, however, **several important exceptions** to this rule. The first three exceptions are set forth in FRE 404(a).

9. **First Exception: Accused May Put Own Character in Issue [§146]**

   A **criminal defendant** may offer evidence of a **pertinent trait of his character** to prove his innocence. [FRE 404(a)(1).] Thus, a defendant charged with murder (a crime of violence) may introduce evidence of his peaceable nature as evidence that he acted in accordance with his peaceable character on the occasion in question, and is therefore innocent. This is often referred to as "putting character **in** issue." Do not confuse this with those cases in which character is **an** issue (that is, when character is an element of a claim or defense).

   a. **Must Be Pertinent Character Trait [§147]**

      The accused may offer evidence only of **a pertinent character trait**. A murder defendant may not offer evidence of his honest character to prove he did not commit the murder.

   b. **Method of Proof: Reputation and Opinion [§148]**

      The defendant may prove his character only by **reputation** and **opinion** testimony. He may not offer evidence of specific acts to prove his good character. [FRE 405.]

   c. **Prosecutor May Rebut [§149]**

      If the defendant offers evidence of his good character, he is said to put "character in issue," and the prosecution may rebut. [FRE 404(a)(1).]

d. **Prosecution Rebuttal: Reputation and Opinion [§150]**

The prosecution may call its **own reputation and opinion witnesses** to testify to the defendant's bad character for the relevant trait. [FRE 405(a).]

e. **Prosecution Rebuttal: Cross-Examination of Defendant's Witnesses [§151]**

The prosecution may ask a **reputation witness** called by the defendant whether she "had heard" about specific acts of the defendant that would reflect badly on the defendant's reputation. The **theory** is that this **tests how familiar the witness is** with the defendant's reputation in the community. If the witness has not heard about such incidents, it undermines her claim that she is familiar with the defendant's reputation. Similarly, the prosecution may ask an **opinion witness** called by the defendant whether she knows about specific acts of the defendant that might bear on her opinion. Again, the **theory** is that the prosecution is simply **testing how well the witness knows** the defendant. [FRE 405(a).]

(1) **Form of Question [§152]**

At common law, the precise form of a question put to a reputation witness on cross-examination was very important. (Remember, opinion witnesses were not permitted at common law.) The question had to be phrased in a manner that tested only the witness's knowledge of community reputation. The correct form was "Have you heard . . . [that the defendant embezzled $10,000 from his daughter's Brownie troop]?" A question asking "Do you know . . . " was improper. Now that opinion witnesses are permitted under the federal rules and in many states, this distinction is of diminished importance and, according to some commentators and case law, has been abandoned in the federal courts. The still widely-used, and probably better, practice is to **ask reputation witnesses "have you heard"** questions and **opinion witnesses "do you know"** questions.

(2) Pertinent Trait Only [§153]

The specific acts referred to in the prosecution's "have you heard" and "do you know" questions must relate to the character trait that the witness testified about on direct examination.

(3) Prosecution Bound by Answer [§154]

Although the prosecution may ask such "have you heard" and "do you know" questions, it **may not introduce evidence to prove that the specific acts actually occurred,** even if the witness answers in the negative. For example, if a defense witness testifies that the defendant has an excellent reputation for peaceableness, the prosecution may ask, "Have you heard that the defendant assaulted an 84-year-old lady in a wheelchair last year?" Even if the witness answers "no," the prosecution is barred from proving that the defendant actually committed the assault.

(4) Limiting Instruction [§155]

Because juries might well infer from the question that defendant did commit the specific act, the defendant is entitled to a limiting instruction that will explain to the jury (futilely) that the question is being asked only to test the witness's familiarity with defendant's reputation and is not evidence that the defendant committed the specific act.

(5) Good Faith Requirement [§156]

Because the jury is unlikely to understand the limiting instruction, "Have you heard" and "do you know" questions are limited to instances of conduct that the prosecution believes in good faith actually occurred.

IMPORTANT CASE: *MICHELSON V. UNITED STATES,* 335 U.S. 469 (1948).
This famous Supreme Court case lays out the common-law rules regarding the admissibility of character evidence. Michelson was accused of bribery and called character witnesses to testify to his

reputation for honesty. The prosecution was then permitted to ask these witnesses "Have you heard [that Michelson committed various acts of dishonesty.]" The opinion makes no attempt to justify the rules of the game on any ground other than "this is the way we've done it and it seems to work pretty well." In fact, Justice Jackson commented that the character evidence rules illustrate the dictum that "the system may work best when explained least."

10. **Second Exception: Accused May Prove Alleged Victim's Character [§157]**

A criminal defendant may offer evidence of his **alleged victim's character to prove that the victim acted in conformity with his character** on the occasion in question. [FRE 404(a)(2).] This exception is used most commonly to buttress a claim that the accused responded in self-defense to the alleged victim's aggression.

   a. **Self-Defense: Victim as First Aggressor Theory [§158]**

   In the victim-as-first-aggressor theory of self-defense, the defendant is contending that the victim struck the first blow. Evidence of the alleged **victim's violent character** is offered, therefore, **to prove that the alleged victim acted in conformity with his violent nature** on this particular occasion; in other words, to prove that the alleged victim **started the fight**. Be sure to **distinguish** this theory of self-defense from the **pre-emptive strike theory** (see §133), under which the defendant claims that he acted before the alleged victim had a chance to act violently. Under the pre-emptive strike theory, therefore, a defendant would not offer evidence of the alleged victim's violent character to prove that the alleged victim acted violently on the occasion in question.

   b. **Method of Proof [§159]**

   The defendant may use only **reputation** and **opinion** testimony to prove the alleged victim's character. [FRE 405(a).] In a few jurisdictions, the defendant may introduce specific acts by the alleged victim.

c. Prosecution Rebuttal—Victim's Good Character [§160]

If the defendant offers evidence of the alleged victim's bad character, the prosecution may rebut by **cross-examining defendant's witnesses** and by **calling its own reputation and opinion witnesses** to testify to the alleged **victim's good character**. In addition, in a **homicide case**, if the defendant offers **any kind of evidence** that the deceased victim was the first aggressor, the prosecution may call reputation and opinion witnesses to testify to the alleged victim's peaceable character. [FRE 404(a)(2).]

d. Prosecution Rebuttal—Accused's Bad Character [§161]

A 2000 amendment to FRE 404 added a second form of prosecution rebuttal. If an accused offers evidence of the **alleged victim's** bad character, the prosecution may respond by offering evidence of the **accused's** bad character for the same trait. Thus, if a defendant offers evidence of the alleged victim's violent character to prove the alleged victim started the fight, the prosecution may offer evidence of the accused's violent character to prove the accused started the fight. The prosecution may use reputation or opinion testimony; specific instances of conduct are not permitted for this purpose.

EXAMPLE

Defendant is on trial for murder. He claims he killed Victim in self-defense, testifying that he shot Victim to only after she tried to stab him. He then calls Friend to testify that, in his opinion, Victim was a very violent person. This is permissible because the evidence is being offered to prove that Victim acted in conformity with her violent character and was trying to stab Defendant. During its rebuttal case, Prosecution calls Witness One to testify that Victim had a reputation for being a very peaceable person, and Witness Two to testify that, in his opinion, Defendant is a very violent person. Both Witness One and Witness Two may testify. This is proper rebuttal by the prosecution.

e. Applicability of Exception in Sexual Assault Cases [§162]

Traditionally, defendants in rape cases took advantage of this exception to offer evidence of the alleged rape victim's character. Every jurisdiction now has a specific rule governing the admissibility of such evidence. This is discussed in §§165-177 below.

11. Applicability of Exceptions to Civil Cases [§163]

FRE 404 was amended in 2006 to make clear that these first two exceptions to the general rule prohibiting character evidence to prove conduct are applicable only in criminal cases.

12. Third Exception: Character to Attack or Support Credibility [§164]

The third exception to the general rule prohibiting character evidence to prove conduct provides that evidence of a witness's character may be used to **attack or support his credibility**. [FRE 404(a)(3).] That is, evidence that a witness has a truthful or untruthful character is offered to prove that the witness is testifying truthfully or untruthfully. This exception applies in both civil and criminal cases. A **special set of rules** governs when and how evidence of character may be used to attack or support credibility. See §497.

13. Evidence of Past Sexual Behavior [§165]

At common law, defendants accused of rape often introduced evidence of the victim's character. That is, they offered evidence that their victim was promiscuous to prove that she acted in conformity with her promiscuous nature and consented to sexual intercourse on this occasion. Such evidence was of dubious probative value and resulted in a great deal of abuse, as rape victims frequently found themselves and their sexual histories the focus of the trial. As a result, every jurisdiction has some **"rape shield" provision** that strictly limits the admissibility of evidence of an alleged victim's past sexual conduct. Many are similar to FRE 412.

a. Criminal Cases: General Rule [§166]

FRE 412 severely limits, in any criminal proceeding **involving alleged sexual misconduct**, the admissibility of evidence of an alleged victim's **other sexual behavior or predisposition**.

(1) Rationale for the Rule [§167]

The rule is premised both on relevancy and public policy concerns. The **relevancy** concerns are that the probative value of this type of evidence is frequently quite low, while the danger of unfair prejudice is frequently quite high. The **public policy** rationale is rooted in the desire to protect the privacy interests of sexual misconduct victims. In addition, many rape victims have been deterred from reporting or pursuing their claims because they feared they would be subjected to an inquiry about their sexual history. FRE 412 and similar state rules are aimed at removing this disincentive to prosecute sexual offenses.

(2) Other Sexual Behavior [§168]

Evidence that any alleged victim engaged in other sexual behavior is **generally inadmissible**. This includes evidence of actual physical sexual contact, activities that imply sexual contact (e.g., use of contraceptives), and reputation and opinion evidence. Note that the rule extends to **any alleged victim** and is not restricted to the complainant in the case.

EXAMPLE

Defendant is charged with sexually assaulting Victim. Prosecution calls Witness (another sexual assault victim of Defendant) to testify to Defendant's modus operandi. Because Witness is also an alleged victim of sexual misconduct, Defendant is prohibited from offering evidence of her other sexual behavior.

(3) Sexual Predisposition [§169]

Evidence offered to prove an alleged victim's sexual predisposition (e.g., evidence of mode of dress, life-style, etc.) is likewise inadmissible.

(4) Not Restricted to Charges of Sexual Assault [§170]

Although the rule will typically apply in cases in which the defendant faces charges of criminal sexual misconduct (e.g., sexual assault), it also reaches cases in which the defendant is charged with an offense that does not contain sexual misconduct as an element but where the defendant's sexual misconduct is relevant to prove motive or as background evidence.

EXAMPLE

Defendant is charged with kidnapping Victim. Prosecution may offer evidence that Defendant sexually assaulted Victim a few days before to establish his motive for kidnapping her.

b. Criminal Cases: Exceptions [§171]

FRE 412(b) enumerates three exceptions under which sexual behavior or predisposition evidence may be admissible.

(1) Source of Semen or Injury [§172]

The accused may offer evidence of specific instances of an alleged victim's sexual behavior to prove that someone other than the accused was the source of semen, injury, or other physical evidence. Note that the use of such evidence does not require any inferences about the alleged victim's character. The other sexual behavior is not being offered to prove the alleged victim's promiscuous character from which the jury would be asked to infer that the alleged victim consented on this occasion. Rather, the evidence is being offered for a more direct purpose. If the alleged victim engaged in sexual behavior with someone other than the accused, that other person might be the source of the semen, injury, or other physical evidence. Of course, the other sexual behavior must have occurred at such a time that it actually tends to rebut or explain the prosecution's physical evidence.

EXAMPLE

Evidence that the alleged victim had intercourse with someone else three weeks prior to the alleged sexual assault will not tend to rebut prosecution evidence that the accused was the source of semen. On the other hand, evidence that the accused had intercourse with someone else the night before the alleged sexual assault would tend to rebut such evidence.

(2) Sexual Behavior Involving Alleged Victim and Accused [§173]

The accused may offer evidence of specific instances of sexual behavior between the accused and the alleged victim **to prove consent**. Thus, evidence that the accused and the alleged victim had previously had sexual relations would be admissible to prove that the alleged act of sexual assault was really consensual. Note that this use of such evidence also does not require any inference about the alleged victim's character. The inference of consent is drawn instead from the nature of the relationship between the alleged victim and the accused. The prosecution may also offer evidence of specific instances of sexual behavior between the alleged victim and the accused to the extent such evidence is admissible as other bad acts evidence. See § 190.

(3) When Constitutionally Required [§174]

Evidence of other sexual behavior or predisposition is admissible when exclusion would violate the accused's constitutional **right to confrontation** or **due process**.

IMPORTANT CASE: *OLDEN V. KENTUCKY*, 488 U.S. 227 (1988).

Olden, a black man, was charged with raping Matthews, a white woman. Matthews testified that she met Olden at a bar. She left the bar with Olden and his friend Harris to go looking for a friend. She testified that Olden then threatened her with a knife and, with Harris's assistance, raped her. Olden sought to elicit the fact that Matthews was then living with

Russell, a black man. Olden's defense was that he and Matthews had consensual sex and that Matthews had concocted the rape story to protect her relationship with Russell, who had seen her emerge from Harris's car and would have otherwise been suspicious of her. The trial court excluded the evidence because it felt that the jury would be prejudiced if it learned that the complainant was involved in an interracial relationship. The Supreme Court reversed. It held that the jury might have received a different impression of Matthews's credibility had Olden been permitted to pursue his proposed line of cross-examination and demonstrate that Matthews had a motive to falsely accuse him of rape.

c. **Civil Cases: Generally [§175]**
The general rule that ordinarily proscribes in criminal cases evidence of an alleged victim's other sexual behavior or sexual predisposition also applies in civil cases involving alleged sexual misconduct. [FRE 412(a).] This includes actions for sexual battery and sexual harassment.

d. **Civil Cases: Exceptions [§176]**
FRE 412(b) allows such evidence to be admitted if it (a) is **otherwise admissible** under the rules (e.g., it does not consist of inadmissible hearsay) and (b) a strict **balancing test** is met. The probative value of the evidence must **substantially** outweigh the danger of unfair prejudice to any party and the danger of harm to any victim. Evidence of an alleged victim's reputation is admissible only if it has been placed in controversy by the alleged victim.

e. **Procedures: Civil and Criminal Cases [§177]**
A party that wishes to offer such evidence must file a **written motion** at least **fourteen days prior to trial**, unless the court for good cause relaxes the time limit. The motion must be served on all parties and must specifically describe the proffered evidence and the purpose for which it is being offered. The alleged victim (or the victim's guardian or representative) must also be notified. The court may not admit such evidence without first conducting an **in camera**

hearing. The parties and alleged victim must be afforded the right to attend and be heard at the hearing.

14. **Fourth Exception: Sexual Assault and Child Molestation Cases [§ 178]**

    FRE 413-415 effectively create another exception to the general rule excluding character evidence when offered to prove conduct. These rules apply in **criminal cases** in which the defendant is charged with **sexual assault or child molestation** or in **civil cases** in which a damage claim is **predicated on the commission of a sexual assault or act of child molestation**.

    a. **Criminal Cases [§ 179]**

       FRE 413-414 govern the criminal cases. They provide that the prosecution may offer evidence that the defendant has committed other such offenses (that is, **other acts of sexual assault or child molestation** respectively) for its bearing on any relevant matter. This means the evidence may be offered to prove defendant's character so that the jury may infer the defendant acted in conformity with his character on the particular occasion and committed the charged act.

    b. **Civil Cases [180]**

       Similarly, FRE 415 governs the admission of such evidence in civil cases. It allows evidence that a party committed **other acts of sexual assault or child molestation** for its bearing on any relevant matter, including as evidence of the party's character.

    c. **Notice Requirement [181]**

       If a party intends to introduce evidence under FRE 413-415, it must provide to its opponent the statements of its witnesses or a summary of the substance of their expected testimony at least **fifteen days prior to trial**. The court may, for good cause, allow disclosure at a later date.

SUMMARY CHART OF CHARACTER EVIDENCE UNDER FRE

S = Specific acts; R = Repudiation; O = Opinion

	1. WHAT	2. MAY	3. HOW
Prosecutor/ Plaintiff	Element of claim/ defense	Yes	S,R,O
	Conduct in Conformity	No	N/A
	Exception: sexual assault/ child molestation	Yes	S
Criminal defendant/ civil defendant	Element of claim/ defense	Yes	S,R,O
Criminal defendant only	Conduct in Conformity — Own character	Yes	R,O
	Conduct in Conformity — Victim's Character	Yes *	R,O
Prosecutor — rebuttal	Conduct in Conformity — Defendant's character	Yes +	R,O #
	Conduct in Conformity — Victim's character	Yes	R,O

*   Except character of rape victim.

\+   To rebut evidence presented by accused of own good character and of alleged victim's bad character.

\#   Prosecution may also cross-examine defendant's reputation witnesses with "Have you heard" questions; opinion witnesses with "Do you know" questions.

M. Habit and Routine Practice Evidence [§182]

The law of evidence distinguishes between a person's character or character traits and a person's habits. Evidence of a person's habit is more probative of his conduct on a particular occasion than is character evidence. Thus, evidence that a person always ran a particular stop sign is good evidence that the person ran that stop sign on the occasion in question, although evidence that he is a "careless" driver is not. Therefore, FRE 406 specifies that evidence of a person's **habit** is relevant to prove that the **person acted in accordance with that habit on a particular occasion.**

1.   **Habit and Character Evidence Distinguished [§183]**
     Habit is typically regarded as a **regular response to a repeated, specific situation**. In contrast, character relates to a generalized description of dispositions or traits such as prudence, honesty, or cautiousness. Usually, the distinction is an easy one to draw: it is the difference, for example, between always locking a particular gate in the front of one's house (a habit) and being "safety-conscious" (a character trait). A habit may be observed whereas a character trait is a matter of opinion.

2.   **Habit and Non-Habit Distinguished [§184]**
     The distinction between habit and character is relatively clear. But habit must also be distinguished from a variety of conduct that a person might engage in that does not rise to the level of habit. Courts look especially at **two factors** in determining whether a person's conduct constitutes a habit: (1) the **specificity** of the conduct and (2) how **volitional** it is.

     a.   **Specificity [§185]**
          The more particularized the conduct, the more likely it will qualify as habit. Evidence that a person has two martinis every weekday evening at a particular bar is more likely to be viewed as habit than is evidence that a person is a frequent drinker who likes martinis.

     b.   **Volitional Nature of the Conduct [§186]**
          The more the person seems to engage in the conduct without a good deal of conscious thought, the more likely it is to be viewed as habit. Evidence that a person routinely bounded up a particular staircase two steps at a time or always turned on a directional signal before turning easily qualifies as habit. Conduct that seems more the product of conscious thought is less likely to qualify as habit, although it is not per se

disqualified. In one case, for example, evidence that a dentist regularly informed patients of the potential risks associated with molar extractions was held to constitute a habit.

3.   Proof of Habit [§187]

Both opinion testimony and evidence of specific instances of conduct may be used to prove habit. A party seeking to prove the existence of a habit must demonstrate that the conduct occurs **frequently** and with **sufficient regularity**. That a person has engaged in a particular conduct one hundred times is, by itself, insufficient to prove habit. That number must be compared to the number of opportunities the person had to engage in the conduct. A habit does not exist if the person had one thousand opportunities to engage in the conduct and did so only one hundred times.

4.   Corroboration and Necessity Limitations Abandoned [§188]

FRE 406 states that habit evidence is admissible "whether corroborated or not and regardless of the presence of eyewitnesses." The quoted language repudiates a restriction many jurisdictions formerly placed on habit evidence. At common law, such evidence had been limited to situations where the use of such evidence was necessitated by the absence of eyewitnesses, or where there was corroboration of the "habit" (routine practice) of a business.

5.   Routine Practice [§189]

The "habit" of an organization is referred to as its **custom** or **routine practice** and is admissible to prove that the organization acted in conformity with its routine practice on the occasion in question.

EXAMPLE

Evidence that a business date-stamps incoming mail within three hours of receipt will be admissible to prove that a letter stamped "March 2" was received on March 2.

N. Other Crimes, Wrongs, or Acts Evidence Admissible For Non-Character Purposes [§190]

Evidence of a person's character ordinarily is inadmissible if offered to prove that the person acted in conformity with his character on a particular occasion. Thus, evidence that a person lied on many previous occasions may not be offered to prove his dishonest nature from which the factfinder is to infer that he committed perjury on the occasion in question. But such evidence may be admissible if it is **offered to prove something other than character from which conduct on a particular occasion is to be inferred**. FRE 404(b) codifies this principle. The first sentence of FRE 404(b) restates the general rule prohibiting character evidence to prove conforming conduct. The second sentence provides, however, that evidence of "other crimes, wrongs or acts" may be admissible if offered for another purpose. It then lists a number of such permissible purposes, which are discussed in §§192-199 below.

1. Rationale [§191]

Remember that evidence of a person's character is ordinarily excluded because its slight probative value as proof of conduct on a specific occasion is outweighed by the danger of unfair prejudice it presents. When evidence of other acts is offered **to prove something other than character**, however, we can no longer say categorically that the balancing of probative and prejudicial value tilts towards exclusion. However, since the danger still exists that the jury may take the evidence as bearing on character, such evidence must be treated with some care.

2. "MIAMI COP" [§192]

Purposes for which other crimes, wrongs, or acts evidence (sometimes referred to as "extrinsic offense" evidence) may be offered may be remembered by the mnemonic device "Miami Cop." **M**otive; **I**dentity; **A**bsence of **M**istake or accident; **I**ntent; **C**ommon plan or scheme; **O**pportunity; **P**reparation. Although this is not an exclusive list, it does cover most of the uses of other crimes evidence.

a. Motive [§193]

If some act by the defendant tends to show that he had a motive for committing the crime in question, evidence of the act is admissible.

EXAMPLE

In Defendant's trial for the murder of Victim, Prosecutor offers evidence that Victim was an eyewitness to another murder committed by Defendant. This is admissible to prove that Defendant had a motive to kill Victim.

b. Identity [§194]

Where the identity of the person who committed the crime is an issue, evidence may be offered that the defendant committed other similar crimes using the same distinctive **modus operandi** as that used by the perpetrator of the charged crime. The non-character theory is that it is likely that the charged and uncharged crimes—all committed in the same distinctive way—were committed by the same person. Therefore, if the prosecution can show that the defendant committed the other crimes, the jury may reasonably infer that the defendant is the person who committed the charged crime. Put another way, the distinctive method of committing these crimes is like the perpetrator's signature or calling card.

EXAMPLE: EVIDENCE ADMISSIBLE

Defendant is charged with sexually assaulting Victim. Victim testifies that she is unable to identify her assailant because he wore a purple and green ski mask and quickly tied a red bandana around her eyes. Prosecutor calls Witness who testifies that she was sexually assaulted a few days after Victim by a man wearing a purple and green ski mask who tied a red bandana around her eyes, but that she was nevertheless able to get a glance at her assailant and it was Defendant. This is admissible to prove that Defendant was Victim's assailant.

EXAMPLE: EVIDENCE INADMISSIBLE

Defendant is on trial for bank robbery in Cleveland. A witness testifies that the bank robber wore a ski mask and carried a gun, but is unable to identify Defendant as the robber. Prosecution offers proof that, wearing a ski mask and carrying a gun, Defendant robbed a bank in Cincinnati several months earlier. Without further evidence about the distinctiveness of the ski mask or gun, a court is likely to exclude such evidence. The use of a ski mask and gun is too common to bank robberies to qualify as a distinctive modus operandi.

c. Absence of Mistake or Accident [§195]

Evidence of a person's other crimes, wrongs, or acts may tend to prove that the person possessed knowledge of what he was doing or of the consequences of his act.

EXAMPLE

Defendant, charged with possession of marijuana, claims that he mistakenly believed the substance he possessed was oregano. To rebut, Prosecutor offers to prove that Defendant was convicted of marijuana possession three years ago. This is admissible.

d. Intent [§196]

Other crimes, wrongs and bad acts are often used to prove intent, but this is the area where the law is probably most confusing. In some instances, it is easy to see how the other crimes evidence is relevant for some inference other than the person's character. For example, other crimes evidence can be used to prove knowledge, from which intent may then be inferred.

EXAMPLE

Defendant is on trial for murdering Victim by poison. Defendant claims that he thought that the pill he gave Victim would merely render her unconscious for a few hours and that he did not intend to kill her. Prosecution offers evidence that Defendant previously killed three people by giving them the same kind of pill. This is admissible to prove that Defendant knew about the pill's lethal nature and, therefore, that Defendant intended to kill Victim.

Other crimes evidence is also frequently used when little or no dispute exists about the physical elements of the crime, but the accused claims a lack of criminal intent.

EXAMPLE

Defendant is arrested while leaving a department store with a watch in his coat pocket. At trial, he admits possessing the watch but claims that he did not intend to steal it. He contends that, unbeknownst to him, it fell into his pocket. The prosecution may be permitted to offer evidence that Defendant has been caught shoplifting four times in the past two years.

> Note that the other crimes evidence in this example seems to prove the defendant's guilt only through an inference about his character. Evidence that he has previously been caught shoplifting four times tends to prove he intended to steal the watch only because the jury may infer from the shoplifting incidents that defendant is the type of person who steals (i.e., that he is dishonest) and that he acted in accordance with his dishonest character on this particular occasion. Despite this, courts routinely admit other crimes evidence in such situations. The probative value of the evidence, combined with the difficulty of otherwise proving the defendant's state of mind, pushes courts to admit such evidence. Courts are less inclined to admit this type of evidence, however, where intent does not appear to be an issue.

EXAMPLE

Defendant is tried for the murder of Victim. He raises an alibi defense. The prosecution will not be permitted to offer evidence that Defendant has committed murder on two other occasions to prove that he intended to kill Victim. Unlike the defendant in the previous example (who conceded he had the watch but claimed he lacked the requisite intent to steal), Defendant here denies any involvement whatsoever with the crime. He does not claim that whoever killed Victim lacked the intent to kill; he simply claims that he was not the killer.

e. Common Plan or Scheme [§197]

The prosecution may offer evidence that the defendant committed another crime, wrong, or act as part of a plan or scheme to commit the charged act.

EXAMPLE

Defendant is charged with killing his mother. The prosecutor offers evidence that Defendant previously killed everyone named in his mother's will (other than himself) as evidence of his scheme to inherit all his mother's wealth. This is admissible.

f. Opportunity [§198]

Evidence of other crimes, wrongs, or acts may be used to prove the defendant had access to the scene of the crime, or the knowledge or capacity to commit the charged crime.

EXAMPLE

In Defendant's prosecution for theft by hacking into the victim's computer despite the existence of a sophisticated firewall, Prosecutor may offer evidence that Defendant had committed other such thefts that required him to neutralize sophisticated firewalls.

g. Preparation [§199]

As with common scheme or plan, evidence of other crimes, wrongs, or acts may be proved to show defendant's preparation for the charged crime.

EXAMPLE

Defendant is charged with murdering elderly hospital patients by injecting them with morphine. Evidence that Defendant stole morphine from the hospital pharmacy may be offered to prove his guilt.

3. "Exceptions" [§200]

Although these uses of other crimes evidence are often referred to as "exceptions" to the general rule prohibiting character evidence, they typically are not. These uses of other crimes evidence do not violate the character rule because the evidence is **not being introduced** for the forbidden purpose, that is, **as evidence of character**

from which conduct is to be inferred. It is being offered as proof of guilt that does not require an inference to be made about the defendant's character.

As discussed under "Intent" above, however, sometimes other crimes evidence is probative only because an inference is being drawn about the defendant's character. The shoplifting hypothetical above is one such example. When courts allow other crimes evidence to be used in this way, they are essentially creating an exception to the general rule against using character evidence to prove conforming character. The courts, however, rarely admit this. Typically they restate the general rule and then add that FRE 404(b) authorizes the admission of other crimes evidence to prove motive, identity, absence of mistake, intent, etc.

This most commonly happens when other crimes evidence is offered to prove **intent**. But it happens in many other instances as well, particularly when the other crimes evidence seems especially compelling. For example, in one case the defendant was charged with attempting to defraud an insurer. The defendant attempted to collect the insurance on his business partner's life after he allegedly killed her by setting their tavern on fire. The court allowed the prosecution to offer evidence that the defendant had previously murdered his wife and collected on her life insurance policy. No distinctive modus operandi was involved that would have justified admitting the evidence to prove identity. Although the court denied it, the evidence was probative because of the inference the jury could draw about defendant's character. This is why the admissibility of other crimes evidence remains such a thorny topic.

4. **Procedural Considerations [§201]**
   Because other crimes evidence may be highly prejudicial to the defendant, certain procedural considerations must be observed.

   a. **Quantum of Proof Required [§202]**
      Other crimes, wrongs, or acts evidence is not restricted to acts for which the defendant has previously been arrested or convicted. Jurisdictions vary as to the strength of the proof necessary to

establish that the defendant committed the other crime, wrong, or act. Some states require the prosecution to produce **clear and convincing** evidence that the defendant had committed the other crime. Others adhere to **a preponderance of the evidence** standard. The United States Supreme Court has adopted a still lower standard for federal courts: whether there is **sufficient evidence for a reasonable juror to find** that the defendant committed the other crime.

IMPORTANT CASE: *HUDDLESTON V. UNITED STATES*, 485 U.S. 681 (1988).

Huddleston was charged with the knowing possession and sale of stolen video cassette tapes. There was no dispute that the tapes were stolen; the only question was whether Huddleston knew that they were stolen. To prove that he did, the prosecution introduced evidence of Huddleston's involvement in a series of sales of allegedly stolen televisions and appliances. On appeal, Huddleston argued that the evidence regarding the sales of the television sets should not have been admitted because the prosecution failed to prove that the sets had been stolen. He argued that other crimes evidence should not be admissible unless the court finds by a preponderance of the evidence that the defendant committed the other crime. The Supreme Court rejected this argument. Admissibility of other crimes evidence is a question of conditional relevancy falling under Rule 104(b). All the trial court should do is determine, after considering all the evidence, whether the jury could reasonably find that the defendant had committed the other crime. Given the low price at which Huddleston offered to sell the televisions, the large quantity he offered for sale, his inability to produce a bill of sale, and his involvement in the sale of other stolen appliances, the jury could reasonably have found that the televisions had been stolen. Thus, the evidence was properly admitted. Any danger that this evidence would be unfairly prejudicial to Huddleston should have been raised by a Rule 403 objection that its probative value was substantially outweighed by the danger of unfair prejudice.

b. Discretionary Exclusion [§203]

Courts may exclude other crimes evidence on the ground that the danger of unfair prejudice substantially outweighs its probative value.

c. Stipulation by Defendant [§204]

One way a defendant might try to alter the balance between probative value and unfair prejudice is by offering to stipulate to the element of the crime that the other crimes evidence would be offered to prove. For example, a defendant might claim that he was not the person who committed the charged crime, but offer to stipulate that whoever did it had the required intent. The defendant would then argue that, having removed the issue of intent from the case, other crimes evidence bearing on intent would no longer have probative value. The Supreme Court has **rejected this stratagem**. (See Important Case: *Old Chief v. United States*, above.) The basic message of *Old Chief* is that the prosecution has the right to prove its case in the manner it sees fit. Except in unusual circumstance (such as those presented by the facts of *Old Chief* itself), a defendant cannot render probative evidence inadmissible by attempting to stipulate an issue out of the case.

d. Notice [§205]

Under FRE 404(b), in a criminal case, **upon request by the accused**, the prosecution must provide **reasonable notice** of the general nature of any other crimes evidence it intends to introduce at trial for any purpose. This notice requirement, however, does not apply to offenses that are inextricably intertwined with the charged offense (e.g., evidence that the accused, charged with bank robbery, commandeered a car to make his getaway).

e. Acquittal [§206]

Evidence of another crime may be offered by the prosecution even if the defendant has already been tried and acquitted for that crime. Evidentiary use of the other crime does not offend the Double Jeopardy Clause. *Dowling v. United States*, 493 U.S. 342 (1990).

IV. Hearsay

A. Hearsay [§207]

Hearsay is probably the most important topic in an evidence course. Certainly, it is one of the most confusing. The basic rule concerning hearsay can be stated simply: Hearsay evidence is inadmissible unless it falls within an exception to the hearsay rule. Therefore, it is crucial to understand (a) what constitutes hearsay, and (b) what comprises the exceptions. This Part deals with the first of these problems: what constitutes hearsay. Part V covers the hearsay exceptions.

Often it is relatively easy to tell whether a particular statement is hearsay; sometimes it is quite difficult. Therefore, the **analysis** is broken down into **two sub parts**. The **first** sub part deals with **basic hearsay** problems. These account for most of the hearsay you are likely to encounter in practice. The **second** sub part deals with **more sophisticated** (complex, bizarre) hearsay problems.

1. Hearsay Defined [§208]

The federal rules define hearsay as: **"A statement, other than one made by the declarant while testifying at the trial or hearing, offered in evidence for the truth of the matter asserted."** [FRE 801(c).] As definitions go, this is not very helpful; in fact, it can be downright misleading at times.

2. The Hearsay Problem [§209]

Whenever a witness testifies at trial, the witness is under oath and can be cross-examined by adverse parties. The witness's credibility can thus be tested, and the jury can decide whether or not to believe the witness's story. Suppose Witness testifies: "John killed Victim." The probative value of that testimony depends upon Witness's **sincerity** (is she lying?), **communicative ability** (does she really mean that John killed Victim?), **perception** (did she accurately observe that John killed Victim?), and **memory** (does she really remember what happened?). John's lawyer can cross-examine Witness in an effort to show that she is deficient in one or more of these respects (i.e., she's lying, near-sighted, has a terrible memory or an even poorer command of the English language).

But suppose Witness testifies: "My friend [who we'll call Declarant] told me John killed Victim." The cross-examiner's job becomes harder. He can cross-examine Witness to test whether Declarant really made that statement to her. But the probative value of the statement ultimately depends on Declarant's credibility — on Declarant's sincerity, communicative ability, perception and memory — and Declarant is not there to be cross-examined. Hearsay problems thus arise **when a witness testifies to an out-of-court statement and the probative value of the statement depends on the credibility of the person who made the out-of-court statement.**

3. **Basic Hearsay: Three-Step Analysis [§210]**
   Most hearsay problems can be answered successfully if you follow these three steps.
   (1) Is there an out-of-court statement? If so,
   (2) What is the statement being offered to prove?
   (3) Does its probative value depend on the credibility of the declarant?

4. **Step One: Is There an Out-of-Court Statement? [§211]**
   A statement may be (a) **oral** or (b) **written**, or (c) it may take the form of **conduct intended as a substitute for words**.

   EXAMPLES
   Witness testifies: (a) "My friend Declarant told me, 'John killed Victim.'" (b) "I received a letter from Declarant that says 'John killed Victim.'" (c) "I asked Declarant whether he knew who killed Victim and he nodded and pointed at a picture of John." In each of these examples, Witness is testifying (in court) to an out-of-court statement made by Declarant.

   a. **Articulating the Statement [§212]**
      In many cases, the statement of the declarant is explicit (e.g., it is placed in quotation marks). In other cases, however, the declarant's statement is masked in a paraphrase and you must try to figure out exactly what the declarant said.

EXAMPLE
Witness testifies: "Denny complained of headaches."
Witness can be cross-examined to be sure that Denny
really complained. Denny, however, is the declarant and it
is his statement that concerns us for hearsay purposes.
Looking at the evidence, it appears that Denny actually
said something like, "My head hurts," or "I have a
headache." That is Denny's out-of-court statement.

5. **Step Two: What is the Statement Being Offered to
   Prove? [§213]**
   This is easy, but crucial. An exam question will either tell
   you what the statement is being offered to prove, or it will
   be apparent from the context.

6. **Step Three: Does the Probative Value of the
   Statement Depend on the Declarant's Credibility?
   [§214]**
   This is really another way of asking whether the statement
   is being offered for the truth of the matter asserted. **If all
   we care about is whether the statement was made by
   the declarant (i.e., we don't care whether the
   declarant was lying or mistaken), IT IS NOT
   HEARSAY. PERIOD. GO NO FURTHER.**
   Remember, not all out-of-court statements are hearsay. If,
   however, we do care about the declarant's credibility (i.e.,
   the probative value of the statement depends on whether
   the declarant was lying or mistaken when he made the
   statement), it is hearsay — subject to the qualifications we
   will study concerning More Sophisticated Hearsay. See
   §223.

B. **Not All Out-of-Court Statements Are Hearsay [§215]**
   If an out-of-court statement is relevant simply because it was
   made (i.e., all we care about is whether the witness who is
   relating the out-of-court statement is accurate when he relates
   the statement), it is not hearsay. There are **several common
   situations** in which this is the case. You do not need to
   memorize these. They all have one thing in common: **the out-
   of-court statement derives its probative value from the
   fact that it was made, not from the credibility of the
   declarant.**

1. **Effect of Statement on Listener [§216]**

    A statement is not hearsay if its importance derives from the effect it had on a person who heard it.

EXAMPLE

Plaintiff sues Defendant, claiming that Defendant maliciously fired him. Plaintiff calls Witness to testify, "I heard Police Chief tell Defendant that Plaintiff had been caught embezzling from his previous employer." This is not hearsay. The probative value of this statement does not depend on the declarant's (Police Chief's) credibility (i.e., whether Plaintiff had actually been caught embezzling). Rather, the mere fact that this statement was made to Defendant tends to prove he was acting in good faith when he fired Plaintiff.

EXAMPLE

Defendant is on trial for murder. He claims he shot Victim because he feared that Victim was about to shoot him. He testifies, "A few minutes before I shot Victim, Friend told me that Victim had a gun and was looking for me so he could kill me." This is not hearsay. The probative value of the statement does not depend on the declarant's (Friend's) credibility (i.e., whether Victim actually had a gun and was looking to kill Defendant). Rather, if Friend said this to Defendant (and Defendant can be cross-examined about that), it would tend to prove that Defendant reasonably feared that Victim was about to shoot him.

2. **State of Mind of Declarant [§217]**

    If the state of mind of a declarant is relevant to the case, a statement made by him may be circumstantial evidence of his state of mind, regardless of its truth.

EXAMPLE

The issue in a case is whether Defendant and Friend were on good terms. Witness testifies that he heard Friend say to several people, "Defendant is a compulsive liar. You can't believe a word he says." This is not hearsay. This statement by Friend is circumstantial evidence of Friend's negative attitude toward Defendant. Whether Defendant is a liar or cannot be believed is of no consequence. If Friend had been on good terms with Defendant, he would not go around making such statements.

3. Legally Operative Facts [§218]

The substantive law imbues some statements with legal significance. That is, the fact that the declarant made such a statement has legal significance, regardless of whether the declarant was lying or mistaken. For example, **transactional words**, such as words of contract (e.g., offers, rejections, acceptances, terms), statements of donative intent accompanying the delivery of a "gift" (e.g., "I want you to have this car"), and statements indicating open or hostile possession (as proof of adverse possession) are not hearsay. Similarly, **statements that are themselves actionable**, such as words of libel or slander, publicly uttered obscenities, and copyrighted passages, are not hearsay. These are also referred to as **verbal acts, operative utterances,** or words of **independent legal significance.**

EXAMPLE

To prove that Defendant guaranteed payment on a loan made to his son, Plaintiff testifies that Defendant told him, "If you make this loan to my son, I will guarantee payment if he defaults." This is not hearsay. The probative value of this statement flows from the fact that Defendant made it. By making such a statement, Defendant created for himself a legal obligation to pay his son's debt if his son defaulted.

EXAMPLE

Plaintiff sues Defendant for slander. Plaintiff calls Witness to testify that she heard Defendant say, "Plaintiff is a liar and a thief. He stole more than $10,000 from me." This is not hearsay. It is being offered only to prove that Defendant uttered these words, which constitute the slander against Plaintiff. (Plaintiff is obviously not offering this out-of-court statement to prove that he is a liar and a thief; he's claiming that the statement defamed him.)

4. Impeachment and Rehabilitation [§219]

The prior statements of a witness may be offered to impeach the witness's credibility (by showing he has previously told a different story) or to rehabilitate him (by showing he has told the same story before). In both instances, the prior out-of-court statements of the witness are not being offered for their truth and are not hearsay.

There are, however, **special rules** dealing with the use of such prior statements. These are discussed at §376 et seq., §475 et seq., and §521.

EXAMPLE

Witness testifies that he saw Defendant shoot Victim. On cross-examination, defense counsel asks, "Right after the shooting, didn't you tell the police that it was Jones, not Defendant, who shot Victim." This is not hearsay. The statement is being offered merely to show that Witness (who is also the declarant here) has told a different story about the same event and that, as someone who changes his story, he lacks credibility. The probative value of the statement thus flows from the fact that the statement was made, and does not depend on a judgment about whether Witness was being truthful when he made the statement to the police.

C. Definition: "Out of Court." [§220]

Any statement other than one made by a witness while testifying at the **present** hearing is an "out of court" statement. "Out of court" means out of **this** court. Thus, a statement made at a previous court hearing is an "out-of-court" statement. The term "extrajudicial statement" is synonymous with "out-of-court statement."

D. Definition: "Declarant." [§221]

The declarant is the person who made the out-of-court statement. **A witness and declarant may be the same person.** With a few exceptions discussed later, it makes no difference whether a witness is relating her own or some other person's out-of-court statements. The hearsay analysis is the same for both. Remember, hearsay is defined as a statement, "other than one made by the declarant while testifying at trial" offered for the truth of the matter asserted. You may think that it doesn't make a lot of sense to treat a witness's own out-of-court statements as hearsay. After all, the witness can be cross-examined about them. You're right — it doesn't make a lot of sense. But, with a few exceptions discussed later, that's the rule.

1. Declarant Must Be a Person [§222]

When a witness testifies that a bloodhound sniffed a hat dropped at the scene of a crime, then sniffed several men in a line-up and barked vigorously at the defendant, the witness is testifying to the dog's out-of-court "statement." Similarly, when a police officer testifies that he pointed his radar gun at defendant's car and the radar gun flashed "77 mph," he is testifying to the radar gun's out-of-court "statement." But neither is hearsay. **The hearsay rule reaches only statements made by persons**. This makes sense because it would do no good to call the bloodhound or radar gun into court for cross-examination. Before testimony about the barking may be introduced, however, evidence will have to be presented regarding the bloodhound's competence to track scents and his handler's competence in interpreting the dog's reactions. In the case of the radar gun, evidence will have to be presented that the gun was in good working order and was operated properly. But these are not hearsay problems.

EXAMPLES

(1) To prove that Defendant was driving while intoxicated the night of May 1, Plaintiff calls Witness to testify, "I saw Defendant down six double scotches and drive off that night."

Not hearsay. There is no out-of-court statement. Witness is testifying in court as to her out-of-court observations, not as to any out-of-court statement.

(2) To prove that Defendant was driving while intoxicated the night of May 1, Plaintiff calls Wife to testify, "My husband told me he saw Defendant down six double scotches and drive off that night."

Hearsay. Husband's out-of-court statement to Wife is being offered to prove that Defendant was drunk on the night in question and the probative value of Husband's statement depends on his credibility (i.e., we care about whether he was mistaken or lying when he made the statement to his wife).

(3) To prove that Brother survived Sister, Witness testifies, "I saw the crash in which they were killed. I rushed over, saw that Sister was dead and then heard Brother say, 'I am alive.'"

Not hearsay. Although Brother made the out-of-court statement, "I am alive," this is not hearsay because the probative value of the statement flows from the fact that Brother spoke (hence was alive) after Sister died. The content of what he said is unimportant. The statement would have been just as probative if Brother had said, "I am dead." This hypo illustrates why the definition of hearsay may be quite misleading. Brother's statement — "I am alive" — appears to be offered for the truth of the matter asserted (i.e., that Brother was still alive). However, it is not hearsay because the probative value of the statement derives solely from the fact that it was made and does not depend on Brother's credibility.

(4) To prove the existence of an oral contract between Plaintiff and Defendant, Witness testifies, "I heard Defendant say to Plaintiff, 'I will sell you this bike for $10.'"

Not hearsay. Defendant's statement constitutes an offer and therefore qualifies as a legally operative fact.

(5) To prove that there was a puddle in the aisle of defendant supermarket, Witness testifies, "I heard Customer tell the store manager that she almost slipped in a puddle on Aisle 6."

Hearsay. Because the statement is offered to prove there was a puddle, the probative value of Customer's out-of-court statement depends on her (Customer's) credibility.

(6) To prove that the store manager had been put on notice that there was a puddle in the aisle, Witness testifies, "I heard Customer tell the store manager that she almost slipped in a puddle on Aisle 6."

Not hearsay. Now this statement is offered to show its effect on the listener (store manager). Customer's statement puts him on notice, even if it turns out to be false.

(7) To prove Defendant committed a crime, Police Officer testifies that Victim pointed out Defendant in a line-up.

Hearsay. Victim's statement is conduct intended as a substitute for words, the probative value of which clearly depends on whether Victim is mistaken or lying. In other words, it is an out-of-court statement (conduct) offered to show that

Defendant was the one who committed a crime, the truth of which depends on Victim's sincerity, perception, and memory.

(8) To prove that Defendant ran a red light, Witness testifies, "I told my wife I saw Defendant run the light."

Hearsay. The witness is relating his own out-of-court statement and so is both the declarant and the witness. But the fact that he is under oath and available for cross-examination does not change the hearsay analysis. It is still an out-of-court statement offered to prove the truth of his out-of-court statement to his wife. Note that there would be no hearsay problem had he simply testified, "I saw Defendant run the light."

E. More Sophisticated Hearsay Problems [§223]

The three-step analysis outlined above will always identify statements that clearly are **not hearsay**. If the probative value of the statement does not depend on the declarant's credibility, it is not hearsay. Unfortunately, the converse is not always true. **A statement whose probative value does depend on the declarant's credibility is usually, but not invariably, hearsay.** Whether such a statement is considered hearsay depends on the precise way in which the jurisdiction defines hearsay. The common law defined hearsay broadly; the federal rules (and many state codes) define it more narrowly.

We can see how the common law and federal rules definitions of hearsay differ by categorizing various kinds of out-of-court statements or conduct. **In each of the five categories below, the probative value of the declarant's out-of-court statement or conduct depends on the declarant's credibility.** Under the common-law definition of hearsay, all five categories of statements or conduct are hearsay. Under the federal rules (and many state codes), however, only the first two are hearsay; statements or conduct that fall in Categories 3, 4, and 5 are not included within the definition of hearsay.

1. Category 1: Explicit Verbal Assertions [§224]

Verbal statements (oral or written) that assert directly what they are introduced to prove

EXAMPLE

To prove that it was raining, Witness testifies that Declarant said, "It is raining outside."

2.   **Category 2: Non-Verbal Conduct Intended as an Assertion [§225]**
     When a person chooses to communicate by a sign or gesture rather than a verbal statement and the act is offered as evidence of the fact that the person intended to communicate.

EXAMPLE

To prove that it was raining, W testifies, "I asked Declarant what the weather was like and he made a gesture as if he were opening an umbrella."

3.   **Category 3: Non-Verbal Conduct Not Intended as an Assertion [§226]**
     People often act with no intent to communicate a message. Nevertheless, if an act is offered as evidence that the actor believed something and that his belief was accurate, its probative value depends on his credibility.

EXAMPLE

To prove that it was raining, Witness testifies, "I saw Declarant open up his umbrella as he stepped out into the street." This tends to prove it was raining only if we believe that Declarant thought it was raining and was accurate in that belief.

4.   **Category 4: Non-Assertive Verbal Conduct [§227]**
     The declarant uses words but does not intend to make an assertion. Nevertheless, his statement is offered as evidence of something implicit in the statement.

EXAMPLE

To prove that it was raining, Witness testifies, "Just before Declarant left he asked, 'Does anybody have an umbrella I can borrow?'" Although Declarant did not intend to assert it was raining, we may infer from his question that it was raining. But the probative value of this inference flows from his belief that it was raining and the accuracy of that belief.

5. Category 5: Verbal Assertions Used Inferentially [§228]

Although the declarant makes a verbal assertion, his statement is offered to prove something implicit in his statement rather than the truth of the statement itself.

EXAMPLE

To prove it was raining, Witness testifies, "Just before Declarant left he said, 'Darn it. I forgot my umbrella.'" This statement is not being offered to prove he forgot his umbrella, but for the unspoken, implicit statement, "it's raining."

6. Common-Law View [§229]

It is frequently said that the common-law view was that **hearsay comprised all five of the above categories**. This statement is usually based on a famous English case, *Wright v. Tatham*, 5 C. & F. 670 (1838). In that case, the court ruled that letters written to a testator were hearsay if offered to prove the testator's mental competency. None of the letter writers (the declarants) asserted that the testator was competent. Instead, the letters (which contained assertions about the weather, thanks for the testator's hospitality, etc.) were offered to show that the letter writers believed the testator was competent (why else would they write such letters to him?) and for the further inference that the letter writers' belief was accurate. Because the probative value of the letters ultimately depended on the accuracy of the letter writers' belief, the court held that they constituted hearsay.

One of the opinions (by Baron Parke) includes what is now the **famous sea-captain hypothetical**. Suppose, to prove a boat's seaworthiness, a party offered evidence that a sea captain inspected the boat and then took his family sailing in it. This would be an example of category 3 above. It is non-verbal conduct, and the sea captain did not intend it as an assertion. He was not trying to communicate his belief that the boat was seaworthy; he only wanted to go sailing with his family. But if offered as proof that the boat was seaworthy, this evidence is probative only if the factfinder infers that the sea captain believed the boat was seaworthy and that his belief was accurate. Baron Parke said this is hearsay. This is the basis of the common-law view that hearsay includes all five categories; that is, all instances in which the probative value of the declarant's out-of-court statement (or actor's out-of-court conduct) depends on the declarant or actor's credibility.

7. **Federal Rules [§230]**

The federal rules take a **narrower view** of hearsay. Rule 801 states that **non-verbal conduct not intended as an assertion** is not a "statement" and thus is **not hearsay**. This **eliminates Category 3** from the definition of hearsay. Moreover, since Rule 801 defines hearsay as a "statement . . . offered for the truth of the matter asserted," **if there is no assertion (Category 4) or a statement is being offered to prove something other than what was asserted (Category 5), it is not hearsay**.

The decision to draft the federal rules in this way and thus to limit the scope of the hearsay rule was quite deliberate. The drafters' view was that **when someone acts (non-verbal conduct) without intending to make an assertion (category 3), the danger of insincerity is diminished**. Someone who inspects the boat and then goes sailing with his family is more likely to be accurate about the boat's seaworthiness than someone who simply asserts, "the boat is safe." Actions speak louder than words. Although the danger of inaccuracy is not eliminated (the sea captain could be incompetent or desirous of drowning his family), it is not substantial enough to justify categorically excluding such evidence. The drafters then expressed the **same view with respect to statements falling within category 4 (non-assertive verbal conduct) and category 5 (verbal assertions used inferentially)**. In other words, the drafters' position was that the definition of hearsay should be limited to those situations where the declarant intended (by words or conduct) to assert X, and the proponent is offering the declarant's words or conduct to prove X.

IMPORTANT CASE: *UNITED STATES V. ZENNI,* 492 F.Supp. 464 (E.D.Ky. 1980).
This case illustrates that under the federal rules, some out-of-court statements whose probative value depends on the

declarant's credibility are not hearsay. Defendant was prosecuted for illegal bookmaking activities. During a legal search of his premises, government agents answered the telephone several times and heard unknown callers state directions for placing bets on various sporting events. The government offered these out-of-court statements as proof that the defendant's premises were used in betting operations. In other words, the government offered the callers' statements (such as "Put $2 to win on Paul Revere in the third at Pimlico") as proof that the callers believed the defendant ran a bookmaking operation and that their belief was correct. The court held that this was not hearsay. The callers' statements were in the form of commands or directives and were not assertions (i.e., these were Category 4 statements). Therefore, under the federal rule, they were not hearsay.

8. Problems [§231]

Unfortunately, it is not always so easy to tell whether there is an assertion (i.e., did the speaker intend to assert something) or exactly what the speaker intended to assert. For example, suppose that in response to the question, "Is defendant a bookie?" the declarant replied, "Is the Pope Catholic?" Presumably, the declarant intended this reply (non-assertive in form) as an assertion and it should be treated as hearsay. Or, to continue with popes, suppose, to prove the testator's mental incompetence, evidence is offered that testator frequently said, "I am the Pope." One could argue that it is not hearsay because it is not offered to prove the truth of what was asserted (i.e., that testator really was the Pope). If, however, you view the statement as asserting "I believe I am the Pope," it is being offered to prove the truth of the assertion. Courts (and evidence professors) are split as to whether such statements should be considered hearsay.

9. Suggested Analysis [§232]

Start with the basic three-step analysis. If you conclude that the probative value of the out-of-court statement does not depend on the declarant's credibility, it is not hearsay, regardless of whether you are working under the common law or the federal rules. Complications arise only when the probative value of the statement depends on the declarant's credibility. In that case, if you are asked whether it is hearsay under the common law, the answer is yes. If you are asked whether it is hearsay under the federal rules, you must look to see if the statement is being offered to prove what the declarant actually said or intended to communicate. If so, it is hearsay. If not, it is not hearsay.

EXAMPLES

(1) To prove that Defendant assaulted Victim, a little girl, Plaintiff offers testimony that when Victim saw Defendant in a line-up she ran to her mother and clung to her skirt.

Not hearsay under the federal rules. See Category 3. The girl did not intend by her conduct to make an assertion (i.e., to communicate "He's the one"). *Hearsay under the common law.*

(2) To prove that Defendant assaulted Victim, a little girl, Plaintiff offers testimony that when Victim saw Defendant in a line-up, she said, "Mommy, don't let that man near me."

Not hearsay under the federal rules. See Category 4. The statement is not an assertion by Victim and is not being offered for the truth of the matter asserted. *Hearsay under the common law.*

(3) To prove that Dr. Defendant checked in on Patient Plaintiff earlier in the day, Nurse testifies, "I saw Dr. Defendant and he told me, 'Patient Plaintiff is doing fine.'"

Not hearsay under the federal rules. This is a verbal assertion used inferentially. Dr. Defendant did not assert that he saw Patient Plaintiff, which is what the statement is being offered to prove. Thus, even though the probative value of Dr. Defendant's out-of-court statement depends upon his credibility (the accuracy of the implied statement "I checked in on Plaintiff"), it falls within Category 5 and is not hearsay. *Hearsay under the common law.*

F. Nonhearsay By Exemption [§233]
Recall that in the discussion of basic hearsay we saw that a witness's own out-of-court statements are considered hearsay if offered for the truth of the matter asserted. We said that this did not make a lot of sense. Consequently, some such statements have been exempted from the definition of

hearsay. Thus the federal rules and most modern codes declare that **certain types of prior statements of current witnesses are not hearsay.** In addition, **admissions by party opponents** are defined as nonhearsay. These will all be briefly mentioned here, but discussed in greater detail in later sections.

1. **Prior Statements of Witnesses [§234]**
    The prior out-of-court statement of a trial witness is not considered hearsay if the witness is **subject to cross-examination** about the particular statement and it falls into one of the three following categories.

    a. **Prior Inconsistent Statements [§235]**
        The witness's out-of-court statement is **inconsistent** with her trial testimony and the out-of-court statement was (a) given **under oath,** (b) subject to the **penalty of perjury,** (c) at some **other trial, hearing, proceeding,** or in a **deposition.** [FRE 801(d)(1)(A).] See §§379, 483.

    b. **Prior Consistent Statements [§236]**
        The witness's out-of-court statement is **consistent** with her trial testimony and is offered to **rebut a charge of recent fabrication or improper motivation or influence.** [FRE 801(d)(1)(B).] See §§380, 529.

    c. **Prior Statement of Identification [§237]**
        The witness's out-of-court statement was one of **identification of a person** made after perceiving the person. [FRE 801(d)(1)(C).] See §381.

2. **Admission by Party Opponent [§238]**
    At common law, admissions by a party opponent are considered exceptions to the hearsay rule. The federal rules and most state codes now define admissions as nonhearsay. [FRE 801(d)(2).] See §245.

G. **Multiple Hearsay [§239]**
    Multiple hearsay is sometimes referred to as "hearsay within hearsay" or "totem pole hearsay." This problem arises when

evidence contains at least two separate out-of-court statements, each of which is offered for its truth.

EXAMPLE: ORAL ASSERTIONS.

Witness testifies: "My neighbor, June, told me that her husband Ward told her that he transferred $10,000 to National Bank." Witness is the witness; there are two declarants and two out-of-court statements: (1) June is the declarant of the statement (to Witness), "Ward told me that he transferred $10,000 to National Bank." (2) Ward is the declarant of the statement (to June), "I transferred $10,000 to National Bank."

EXAMPLE: WRITING

Sometimes multiple hearsay comes in the form of a writing that incorporates an oral statement. Suppose Plaintiff offers a hospital record prepared by Dr. Feelgood which states: "Klutz says he fell off a scaffold." Again there are two declarants and two out-of-court statements: (1) Dr. Feelgood is the declarant of the statement (made in the record), "Klutz said, 'I fell off a scaffold.'" (2) Klutz is the declarant of the statement (to Dr. Feelgood), "I fell off a scaffold."

1. **Approach to Multiple Hearsay [§240]**

   In dealing with multiple out-of-court statements, you must **analyze each one separately**. First, determine whether each statement is hearsay. Thus, in the first example, you would ask whether the probative value of June's statement to Witness ("Ward told me he transferred $10,000 to National Bank") depends on June's credibility. If so, it is hearsay. Then ask if the probative value of Ward's statement to June ("I transferred $10,000 to National Bank") depends on Ward's credibility. If so, it is hearsay.

   Multiple hearsay will be admissible only if you have a **hearsay exception for each layer** of hearsay. Therefore, if both Ward's and June's statements are hearsay, you will need a hearsay exception for Ward's statement and one for June's; otherwise Witness's testimony may not be offered to prove Ward transferred $10,000 to National Bank.

H. Limited Admissibility [§241]

Whether a given statement is hearsay depends on what it is being offered to prove. Therefore, it should be clear that a single statement may be hearsay if offered for one purpose and not hearsay if offered for another purpose. When a statement is hearsay for one purpose and not hearsay for another purpose (relevant to the case), the court will ordinarily admit the evidence and, upon request from objecting counsel, give a **limiting instruction** to the jury.

EXAMPLE

Witness testifies, "Shortly before Plaintiff fell, I heard Customer tell Store Manager the floor was slippery on aisle 6." This statement is hearsay if offered to prove the floor was slippery, but not hearsay if offered to prove Store Manager was put on notice. If notice is an issue in the case, the court will admit such testimony and instruct the jury to consider it only as evidence of notice.

I. Silence [§242]

Whether a person's silence should be treated as hearsay is easy to analyze under the federal rules. Silence is a form of non-verbal conduct. Therefore, if it is **intended as an assertion** (e.g., silence in response to the statement, "Say something if I am wrong"), it falls within Category 2 and is hearsay. If it is **not intended as an assertion**, it falls within Category 3 and is not hearsay. Under the broader definition of hearsay at common law, it can more easily be viewed as hearsay since the jury is being asked to infer that the silence represents the person's belief about something and that the belief is correct. Nevertheless, once a common-law court concludes that a person's silence is sufficiently probative, it rarely excludes it on hearsay grounds.

V. Hearsay Exceptions

A. Hearsay Exceptions in General [§243]

Hearsay is inadmissible unless it falls within one of the exceptions to the hearsay rule. [FRE 802.] In fact, there are numerous exceptions to the hearsay rule, some of which are obscure and rarely the subject of examination. Most hearsay exceptions are **justified on the ground that particular classes of statements possess inherent guarantees of reliability**: the circumstances are such that the declarant is unlikely to be lying and/or the dangers of misperception or faulty memory are significantly reduced. When a statement is made under such circumstances, the absence of cross-examination is less crucial to reliability and fairness.

1. **Mnemonic Device: [§244]**
   You can remember all the important hearsay exceptions with the mnemonic **BAD SPLITS, PEPPI F.**

   B — Business records
   A — Admission by party opponent
   D — Dying declaration

   S — Spontaneous statements (excited utterance and present sense impression)
   P — Past recollection recorded
   L — Learned treatise
   I — Interest, Declaration against
   T — Testimony, Former
   S — State of mind or condition

   P — Public records
   E — Equivalency (residual, catch-all)
   P — Prior inconsistent statement
   P — Prior consistent statement
   I — Identification

   F — Forfeiture

   Technically, not all of these are hearsay exceptions. As mentioned earlier (see §§234-238), **admissions by a party opponent** and certain **prior statements by a witness** (the last three "exceptions" listed in PEPPI) are defined in the federal rules and many state codes as **nonhearsay**. As a practical matter, however, it makes no difference whether the evidence gets in because it falls within a hearsay exception or because it is considered "nonhearsay."

B. **Admission by Party Opponent [§ 245]**
   This is the most important "exception" and the one you should always look for first. A party may not object on hearsay grounds when his **opponent** offers a statement made by the party. That is, Plaintiff may offer any statement made

by Defendant without worrying about a hearsay objection; Defendant may offer any statement made by Plaintiff. There are several idiosyncrasies about the admissions "exception" that should be noted.

1. **Not an Exception [§246]**
   At common law, admissions by a party opponent were considered a hearsay exception. The federal rules [FRE 801(d)(2)] and many state codes now define admissions as nonhearsay.

2. **Not Based on Reliability [§247]**
   Unlike most hearsay exceptions, the admissions "exception" is not justified on the ground that such statements are reliable. Instead, party admissions are admitted because a party should not be allowed to object to his own statements on the ground that he can't cross-examine the declarant (i.e., himself). The theory is one of **responsibility** or **estoppel**: "you said it, you explain it." **Two consequences** flow from this.

   a. **Limited Admissibility [§248]**
      An admission of a party opponent is admissible under this "exception" only as evidence **against the party who made the statement**. This is important in multi-party litigation.

      EXAMPLE
      In a prosecution against A and B for assault, A's out-of-court statement, "B and I really roughed up Victim" may be offered by the prosecution against A as his admission, but it is not admissible against B under this "exception."

   b. **Personal Knowledge Not Required [§249]**
      The personal knowledge requirement (see §423) does not apply to a party-opponent's statements. A party-opponent's statement is admissible even if he had no firsthand knowledge of the facts asserted.

3. **An Admission Does Not Have to be an Admission [§250]**
   An admission by a party opponent does not have to be an actual admission. **Any statement** of a party opponent

falls within this exception even if the party wasn't admitting (i.e., confessing) to anything at the time the statement was made. In fact, the statement may have been self-serving at the time it was made. Do not call this the admission against interest exception (there is no such thing) and do not confuse this with the declaration against interest exception. Think of it as the statement by party opponent exception. Remember, a party may offer his opponent's statements pursuant to this exception, but not his own statements.

4. Three Different Kinds of Admissions [§251]
There are three different kinds of admissions: (a) a party's own statements; (b) adoptive admissions; and (c) vicarious admissions.

a. Party's Own Statements [§252]
Anything a party says may be offered by his opponent. This includes statements concerning matters about which the party lacked personal knowledge (e.g., Defendant's statement as to how an accident occurred is admissible against her even if it can be shown that Defendant did not see the accident) and expressions of opinion (e.g., "I'm sorry, I was careless, the accident was my fault.").

(1) Statements in Pleadings [§253]
A party's superseded pleadings or pleadings in other actions are admissible against the party as admissions. Moreover, procedural rules dictate that matters admitted in the live pleadings or stipulated to on the record may be considered **judicial admissions** that are conclusive in the proceeding in which they are made. A defendant's plea in a criminal case will qualify as an admission by a party opponent if offered against him in subsequent collateral litigation (e.g., a civil damage action brought by the victim of a criminal assault). However, certain pleas (a withdrawn plea of guilty or a plea of nolo contendere) are rendered inadmissible against the defendant because of an independent rule of evidence that prohibits the use of such pleas on policy grounds. See §108.

(2) Admissions by Conduct [§254]

When a party acts in such a way that an inference may be drawn that she believes herself to be criminally or civilly liable (i.e., manifests "consciousness of guilt"), the act is often deemed a party admission. Examples of such acts include: (a) flight after the commission of a crime; (b) assumption of a false name; (c) resisting arrest; (d) attempting to bribe an arresting officer, witness or juror; (f) fabrication or destruction of evidence; (g) attempting to commit suicide; and (h) refusing to take a breath test. Note, however, that none of these would be considered hearsay under the federal rules because none of this conduct was intended by the party to communicate her consciousness of liability. The real question is one of relevancy.

b. Adoptive Admissions [§255]

A party can, in effect, **adopt a statement made by another person** as her own, and the other person's statement will be treated as the admission of the party. A statement may be adopted by a party either **explicitly** or **tacitly**.

(1) Explicit Adoptions [§256]

A party may expressly manifest a belief in another person's statement, either before or after the person actually makes the statement.

EXAMPLE

Plaintiff calls Witness. Witness testifies that Joe told him that the accident occurred when an overhanging tree limb suddenly broke, and that Defendant heard Joe's statement and said, "That's right."

EXAMPLE

Plaintiff calls Witness. Witness testifies that Defendant told him, "Ask Joe how the accident happened. He knows." Joe's statement to Witness would be considered an adoptive admission by Defendant.

(2) Tacit Admissions [§257]

When a statement is made in a party's presence and contains an assertion that a reasonable person would, under the circumstances, deny if it were not true, the party's failure to deny is construed as an adoption of the assertion. This kind of admission is called a "tacit," "adoptive," or "implied" admission, or an "admission by silence." This type of admission will be found only when it is reasonable to view the party's **silence as constituting assent** to the truth of the assertion made in her presence. Has the party, by her silence, manifested a belief in the statement? If there are other plausible reasons that explain the failure to deny, the party's silence does not amount to a tacit admission.

EXAMPLE: TACIT ADMISSION

To prove that Defendant failed to deliver goods by June 1 as promised, Plaintiff testifies, "I called up Defendant on June 2 and said, 'those goods still haven't arrived and they were supposed to be here yesterday,' and Defendant said nothing in response."

EXAMPLE: NOT A TACIT ADMISSION

To prove that Defendant stole a lamp, Prosecution calls Witness to testify that she heard Stranger say to Defendant, "you stole my friend's lamp," and that Defendant walked away from Stranger without responding. The evidence shows that Defendant was in a hurry and did not know Stranger. Under these circumstances, it is not reasonable to view Defendant's silence as indicating assent to Stranger's statement.

(3) Constitutional Limitations on Tacit Admissions [§258]

The Supreme Court has held that the constitution bars the prosecution from using an accused's failure to respond to accusations **after being arrested and given his _Miranda_ warnings** as a tacit admission against him. _Doyle v. Ohio_, 426 U.S. 610 (1978). As a constitutional matter, however, an accused's **pre-arrest silence** may be

used against him. Thus, a defendant who claims
self-defense at trial may be impeached by
showing that he never raised any claim of self-
defense in the two weeks between the killing and
his apprehension. *Jenkins v. Anderson*, 447 U.S. 231
(1980). The constitution does not prohibit the
prosecution from using a defendant's silence in
the period **after being arrested but before
being given a Miranda warning.** *Fletcher v.
Weir*, 455 U.S. 603 (1982). But many courts refuse
to admit such evidence on the ground that a
defendant's post-arrest silence, even before a
Miranda warning is given, does not amount to a
tacit admission.

c. **Vicarious Admissions [§259]**

Statements by a non-party—an **employee, agent,** or
co-conspirator of a party— may be **attributed to**
and used against the party under certain
circumstances. In these cases the party is not the
declarant, but because of the special relationship
between the party and the declarant, it is fair to
attribute the statement to the party and require the
party to explain or clarify the statement.

d. **Vicarious Admissions by Agents and Employees
[§260]**

A statement by a **party's agent or employee** may be
considered the admission of the party. The federal
rules and most states have expanded the scope of this
type of admission.

(1) **Common-Law View [§261]**

Under the common law, an agent's statement is
considered the party's admission only if the agent
was **authorized to speak on behalf of the
party.** An agent's authority to speak is not
necessarily congruent with his authority to act.
For example, Driver may be authorized to drive
Defendant Co.'s truck, but not authorized to
speak for Defendant Co. about the truck's
mechanical condition. The proponent of this type
of vicarious admission must establish Driver's

express or implied authority to speak for Defendant Co.

(2) Federal Rules [§262]

The federal rules consider statements made by **someone authorized by a party to speak** to be the party's admissions. [FRE 801(d)(2)(C).] In addition, under the federal rules, a statement by a party's **agent or employee** will be considered the party's admission if the statement (a) **concerned a matter within the scope of the declarant's agency or employment** and (b) was made while the **declarant was still an agent or employee**. No authority to speak is required. [FRE 801(d)(2)(D).]

EXAMPLE

Plaintiff sues Tech Co., claiming that he was fired in violation of age discrimination laws. He calls Witness, who testifies that he heard two different Tech Co. employees make statements about Plaintiff's firing. Employee 1, who works in the mailroom, told Witness, "Plaintiff was fired because they wanted to bring in younger people." Employee 2, Plaintiff's supervisor, told Witness, "Plaintiff is doing a top-rate job. He's my best employee." Employee 1's statement is inadmissible. As a mailroom employee, he was not authorized to speak on behalf of Tech Co. Nor does his statement concern a matter within the scope of his mailroom duties. Employee 2's statement is admissible. Regardless of whether he was authorized to speak on Tech Co.'s behalf, his statement concerns a matter within the scope of his duties, and he made the statement while still in Tech Co.'s employ.

(3) Personal Knowledge Requirement [§263]

Recall that a party may not object on the ground of lack of personal knowledge when it is his own statement that is being offered by his opponent. Courts generally reach the same conclusion when the statement offered is a vicarious admission. *Mahlandt v. Wild Canid Survival & Research Center, Inc.*, 588 F.2d 626 (8th Cir. 1978).

e. **Co-Conspirator Admissions [§264]**

A statement made by a party's co-conspirator is admissible against the party as a vicarious admission. The proponent of such a statement must show (a) that the **declarant and the party were co-conspirators**; and that the statement was made (b) **during the pendency** of the conspiracy (i.e., while the conspiracy is ongoing) and (c) **in furtherance of** the conspiracy. [FRE 801(d)(2)(E).] The statement of one co-conspirator is admissible against all other members of the conspiracy, even those who joined after the statement was made and those who had no contact with or did not even know the existence of the declarant.

(1) **Proof of Conspiracy [§265]**

Many common-law courts required that the existence of the conspiracy be proved by evidence other than the co-conspirator's hearsay statements. In 1987, however, the Supreme Court held that such hearsay statements may themselves be considered by the court in deciding whether the proponent has established the requirements for this hearsay "exception." *Bourjaily v. United States*, 483 U.S. 171 (1987). A 1997 amendment to FRE 801 codified this holding and applied it to other vicarious admissions. See §268. The existence of the conspiracy need only be established by a **preponderance of the evidence**.

(2) **Admissible in Non-Conspiracy Cases [§266]**

Note that the admission by co-conspirator "exception" can be used even if the party is not being prosecuted for conspiracy. As long as the proponent of the evidence establishes the requirements for the "exception," it can be used regardless of the kind of case.

(3) **Confessions to Police [§267]**

A confession made by a member of a conspiracy to the police will not qualify for admission against fellow conspirators under this "exception."

Remember: an admission by co-conspirator must be made in furtherance of the conspiracy. Confessions to police rarely further a conspiracy's goals.

f. **Preliminary Question of Fact [§268]**

Before admitting hearsay under any of the vicarious admission provisions, the court must determine that the elements of the provision have been met. The proponent of the hearsay has the burden of proving this by a **preponderance of the evidence**. A 1997 amendment to FRE 801 permits the court to consider the contents of the hearsay statement itself in making this determination. But the hearsay statement itself **may not be considered sufficient evidence** to support such a determination. The proponent must also produce some independent evidence.

EXAMPLE

Prosecution calls Witness to testify that Cohort told him, "Defendant and I are working together to sell the drugs. He gets them from Supplier, and I sell them on the street. I want you to help me." The court may consider this statement as evidence that Cohort (the declarant) and Defendant were co-conspirators and that the statement was made during the pendency and in furtherance of the conspiracy. But this statement by itself may not be considered sufficient evidence to establish that it is an admission by co-conspirator. Prosecution must produce other evidence to show that Cohort and Defendant were conspiring to sell drugs.

g. **Admissions by Parties in Privity [§269]**

Although not included in the federal rules, the common law and some states treat statements **made by someone in privity with the party** as the vicarious admission of the party.

EXAMPLE

Plaintiff sues Defendant over title to Blackacre. Witness testifies that Father, from whom Defendant inherited Blackacre, stated, "I stole Blackacre from Plaintiff." This would be admissible in many jurisdictions as an admission by someone in privity with Defendant.

C. Hearsay Exceptions: Availability Immaterial [§270]

Some hearsay exceptions apply only if the declarant is unavailable to testify at trial. Most exceptions, however, can be used regardless of the declarant's availability. The material immediately below covers the major hearsay exceptions for which the declarant's availability (or lack of availability) is immaterial. These exceptions are found in FRE 803.

D. Spontaneous Statements [§271]

Statements that the declarant makes spontaneously (i.e., before he has had an opportunity to think about what to say) are said to be reliable. Two related hearsay exceptions fall within this rationale: (a) **excited utterances** and (b) **present sense impressions**.

1. Excited Utterances [§272]

Both the federal rules [FRE 803(2)] and the common law recognize the excited utterance exception. The exception covers statements (a) made while the declarant was **under the stress of excitement** caused by a startling event or condition (b) that **relate to the event or condition**. In the past, this was sometimes referred to as "res gestae," but that term is now in disfavor.

a. Rationale [§273]

The stress under which the statement is made is deemed to ensure **spontaneity** and thus reduce the possibility of fabrication.

b. Must Relate to Startling Event [§274]

The statement must **relate** to the **startling event or condition**. This encompasses not only statements that describe or explain the event, but statements that relate to it in any way. Suppose Declarant is involved in a wreck and blurts out, "I'm in a hurry. I'm trying to reach an important customer." Although the fact that Declarant was trying to reach an important customer does not describe or explain the startling event (the accident), it relates to it and will, therefore, qualify as an excited utterance. Be sure to contrast the scope of the excited utterance exception with the present sense impression. See §282.

c. **While Under Stress of Excitement [§275]**

The statement must be made before the declarant has had time to reflect. Therefore, excited utterances are usually made soon after the exciting event. However, there is **no time requirement** for excited utterances. Thus, a statement made immediately after a period of unconsciousness may qualify as an excited utterance, even if the unconsciousness lasted for hours or days. Particularly in child abuse cases, some courts have been quite lenient in finding that statements made by the child victim several hours, and even days, after the event qualify as excited utterances.

d. **Spontaneity Requirement [§276]**

The typical excited utterance occurs when a declarant spontaneously blurts out a statement while in the throes of excitement (e.g., "That man just shot the boy!"). But the exception goes beyond such unprompted statements. Statements made in response to a question (e.g., "What happened?") may be admitted as excited utterances. Whether a statement was made in response to a question is simply a factor the court will consider in determining whether the statement was sufficiently spontaneous. The crucial consideration is whether the statement was made while the declarant was still under the stress of the startling event.

e. **Identity of Declarant Immaterial [§277]**

The declarant often is, but need not be, involved in the startling event; he may be a bystander. In addition, the declarant need not be identified. Thus, Witness may testify, "Someone yelled, 'The blue car ran the red light.'"

f. **Proof of the Startling Event [§278]**

The court may consider the contents of the statement itself as evidence of the existence of the startling event and the declarant's spontaneous reaction to the event. Independent evidence of either is not required, although the existence of such independent evidence makes it more likely that the court will find that the proponent of the statement has met the burden of demonstrating that it qualifies as an excited utterance.

2. **Present Sense Impression [§279]**
The federal rules contain an exception for statements that (a) **describe or explain** an event or condition (b) made **while the declarant was perceiving** the event or condition **or immediately thereafter**. [FRE 803(1).] This exception was not recognized until a Texas court adopted it in 1942. By the time the federal rules were promulgated, many courts had embraced this exception.

a. **Rationale [§280]**
The **spontaneity** of the statement ensures that the declarant will not have had time to think about what she was going to say, and thus guarantees sincerity. In addition, the danger of memory loss is negligible. Finally, some courts stress that the person who heard the statement is usually in a position to verify its accuracy.

b. **Time Factor [§281]**
The statement must be made while the event or condition is **being perceived or immediately afterwards**. Only a slight time lapse is allowed.

c. **Must Describe or Explain the Event [§282]**
Unlike excited utterances, which may "relate" to the exciting event, present sense impressions must "describe or explain" the event. Thus, present sense impressions are limited to statements like, "The blue car just ran the red light."

d. **Corroboration [§283]**
Because the present sense impression exception is based in part on the ability of the person who heard the statement to verify its accuracy, a few courts have required the witness to have been in a position to corroborate the statement. But the federal rules and most courts impose no such requirement.

EXAMPLE
Witness testifies, "Victim and I were chatting on the phone. Victim said to me, 'I've got to go. Defendant's at the door.'" Those courts that apply a corroboration

requirement will exclude such testimony because Witness was not in a position to verify the accuracy of Victim's statement. Federal courts and states that do not apply a corroboration requirement will not hold the statement inadmissible simply because it is uncorroborated. The trial judge may, however, consider the lack of corroboration in determining whether the proponent of the hearsay statement has established that the statement really meets the requirements of the present sense impression exception.

E. State of Mind: Mental or Physical Condition [§284]

The common law and the federal rules recognize a hearsay exception for certain statements by a declarant relating to her **then-existing** mental, emotional, or physical condition. [FRE 803(3).] A **related exception** covers statements made for the **purpose of medical diagnosis or treatment**. [FRE 803(4).]

1. Present State of Mind [§285]

The state of mind exception covers statements of **presently-existing** intent ("I plan to go to the store tomorrow"), belief ("I think my brakes are bad"), attitude ("I don't like him"), motive ("I owe him one"), mental feeling ("I am bored studying evidence"), pain ("my head hurts") and bodily health ("I have the flu").

a. Rationale [§286]

A statement relating a present state of mind or physical condition raises no problems of memory or perception. Moreover, since a person's state of mind is often difficult to prove, there is frequently a need for such direct evidence.

b. Proper Uses of Present State of Mind: To Prove State of Mind Itself [§287]

Where a person's intent, knowledge, belief, attitude, or physical condition is itself a relevant issue, any statement made by the person that directly reveals the intent, knowledge, etc. is admissible. Note that the exception requires only that the statement express the declarant's state of mind at the time the statement is made.

EXAMPLE

In an alienation of affections case, to prove that Wife no longer loved Husband, Witness testifies, "Wife told me, 'I hate my Husband.'" This is admissible as a statement of her then-existing state of mind toward Husband. Her statement could also be used to infer that she felt that way toward Husband earlier or later in time.

c. **Proper Uses of Present State of Mind: To Prove Conduct of the Declarant [§288]**

People follow through on their intentions with sufficient frequency to justify the inference that someone who announces her intent to do something or go somewhere actually did that thing or went to that place. Therefore, a declarant's statement of her **existing intent to do something in the future** is admissible under the state of mind exception to prove she actually carried through with her plans.

IMPORTANT CASE: *MUTUAL LIFE INS. CO. V. HILLMON*, 145 U.S. 285 (1892).

In one of the most famous evidence cases, the Supreme Court first held that a statement of an existing intent to do something in the future is admissible under the state of mind exception to prove the declarant actually followed through with his plans. Sallie Hillmon sued several insurance companies to recover on policies on the life of her husband, John Hillmon. The companies claimed that Hillmon had fraudulently staged his "death." They sought to prove that the body found at Crooked Creek was not Hillmon's, as Sallie claimed, but was that of one Adolph Walters. To support their theory, they offered letters written by Walters to his family two weeks before the body was found, in which Walters said that he planned to go west (where Crooked Creek is located) with Hillmon. The Supreme Court held that the letters were admissible under the state of mind exception as evidence that Walters carried out his stated intent to travel west with Hillmon.

EXAMPLE

To prove that she was in Cincinnati on June 12, Defendant calls Witness to testify, "On May 25,

Defendant told me that she was planning to go to Cincinnati the morning of June 12." This is admissible as a statement of Defendant's existing intent to do something in the future.

d. Improper Use of Present State of Mind: To Prove Truth of Underlying Facts [§289]

A statement of a currently-existing memory or belief may not be used to prove the truth of the **facts remembered or believed**. For example, in the famous case of *Shepard v. United States*, 290 U.S. 96 (1933), the prosecution called a nurse to testify that the victim said to her, "Dr. Shepard has poisoned me." The prosecution argued that this statement qualified under the state of mind exception as a statement of the wife's then-existing belief (that Dr. Shepard had poisoned her). The Court rejected this argument, holding that the state of mind exception does not reach "backward looking" statements (i.e., statements about past events). If it did, the hearsay rule would be eviscerated, because every out-of-court statement could be cast as a statement of the declarant's then-existing belief.

Nor may a statement of a present state of mind be used to prove the truth of the **facts underlying the belief.** For example, Victim's statement, "I am afraid of Defendant" would not be admissible to prove that Defendant had actually done anything (such as make threats) that might have induced such a state of mind. The statement would, however, be admissible to prove Victim did not voluntarily go out alone with Defendant.

(1) Exception: Statements Relating to a Will [§290]

A statement of memory or belief may be offered to prove the fact remembered or believed if it relates to the **execution, revocation, identification, or terms** of the declarant's will. Thus, Testator's statement "I disinherited my son because he flunked Evidence" would be admissible under this exception.

e. **Controversial Use of Present State of Mind [§291]**

This exception covers statements made by a declarant about her **own beliefs, feelings, intentions, physical sensations**, etc. It does **not** cover statements made by a declarant about **someone else's beliefs, feelings, intentions**, etc. Controversy may arise, however, when a party offers a declarant's statement about her own intention to do something that also explicitly or implicitly refers to someone else's intention to do something. For example, Declarant's statement, "I am going downtown tonight to meet Sam" is clearly a statement of Declarant's intention to go downtown and is admissible to prove that she went downtown that evening. But her statement also implies that Sam intended to go downtown that evening. Many, but not all, courts would admit this statement to prove that Sam went downtown. See *United States v. Pheaster*, 544 F.2d 353 (9th Cir. 1976).

f. **State of Mind Exception Distinguished From State of Mind Nonhearsay [§292]**

An out-of-court statement may sometimes provide **circumstantial proof of the declarant's state of mind**. That is, the fact that the declarant made a particular statement may reveal how the declarant feels about something or someone, regardless of whether the statement is true. Such out-of-court statements are **not hearsay** because they are not offered for their truth. In contrast, if a declarant makes a direct assertion about her state of mind, and that assertion is being offered for its truth, (i.e., to prove that the declarant possessed the state of mind asserted), the statement is hearsay, but admissible under the state of mind exception.

EXAMPLE

If Father tells numerous people, "My son is a spendthrift bum who will never amount to anything," the statement is not hearsay if offered only as circumstantial evidence that the father desires to disinherit the son. No one is trying to prove the son is a bum. The fact that the father made that statement tends to prove that he is not well disposed

toward his son. On the other hand, if Father says to
Mother, "I won't leave Son a dime," the statement is a
direct assertion of his intentions and bears on the issue of
the son's inheritance only if it is true. It is hearsay, but
comes in as a statement of a present state of mind.

2. **Statements for Purpose of Medical Diagnosis or
   Treatment [§293]**
   The federal rules and many states depart from the
   common law by including a special hearsay exception for
   statements made for the purpose of medical diagnosis or
   treatment. The exception covers not only statements as to
   present symptoms and sensations, but also statements
   regarding **medical history** and past symptoms and
   sensations. In addition, certain statements relating to the
   cause of the condition are admissible under this
   exception. [FRE 803(4).]

   a. **Statements of Present Symptoms, Etc [§294]**
      The state of mind exception [FRE 803(3)] generally
      covers statements of present symptoms, pain,
      sensations, or physical condition. Under common
      law, however, courts generally did not admit such
      statements if they were made to a **non-treating
      physician** (typically, a physician consulted for
      purposes of litigation). Nevertheless, juries often
      learned of such statements since doctors testifying as
      experts were allowed to refer to such statements to
      explain the basis of their opinion. Consequently, the
      FRE and most states reject the common-law rule and
      admit such statements, **even if made to a
      consulting physician.** The danger that the litigant
      might make exaggerated claims of pain and symptoms
      to a non-treating physician may be considered by the
      jury in deciding how much weight to give the
      evidence.

   b. **Statements of Past Symptoms, Etc [§295]**
      Statements regarding a person's medical history, past
      symptoms, pain or physical condition ("My back hurt
      all last month") are admissible if made **for purposes
      of either diagnosis or treatment.** If made to a
      treating physician, reliability is ensured by the desire
      to obtain effective treatment. If made to a non-

treating physician, admission is justified on the ground that the jury will learn about the statement anyway, since the physician will be able to refer to it in explaining the basis for her opinion. The common-law rule does not allow this type of statement, whether made to a treating or non-treating physician.

c. **Statements of Cause [§296]**

The federal rule and most states also depart from the common law in allowing a statement regarding the **cause** or **external source** of the pain, symptom, condition, etc. insofar as it is **pertinent to the diagnosis or treatment**.

EXAMPLE
Patient's statement to Doctor, "My neck pains began after I was rear-ended by a blue '57 Chevy that went through a stop sign" will not be admissible to prove the identity of the car or negligence of the driver that rear-ended Patient. Neither the make of car nor the negligence of the driver is pertinent to Patient's diagnosis or treatment. The fact that Patient was rear-ended may, however, be pertinent, and that part of the statement may be admissible.

d. **Declarant Need Not Be the Patient [§297]**

The exception does not state that the declarant must be the patient; it requires only that the statement be made for purpose of medical diagnosis or treatment. Thus, a parent's statement to her child's doctor regarding the child's medical history is admissible under this exception.

e. **Need Not Be Made to a Doctor [§298]**

The exception covers statements made to hospital attendants, ambulance drivers, nurses, etc. if they are made for the purpose of receiving medical diagnosis or treatment.

f. **Child Abuse Cases [§299]**

This exception has been interpreted liberally by many courts to embrace statements made by child-abuse victims to physicians. Many courts now hold that statements regarding the identity of the assailant are pertinent to diagnosis and treatment and thus admissible.

F. Business Records [§300]

A written record qualifies for the business records exception if it was (a) the regular practice of the business to **keep** such records and the records were made: (b) in the **regular course** of the business; (c) **at or near the time** of the event or condition recorded; and (d) by an employee with **personal knowledge** of the event or upon information provided by someone with a business duty to report the information. Even if these four requirements are met, however, the record will not qualify if the source of information or the method or circumstances of its preparation indicate a **lack of trustworthiness**. [FRE 803(6).]

1. Mnemonic Device: "KRAP" [§301]

To remember the four elements of the business record exception, take the first letter of the first boldfaced word in §300 for each of the four requirements: **K**eep; **R**egular course; **A**t or near the time; **P**ersonal knowledge.

2. Rationale [§302]

Business records qualify for a hearsay exception because of their **reliability**. If businesses rely upon such records in their day-to-day affairs, it is reasonable to assume that they have sufficient incentive to ensure their accuracy.

3. Analysis of Elements: Personal Knowledge [§303]

This is the most common kind of business record problem. Many business record statutes (especially those drafted pre-FRE) provide that the entrant's (i.e., the person who made the record) lack of personal knowledge of the facts recorded goes to the weight, not the admissibility, of the business record. But such language was designed to obviate the need to produce as witnesses every member of a business organization who might have had a part in gathering or transmitting the information entered in the record. As a result, such statutes are not read literally. Rather, it is now well accepted that if the maker of a business record obtains from another person the information recorded, a double hearsay problem arises. Whether the record is admissible depends on the source of the information recorded and the applicability of other hearsay exceptions.

EXAMPLE

Plaintiff offers Police Officer's report, which states, "Shortly after the accident I spoke with Bystander. She told me that the motorcycle ran a red light." If offered to prove the motorcycle ran a red light, this report constitutes double hearsay: the police officer's written statement ("Bystander told me the motorcycle ran a red light") and Bystander's statement to Police Officer ("The motorcycle ran a red light"). This will be admissible only if a hearsay exception can be found for both Police Officer's written out-of-court statement and Bystander's out-of-court statement to Police Officer. *Johnson v. Lutz*, 253 N.Y. 124, 170 N.E. 517 (1930).

a. Entrant Has Personal Knowledge [§304]
If the maker of the record has personal knowledge of the recorded facts, the personal knowledge requirement is fulfilled.

EXAMPLE

Police Officer Smith files a report that states, "I saw the motorcycle run the red light and crash into the truck." There is only one declarant and one level of hearsay. The police officer is the declarant; his written out-of-court statement is the only hearsay. His statement of how the accident occurred is based on his personal knowledge. If the report meets the other requirements of the business record exception, it will be admissible.

b. Information From Someone With Business Duty to Report [§305]
Even if the maker of the record lacks personal knowledge of the recorded facts, if the information comes from someone else who has **a business duty to report** the information, the personal knowledge requirement is fulfilled. This is to align the business record exception with modern business practices in which information may be transmitted through several employees before it is actually recorded (e.g., sales clerk to manager to head of bookkeeping to entrant).

EXAMPLE

Police Officer Smith files a report that states, "Officer Jones told me that she saw the motorcycle run the red light and crash into the truck." There are two declarants: Officer Smith and Officer Jones. Both of their statements are hearsay if the report is offered to prove that the motorcycle ran the red light. But since Officer Jones had a business duty to report what she knew about the accident to Officer Smith, the business record exception covers both her oral statement to Officer Smith and Officer Smith's written out-of-court statement.

c. **Information From Someone Without Business Duty to Report [§306]**

   If the maker of the record lacks personal knowledge of the recorded facts and the information comes from someone who is not under any obligation to report the information (e.g., a bystander), the evidence will be inadmissible **unless another hearsay exception can be found** for the other person's statement.

EXAMPLE

Police Officer Smith files a report that states, "Bystander came running up to me and screamed excitedly, 'The motorcycle ran the light.'" Although this is double hearsay if offered to prove the motorcycle ran the light, Bystander's statement qualifies as an excited utterance and Officer Smith's statement qualifies as a business record. The report, therefore, is admissible.

EXAMPLE

Police Officer Smith files a report that states, "Motorcyclist told me that he ran the light." If offered against Motorcyclist, this is admissible because Motorcyclist's statement is an admission by a party opponent and Officer Smith's statement qualifies as a business record.

d. **Recorded Information Not Offered For Its Truth [§307]**

   The multiple hearsay problem arises only if the recorded information that comes from someone other than the entrant is offered for its truth. That is, if the record is offered merely to show that the "informer" made the statement, there is only one level of hearsay.

EXAMPLE

Police Officer Smith files a report that states, "Bystander told me, 'The motorcycle ran the light.'" If this is offered merely to prove that Bystander made this statement (not to prove that the motorcycle ran the light), Bystander's statement is not hearsay. Officer Smith's statement is hearsay, but qualifies as a business record.

4. **Analysis of Elements: Regular Course of Business [§308]**

In order to assure reliability of the record, it must be the type of record regularly kept by the business and it must have been recorded in routine fashion.

5. **Analysis of Elements: Lack of Trustworthiness [§309]**

Once the proponent of the record shows that the four requirements of the business record exception are met, the record will be admitted unless the opponent can show that the **source of information** or the **method or circumstances** surrounding its making indicate a **lack of trustworthiness**.

a. **Records Made in Contemplation of Litigation [§310]**

In *Palmer v. Hoffman*, 318 U.S. 109 (1943), the defendant railroad offered as a business record an accident report containing the statement of a railroad engineer, recorded by the railroad's investigator as part of his regular practice to investigate accidents. The Supreme Court held the report inadmissible. The Court viewed the accident report as lacking in trustworthiness, noting that its primary utility was in litigating, not railroading.. Since then, courts have been suspicious of records that are **made with an eye toward litigation**. Such records tend to lack the reliability that other, more traditional business records possess. Occasionally, however, a court finds that an accident report was made under circumstances that betoken no lack of trustworthiness and admits it.

6. **Diagnoses and Opinions [§311]**

   Many pre-FRE business record statutes permitted business records that memorialized "acts, events, or conditions," and some courts interpreted this to exclude opinions or diagnoses contained in hospital records. The federal rule and most states now provide that business records may include diagnoses and opinions.

7. **Definition of Business [§312]**

   Business is defined broadly enough to include any organization, entity, or association, whether or not for profit.

8. **Laying the Foundation [§313]**

   In order to qualify a record as a business record, the proponent must establish that the elements of the exception ("KRAP") are met. This may be done by **any person who knows how the records are made and kept**. The sponsor of the record may, but need not, be the maker or the custodian of the record. Note that the record's sponsor is not required to possess personal knowledge of the contents of the record, or even of the circumstances in which the particular record was made. The sponsor can satisfy the requirements of the business record exception by testifying to the manner in which records of that particular type are made.

   In addition, the record must be authenticated. That is, it must be shown that the record is what it purports to be (e.g., a record of the XYZ Corp.). See §575 et seq.

9. **Absence of Record to Prove Non-Occurrence [§314]**

   The federal rules [FRE 803(7)] and most states allow reference to business records to prove the non-occurrence of an event. The **absence of any record** of an event among regularly kept records is admissible to prove the event did not occur so long as the event was the type of event the business would have been expected to record had it occurred.

EXAMPLE

Auto Dealer offers its sales records for the month of March, which fail to list any sale to Plaintiff. If Auto Dealer qualifies the sales records under the business record exception (i.e., meets the KRAP requirements), the record will be admissible to prove that Auto Dealer did not make a sale to Plaintiff in March.

G. Public Records and Reports [§315]

The federal rules and many states now have an expansive exception for public records. This exception is justified primarily by the assumption that public officials will perform their duties properly. Under FRE 803(8), the **records and reports of a government agency** are admissible if they set forth information falling within one of three categories.

1. Activities of the Agency [§316]

Records setting forth the **agency's own activities** (e.g., Treasury Department records of receipts and disbursements) are admissible. [FRE 803(8)(A).]

2. Matters the Agency is Required to Observe and Report [§317]

Records setting forth **matters that the agency is required by law to observe and report** (e.g., rainfall records of the Weather Bureau) are admissible. This involves the recording of public officials' own first-hand observations. [FRE 803(8)(B).]

a. But Not in Criminal Cases [§318]

This part of the public records exception is qualified. It excludes **in criminal cases matters observed by police officers and other law enforcement personnel**. [FRE 803(8)(B).] Courts have tended to give a broad reading to the term "law enforcement personnel." In *United States v. Oates*, 560 F.2d 45 (2d Cir. 1977), for example, the Second Circuit held that a Customs Service lab chemist qualified as "law enforcement personnel." Therefore, the lab report that found the substance seized from the accused was heroin could not be offered under the public records exception.

    b. Well, Sometimes in Criminal Cases [§319]

Notwithstanding the language of FRE 803(8)(B), the courts have admitted records of matters observed by law enforcement personnel in criminal **cases where the matters observed are ministerial in nature;** that is, routine, objective observations made as part of the everyday functioning of the office. For example, courts have admitted Customs Service computer records of license plate numbers of cars crossing the border, reports listing the serial numbers on firearms, and calibration reports of breathalyzer maintenance operators.

    c. Can't Slip It In Through Business Record Exception [§320]

Courts do not allow prosecutors to use the business record exception to circumvent the provision of the public records exception excluding law enforcement records in criminal cases. Thus, if a court finds that a law enforcement record is inadmissible because of this provision in the public records exception, it will not allow the record to be offered under the business records exception. *United States v. Oates*, 560 F.2d 45 (2d Cir. 1977).

3. Factual Findings [§321]

Reports setting forth **factual findings** that result from an **authorized governmental investigation** are admissible (a) in **civil cases** and (b) **against the government in criminal cases**. [FRE 803(8)(C).]

    a. Includes Conclusions As To Fault [§322]

The Supreme Court has held that the term "factual findings" includes conclusions as to fault (e.g., that pilot error caused an airplane crash). *Beech Aircraft Corp. v. Rainey*, 488 U.S. 153 (1988).

    b. Excluded If Not Trustworthy [§323]

The opponent of a public report setting forth factual findings may convince a court to exclude the report by demonstrating that **the sources of information or other circumstances** (e.g., the bias or inexperience of the investigator) indicate a **lack of trustworthiness**.

4. Vital Statistics [§324]

A related hearsay exception covers public records of births, deaths, and marriages. [FRE 803(9).]

5. Absence of Record to Prove Non-Occurrence [§325]

As is the case with business records, the absence of a public record about an event may be used to prove **the non-occurrence of the event** if reports of such an event are regularly made. [FRE 803(10).]

H. Learned Treatises [§326]

The common law allows a cross-examiner to impeach an expert witness by pointing out discrepancies between the witness's testimony and statements made in a treatise or article that the witness has relied on. See §570. The federal rules and many states now have a hearsay exception for statements contained in **published treatises, periodicals, or pamphlets** concerning history, medicine or any other science or art. FRE 803(18) contains three important restrictions.

1. Must Be Presented in Connection With Expert Testimony [§327]

Statements in learned treatises, periodicals and pamphlets may be used only to the extent that they are **called to the attention of an expert on cross-examination** or **relied upon by an expert in direct exam**.

2. Must Be Established as Reliable Authority [§328]

The proponent of a learned treatise must establish that it is reliable authority. Ordinarily, the proponent does this through the **testimony of the witness** in connection with whose testimony the learned treatise is offered. But the proponent may also establish the authoritative nature of the treatise through the testimony of **another expert**. The proponent may also ask the court to take **judicial notice** of a treatise's status as reliable authority, but this is rarely done.

3. May Not Be Introduced as an Exhibit [§329]

The learned treatise exception allows the proponent only to read into evidence statements contained in learned treatises. The treatise **may not be introduced** as an exhibit.

I. Past Recollection Recorded [§330]

The Past Recollection Recorded exception (PRR) allows a statement previously recorded by a witness to be used at trial when the witness can no longer remember what happened.

1. Elements of PRR [§331]

A recorded statement concerning a matter is admissible as PRR if the following six requirements are met: (a) the **declarant testifies** at trial; (b) he once had **personal knowledge** about the matter; (c) he now has **insufficient recollection** to testify fully and accurately about it; (d) he **made or adopted** the statement (e) while the event was still **fresh in his memory**; and (f) it **accurately reflected his knowledge** at the time. [FRE 803(5).]

a. Insufficient Recollection [§332]

PRR may be used only when necessary. Thus, the witness's **ability to remember the facts in question must be exhausted**. If, after reading the statement, the witness states that his memory has been jogged and that he now remembers the facts, PRR cannot be used. (At that point, the witness's recollection has been refreshed. See §337.)

b. Made or Adopted the Statement [§333]

Even if the witness did not create the writing himself, if it was created at his direction (e.g., dictation) or adopted by him (e.g., he reads over and approves the content of someone else's statement), it may qualify as PRR.

2. Rationale [§334]

This exception is justified on the basis of **reliability** and **necessity**. The witness/declarant provides assurances that, when he recorded the information, it was fresh in his mind and he recorded it accurately. Thus, the witness vouches for the record's reliability. The use of PRR is necessary because the witness/declarant no longer remembers the facts.

3. May Only Be Read Into Evidence [§335]

A memo that qualifies as PRR **may not be introduced** as an exhibit. Since it is a substitute for the witness's testimony, the proponent may only have the PRR read to the jury. However, the **opposing party is entitled to examine the memo and introduce it** (e.g., to show that there are erasures or irregularities that cast doubt on its reliability).

4. **Availability of the Declarant Really is Required [§336]**

Although PRR is included among the hearsay exceptions in FRE 803 for which the availability of the declarant is said to be immaterial, PRR requires that the declarant be a witness. (He must testify that he doesn't remember, that he made or adopted the memo, etc.)

5. **Present Recollection Refreshed Distinguished [§337]**

Past Recollection Recorded is often confused with the similar-sounding Present Recollection Refreshed. Remember, **Past Recollection Recorded** is a **hearsay exception** that allows the use of a previously written statement by a witness who can no longer remember what happened. **Present Recollection Refreshed** merely refers to the technique and procedures surrounding an **attempt by counsel to jog a forgetful witness's memory**. This often involves showing the witness a writing that he (or someone else) created, in the hope that the witness will say, "Oh yes. Now I remember." Present Recollection Refreshed does not involve a hearsay problem and is covered in §449 below.

J. **Catch-All Exception: Equivalent Trustworthiness [§338]**

The federal rules and about half the states include a **"catch-all"** or **"residual"** hearsay exception. Even if the hearsay statement does not fall within a specific hearsay exception, it will be admissible if it possesses **"equivalent circumstantial guarantees of trustworthiness."** (Hence, "equivalency" in the mnemonic. See §244.) In addition to finding "equivalency," the court must find that **four requirements** are met.

1. **Must Be Material [§339]**

The statement is offered as evidence of a **material fact**. (Since evidence must be relevant to be admissible, this adds nothing.)

2. Must Be Necessary [§340]

The statement must be more probative on the point for which it is offered than any other evidence that the proponent can reasonably be expected to come up with.

3. Must Serve Justice [§341]

Admission of the statement must best serve the general purposes of the rules and the interests of justice. (If the other requirements are met, what are the odds that this requirement won't be met?)

4. Notice Requirement [§342]

The proponent must give the adverse party **notice** of (a) the **intention to offer** hearsay under this exception; and (b) the **particulars** of the statement, including the **name and address of the declarant**. The notice must be given **sufficiently in advance of trial** to afford the opponent a fair opportunity to meet the evidence.

5. Not Included in Either FRE 803 or 804 [§343]

The federal rules list most of the hearsay exceptions in either FRE 803 (availability of the declarant immaterial) or FRE 804 (declarant must be unavailable). The catch-all exception has its own rule—FRE 807. The text of FRE 807 does not list unavailability of the declarant as a requirement. Unavailability, therefore, is not a requirement. But if the declarant is available to testify, a court may be less inclined to find that the hearsay statement is more probative than other evidence that the proponent can procure.

K. Hearsay Exceptions: Unavailability Required [§344]

There are certain hearsay exceptions that apply only if the declarant is unavailable. The five hearsay exceptions that apply only if the declarant is unavailable are: **D**ying declarations; **A**gainst interest declarations; **F**amily and personal history statements; **F**orfeiture by wrongdoing; **T**estimony, former. Use the mnemonic "DAFFT" to remember them.

1. Unavailability Defined [§345]

The federal rules and most states declare that a declarant is "unavailable" if she (a) is too **ill** to testify or is **dead**; (b) validly asserts a **privilege** not to testify; (c) **refuses to testify** despite being ordered by the court to do so; (d) testifies to a **lack of memory**; or (e) is **absent** and the proponent of the statement **cannot procure her attendance** (i.e., the declarant is outside the court's subpoena power) **or testimony** (i.e., the proponent can't take her deposition). [FRE 804(a).]

a. **Mnemonic: "PRIMA" [§346]**
    You can remember the five grounds for unavailability by "PRIMA": **P**rivilege; **R**efusal to testify; **I**ll or dead; **M**emory; **A**bsent.

b. **Absence as Ground For Unavailability [§347]**
    If the proponent of a statement tries to show that the declarant is unavailable on the ground that she is absent, the proponent must show that the **declarant's attendance at trial cannot be procured**. In addition, except when the proponent is offering the statement under the former testimony or forfeiture exceptions, the proponent must establish that he **could not take the declarant's deposition**. [FRE 804(a)(5).]

c. **Proponent Cannot Procure Unavailability [§348]**
    If the proponent of the statement acts to prevent the declarant from testifying, the proponent cannot claim the declarant is unavailable. [FRE 804(a).]

EXAMPLE
Defendant seeks to offer a statement by Declarant under the declaration against interest exception, which requires a showing that the declarant is unavailable. Declarant is unavailable because Defendant paid for him to take a trip to a remote jungle in South America. Since Defendant procured Declarant's unavailability, he cannot claim Declarant is unavailable. Therefore, he will not be able to offer Declarant's statement under the declaration against interest exception.

L. **Dying Declarations [§349]**
    Statements made by a person who believes his death is imminent are said to be reliable because the person would not want to go to his maker "with a lie on his lips." This is, in a

nutshell, the traditional explanation for the dying declaration exception.

1. **Common-Law Version [§350]**

   Skeptical of the reliability of dying declarations, the common law requires not only that (a) the declarant **believe his death is imminent**, but also (b) that the **statement concern the causes and circumstances of the impending death**. In addition, the common law allows dying declarations to be admitted (c) only in the **homicide prosecution of the declarant's killer**. This latter requirement makes clear that the common law requires (d) that the declarant be **dead**. It also shows that common-law courts view the **need for the evidence** as a major justification for the exception.

2. **Federal Rules [§351]**

   Under FRE 804(b)(2), a statement qualifies as a dying declaration if (a) the declarant made the statement while **believing his death is imminent**; (b) the statement **concerns the causes or circumstances of what he believed to be his impending death**; (c) the declarant is **unavailable** and (d) the statement is offered in a **civil case** or **any homicide prosecution**.

   a. **Federal Rule Compared With Common Law [§352]**

      FRE 804(b)(2) broadens the dying declaration exception in two ways. First, although the declarant must be unavailable, he **need not be dead**. Second, dying declarations are admissible in all **civil cases** and **criminal homicide prosecutions**. Several states have expanded the exception still further and allow dying declarations in all cases, civil and criminal.

   EXAMPLE

   Victim 1 and Victim 2 are shot by an assailant. Victim 1 tells Witness, "I'm a goner — Defendant shot us," and lapses into unconsciousness. Victim 1 does not die but remains in a coma. At Defendant's trial for the murder of Victim 2 (who does die), Witness's testimony as to Victim 1's statement would be admissible under the federal rules but not under the common law.

b. Statement Must Concern Circumstances of Death [§353]

The statement must relate to the causes or circumstances surrounding the declarant's death (or what he believed to be his imminent death). If the declarant is dying of cancer, his statement, "Defendant killed my friend Joe," will not qualify as a dying declaration.

c. Declarant Must Believe Death is Imminent [§354]

All jurisdictions require that the statement be made with a conscious, hopeless expectation of impending death. In a law school exam, it must be made fairly clear that such an expectation exists. Remember that the court decides whether a statement qualifies under a hearsay exception, so the court must be satisfied that the declarant believed his death was imminent.

M. Declaration Against Interest [§355]

Under common law, a statement qualifies for the declaration against interest exception if it was (a) against the declarant's **pecuniary** (financial) or **proprietary** (property) interest (b) **at the time the statement was made**; and (c) the declarant is **unavailable**. The federal rules and most states have broadened this exception slightly by including statements that are against a declarant's **penal** interest as well. [FRE 804(b)(2).]

1. Rationale [§356]

This exception is premised on the notion that a person ordinarily doesn't say something adverse to her own interest unless it is true. The unavailability requirement assures that this hearsay exception will be used only when necessary.

2. Analysis of Elements [§357]

a. Unavailability [§358]

Declarations against interest are admissible only when the declarant is unavailable.

b. When Made [§359]

The statement must have been against the declarant's interest **at the time the statement was made**. Look at the factual context of the statement to determine whether it is against interest and whether the declarant knew it. Statements that on their face appear to be against interest may not be so if other facts indicate that the declarant had not thought of possible adverse consequences or may have viewed the statement as self-serving.

c. Pecuniary or Proprietary Interest [§360]

A statement is against a person's pecuniary or proprietary interest when the person acknowledges facts that might adversely affect her **financial** well-being (e.g., "I owe X $100" or a receipt acknowledging payment) or limit her **property** rights (e.g., "I don't own Blackacre; X does").

d. Civil Liability [§361]

The federal rules and many states also include statements that would tend either to **subject the declarant to civil liability** (e.g., "the accident was my fault") or **render invalid a claim by the declarant** against another (e.g., "I knew the salesman was lying through his teeth when he told me the car had only 40,000 miles on it").

e. Criminal Liability [§362]

The federal rules and many states now allow the use of declarations against penal interest, i.e., statements that **tend to subject the declarant to criminal liability**. Traditionally, courts did not allow such statements because of the fear that criminal defendants could too easily establish reasonable doubt by getting a friend to testify, "I heard X say that he committed the crime." Consequently, the federal rules allow the use of declarations against **penal** interest to **exculpate** (exonerate) an accused only when **corroborating circumstances clearly indicate the trustworthiness** of the statement. The federal rule places no such limitation on the use of declarations against penal interest offered to **inculpate** an accused (e.g., "Accused and I committed the crime"). Nevertheless, the Supreme Court's reading of this exception and the Confrontation Clause place limits on the prosecution's ability to use inculpatory declarations against penal interest. See §§404-410 below.

f. Social Interest [§363]

A few states allow statements by a declarant that would tend to subject her to **hatred, ridicule,** or **disgrace**.

g. "Collateral" Statements—Supreme Court Approach [§364]

In the course of saying something that is disserving to himself, a declarant may also comment collaterally on the involvement or non-involvement of other people. For example, Declarant might say, "I committed the crime with Joe" or "I committed the crime, but Joe wasn't involved." No problem arises when Declarant is the person against whom such a statement is offered: the statement then qualifies as an admission by party opponent, and there is no need even to refer to the declaration against interest exception. But suppose Joe is the one who is on trial. May the prosecution offer Declarant's statement, "I committed the crime with Joe"? It is not Joe's statement, so it cannot be offered against Joe as an admission by party opponent. Can it be offered under the declaration against interest exception? And what if Joe wanted to offer Declarant's statement "I committed the crime, but Joe wasn't involved"? Is that admissible as a declaration against interest?

The problem here is that Declarant's reference to Joe—either to his involvement or non-involvement—may not be disserving **to Declarant**. Three possibilities exist. The reference to Joe may be (a) disserving to Declarant (e.g., revealing his association with Joe may implicate Declarant in other crimes or more strongly in this one); (b) neutral as to Declarant (e.g., exonerating Joe from participation may have no influence on Declarant's liability); or (c) self-serving (e.g., Declarant may be attempting to curry favor with the authorities by implicating Joe).

In *Williamson v. United States,* 512 U.S. 594 (1994), the Supreme Court held that **only those portions of a statement that are actually disserving to the declarant** fall within the declaration against interest exception. Each statement made within the context of an overall confession must be examined individually. The exception applies only to those statements that, when viewed in context, are so disserving that a reasonable person in the declarant's situation would not have made them unless he or she believed them to be true. If they are not disserving to the declarant, they are not admissible as declarations against interest.

EXAMPLE: DISSERVING
After Joe has been charged with murdering Victim, Declarant reveals to his girlfriend that he assisted Joe in the murder. By linking himself with Joe, Declarant has made a statement that is against his own interest.

EXAMPLE: NEUTRAL
Declarant makes a statement, "Joe and I robbed the Seven-Eleven last week. Defendant was not involved." Although the part of the statement in which Declarant acknowledges that he robbed the Seven-Eleven is clearly a declaration against his penal interest, the portion that absolves Defendant of any involvement is neutral as to Declarant's interest. The part that implicates Joe may also be neutral, except insofar as it might tend to subject Declarant to conspiracy charges in addition to the robbery charge.

EXAMPLE: SELF-SERVING
Declarant makes a statement, "Joe and I robbed the Seven-Eleven last week. Joe shot the clerk. I was only standing watch; I didn't even know he had a gun." The first sentence is against Declarant's interest (and perhaps only the part referring to Declarant). The balance of the statement, however, tends to be self-serving.

h. "Collateral" Statements—Other Jurisdictions' Approach [§365]

The Supreme Court's reading of the federal rules' declaration against interest exception is not binding on the states. A state is free to interpret its declaration against interest exception more broadly. Some jurisdictions are more receptive to admitting neutral comments contained in a larger statement against interest or are more apt to find that a collateral statement qualifies as disserving. In criminal prosecutions, however, the Confrontation Clause (found in the Sixth Amendment) places limits on the state's ability to offer hearsay against an accused. See §§404-410.

3. Declarations Against Interest vs. Admissions [§366]

A declaration against interest must be disserving to the declarant at the time the statement is made. An admission by a party opponent need not be. A declaration against interest is admissible only when the declarant is unavailable. Admissions are admissible against a party opponent regardless of the availability of the declarant. (Remember the party opponent may be a corporation and its admission may be made by an employee). Finally, declarations against interest are admitted because they are reliable and so are admissible against all parties to a multi-party action. Admissions are admitted under a responsibility or estoppel theory and so are admissible only against the party opponent.

N. Former Testimony [§367]

The former testimony exception comes into play when the out-of-court statement that is now being offered was itself made as testimony in another hearing or deposition. If certain requirements are met, such statements are deemed sufficiently reliable to be admitted. [FRE 804(b)(1).]

1. Other Hearing or Deposition [§368]

The former testimony must have been given at an earlier trial of the same case, the trial of another case, a deposition taken in connection with the same or another case, or at some other proceeding. It must have been given under oath.

2. **Unavailability Required [§369]**
    The declarant (i.e., the witness in the earlier hearing) must now be unavailable. The preference is still for live testimony.

3. **Opportunity and Motive to Develop the Testimony [§370]**
    Former testimony is admissible only if the party **against whom it is now being offered** had (a) the **opportunity** and (b) the **motive** to develop the testimony in the former hearing in much the same way that it would develop the testimony if the declarant were testifying in the current proceeding. This is what gives the former testimony its aura of reliability: the fact that the party against whom it is now being offered had the chance and the incentive to probe the witness's story at the earlier hearing.

    a. **Predecessor in Interest Okay for Civil Cases [§371]**
        In addition, the federal rules provide that **in civil cases**, even if the party against whom the testimony is now being offered did not have the opportunity and motive to develop the testimony at the earlier hearing, the former testimony is admissible if **a predecessor in interest of the party** had the opportunity and motive to do so. The meaning of predecessor in interest is somewhat cloudy. One reading is that the predecessor in interest must be someone in privity with the party against whom the testimony is now being offered. Federal courts have tended to interpret the requirement more loosely. In the leading federal case, the court essentially required only that the predecessor in interest be someone who had a similar interest in developing the testimony. *Lloyd v. American Export Lines, Inc.,* 580 F.2d 1179 (3d Cir. 1978).

        EXAMPLE: CIVIL CASE
        Arnold and Brenda are injured by Defendant's train in the same accident. They bring separate actions against Defendant. In *Arnold v. Defendant*, Arnold testifies against Defendant. Arnold dies before Brenda's case goes to trial. In *Brenda v. Defendant*, Brenda offers Arnold's former

testimony. It is admissible because Defendant, the party against whom it is now being offered, had the opportunity and motive to develop Arnold's testimony in *Arnold v. Defendant*.

EXAMPLE: CIVIL CASE—PREDECESSOR IN INTEREST

Arnold and Brenda are injured by Defendant's train in the same accident. They bring separate actions against Defendant. In *Arnold v. Defendant*, Witness testifies against Arnold. Witness dies before Brenda's case goes to trial. In *Brenda v. Defendant*, Defendant offers Witness's former testimony. It may be admissible. Although Brenda, the party against whom the testimony is now being offered, did not have the opportunity to develop Witness's testimony (since Brenda was not a party in *Arnold v. Defendant*), Arnold had the opportunity and the same motive to develop the testimony that Brenda would now have. If Arnold is considered Brenda's predecessor in interest (as is likely under the liberal interpretation given by the federal courts), Witness's former testimony would be admissible because this is a civil case.

EXAMPLE: CRIMINAL CASE

Defendant is on trial for an armed robbery he committed with Cohort. The prosecution seeks to introduce the testimony given by Eyewitness in Cohort's trial. Eyewitness died of a heart attack shortly after Cohort's trial. The testimony is inadmissible. Defendant, the party against whom the testimony is now being offered, did not have a chance to cross-examine Eyewitness. Although Cohort had the opportunity and the motive to cross-examine Eyewitness, in criminal cases it must be the person against whom the testimony is now being offered who had the opportunity and motive to do the cross-examination. A predecessor in interest can serve this function only in civil cases.

b. **Former Testimony Need Not Have Been Developed [§372]**

The rule requires only that the party against whom the testimony is now offered (or, in a civil case, a predecessor in interest) have had an **opportunity** to develop the former testimony. The failure to take advantage of the opportunity does not render the exception inapplicable. Of course, the party may now argue that the failure to examine the declarant in the former proceeding is evidence of a lack of motive to develop the testimony in that proceeding.

4. Common-Law Approach [§373]

The majority common-law rule is that former testimony is admissible only if the issues and parties in the former proceeding are identical to those at the trial in which the former testimony is now being offered. As indicated above, the federal rules depart from this approach, and so have many states. But in determining whether a party had similar motive to develop the testimony in the former hearing, courts will consider the degree of similarity between the issues in the present and former hearings.

5. Introduction of Former Testimony [§374]

The normal mode of introducing former testimony is to have counsel or a witness read from the transcript of the earlier hearing. Beware that this involves double hearsay; the transcript is itself the court reporter's out-of-court statement, "This is what the witness said." Typically, the transcript will qualify as a business record.

O. Forfeiture by Wrongdoing [§375]

The forfeiture by wrongdoing exception applies when the party against whom a hearsay statement is offered procured by wrongdoing the declarant's unavailability. The federal rules added this exception in 1997. Before that, the federal courts and many states dealt with this issue as a matter of **waiver**. They simply held that a party who rendered a declarant unavailable to testify—for example, by killing the declarant or "advising" the declarant to leave the jurisdiction—had waived his right to object to the admission of the declarant's hearsay statement. The federal rules now treat this as a **hearsay exception**. It applies when the party against whom the statement is offered **engaged or acquiesced in wrongdoing** that was **intended to, and did, procure** the declarant's unavailability.

P. Statements of Personal or Family History [§376]

This is the last hearsay exception that requires unavailability of the declarant. It is not an important exception, however, and will be covered with other unimportant exceptions in §§384-388.

Q. Prior Statements of a Witness [§377]

Recall that in the discussion of what is hearsay, we saw that a **witness can also be a hearsay declarant**. That is, a witness's own out-of-court statements can be hearsay even though the witness can be cross-examined about those statements. See §221. Because that does not make a lot of sense, the federal rules and many states now **exempt from the hearsay rule three kinds of statements previously made by a witness**. Technically, these are not hearsay exceptions. As is the case with admissions by a party opponent, they are simply **defined as nonhearsay**.

1. Declarant Must Testify and be Subject to Cross-Examination [§378]

These three hearsay exemptions cover only out-of-court statements made by someone who testifies at the current trial. In other words, they cover only statements by a declarant who is also a witness at the current trial. In addition, the declarant/witness **must be subject, at the current trial, to cross-examination about the prior statement**. The Supreme Court has held that a witness is "subject to cross-examination concerning the statement" even when the witness has suffered a memory loss and is unable to respond substantively to questions about the statement. This requirement is ordinarily met when a witness is placed on the stand, under oath, and responds willingly to questions. *United States v. Owens*, 484 U.S. 554 (1988).

a. Certain Prior Inconsistent Statements [§379]

Recall that a witness may be impeached by showing that he has previously made statements inconsistent with his trial testimony. Under FRE 801(d)(1)(A), however, some prior inconsistent statements may be used not only for impeachment purposes, but as substantive evidence as well. If the prior inconsistent statement of the witness was made (a) under **oath**, (b) subject to the **penalty of perjury**, (c) at an earlier **trial, hearing, or other proceeding, or in a deposition**, it is defined as nonhearsay and **may be**

used for its truth. For an example of this, see §483. Note that **grand jury testimony** meets these requirements. Thus, if a witness's trial testimony is inconsistent with his testimony before the grand jury, the grand jury testimony may be used not only to impeach him, but as substantive evidence (i.e., for its truth) as well.

b. Certain Prior Consistent Statements [§380]
A witness may sometimes be rehabilitated by showing that he has previously made statements consistent with his trial testimony. Federal Rule 801(d)(1)(B) provides that certain prior consistent statements are nonhearsay and thus may be used as substantive evidence as well. The prior statement will qualify if it (a) is **consistent** with the witness's trial testimony and (b) is offered to **rebut a charge** (express or implied) that the witness either has recently **fabricated his testimony** or is **testifying from an improper motive or influence**. The prior consistent statement must have been made, however, **before the motive to fabricate** the story or the improper influence arose. See §529.

c. Prior Statements of Identification [§381]
A witness's out-of-court **identification of a person made after perceiving him** is defined as nonhearsay in Federal Rule 801(d)(1)(C). Thus, the fact that a witness earlier picked the defendant out of a line-up is admissible not only to rehabilitate the witness (e.g., if the witness's ability to identify the defendant has been attacked), but also as substantive evidence (i.e., as evidence that the out-of-court identification of defendant is true).

2. Not Really Hearsay Exceptions [§382]
Remember, these three types of prior statements of witnesses are defined as nonhearsay and are technically not hearsay exceptions. This is of no practical importance (except perhaps on a law school exam).

R. Miscellaneous Exceptions [§383]

There are many relatively unimportant hearsay exceptions, most of which never see the light of day on a law school exam. Just in case, here they are.

1. Personal or Family History [§384]

A number of hearsay exceptions may be used to prove matters relating to someone's personal or family history.

a. Statements Regarding Personal or Family History [§385]

Statements concerning either the declarant's own personal or family history or another person's personal or family history are admissible under FRE 804(b)(4).

(1) Declarant's Own History [§386]

This exception covers statements concerning the declarant's own birth, adoption, marriage, divorce, legitimacy, relationship by blood, adoption or marriage, ancestry, or other similar fact. In contrast to the common law, the federal rule does not require the declarant to show that he had personal knowledge about the matter.

(2) Another's History [§387]

The exception also covers statements concerning someone else's personal or family history (the above-stated matters plus the person's death) if the declarant was (a) **related to the other person** by blood, adoption or marriage or (b) was so **intimately associated** with the other's family as to be likely to have accurate information. Personal knowledge on the part of the declarant is required here.

(3) Declarant Must Be Unavailable [§388]

This is one of the exceptions that apply only if the declarant is unavailable to testify.

b. Records of Vital Statistics [§389]

Records of vital statistics—births, fetal deaths, deaths, marriages—are admissible if the report thereof was made to a public office pursuant to the requirements of law. [FRE 803(9).] The person who reported the information need not herself have been a public official.

c. **Records of Religious Organizations [§390]**
Statements contained in a **regularly kept record** of a religious organization **concerning personal or family history** such as births, deaths, marriages, divorces, deaths, legitimacy, ancestry, or relationship by blood or marriage are admissible under FRE 803(11).

d. **Marriage, Baptismal, and Similar Certificates [§391]**
FRE 803(12) creates an exception for statements of fact contained in a certificate that the maker (a) performed a marriage or other ceremony or (b) administered a sacrament. The **maker** of the certificate must be a **clergyman, public official, or other person authorized** by the religious organization or law to perform the act certified. In addition, the certificate must have been made at the time of the act or within a reasonable time afterwards.

e. **Family Records [§392]**
FRE 803(13) creates an exception for statements of fact concerning personal or family history found in family Bibles, genealogies, charts, inscriptions on family portraits, engravings on rings, urns, crypts, or tombstones, or the like.

f. **Reputation [§393]**
FRE 803(19) creates an exception for a person's reputation concerning matters of his personal or family history. The reputation may exist among members of the person's family, among his associates, or in the community.

g. **Judgments [§394]**
Under FRE 803(23), a prior judgment may be used as proof of matters of personal or family history if the particular matter was essential to the prior judgment.

2. Ancient Documents [§395]

If a document is old enough, statements in it are unlikely to have been made with a motive to falsify arising from impending litigation. Therefore, under FRE 803(16) a hearsay exception exists for statements contained in documents that are **at least 20 years old** and that have been **authenticated**. This reduces the common-law time period, which was 30 years.

3. Property Interests [§396]

Several exceptions may be used to prove facts relating to property or interests in property.

a. Records of Documents Affecting Property Interests [§397]

If a record of a document that purports to establish or affect an interest in property is (a) the record of a public office and (b) local law authorizes the recording of such documents in that kind of office, the record may be used as proof of **the contents of the original** recorded document and of its **execution and delivery** by each person by whom it purports to have been executed. [FRE 803(14).]

b. Statements Contained in Documents Affecting Property Interests [§398]

Under FRE 803(15), a hearsay exception is created for statements contained in documents that purport to establish or affect an interest in property **if the matter relates to the purpose of the document** (e.g., a deed recites that the grantors are all heirs of the last record owner). The exception cannot be used, however, if dealings by the property owners since the document was made have been inconsistent with the truth of the statement.

c. Reputation [§399]

FRE 803(20) creates an exception for the reputation in the community as to boundaries of or customs affecting lands in the community.

d. Judgments [§400]

Judgments may be used as proof of boundaries if such matters were essential to the judgment. [FRE 803(23).]

4. Market Reports and Commercial Publications [§401]

"Market quotations, tabulations, lists, directories, or other published compilations, generally used and relied upon by the public or by persons in particular occupations" are admissible. [FRE 803(17).]

5. Reputation [§402]

Reputation evidence may be used for several different purposes. Some are discussed above: reputation for personal or family history and as to land boundaries and customs. Reputation evidence may also be used to prove **events of general history** important to the community, state or nation. [FRE 803(20).] Finally, reputation evidence may be used to prove **a person's character**. [FRE 803(21).] Recall, however, that evidence of a person's character is admissible only for certain purposes.

6. Judgment of Previous Conviction [§403]

Evidence of a final judgment adjudging a person guilty of a **felony** is admissible to prove **any fact essential to sustain the judgment**, with certain limitations. First, this exception applies only if the judgment was entered **after a trial or upon a guilty plea**; it does not apply where the conviction was entered upon a plea of nolo contendere. Second, in criminal cases, the government may not use the fact that some person other than the accused has been convicted of a felony as proof of some fact that was essential to sustain that conviction. The government may, however, use another person's convictions for impeachment purposes.

EXAMPLE: CIVIL CASE

Plaintiff sues Brokerage Firm for damages Plaintiff alleges she incurred as a result of material misrepresentations made by Brokerage Firm's securities analyst concerning Dotcom Co. Plaintiff seeks to prove that the analyst was convicted of securities fraud, a felony, for making material misrepresentations about Dotcom Co. Evidence of the conviction is admissible to prove that the analyst made material misrepresentations about Dotcom Co.

EXAMPLE: LIMIT IN CRIMINAL CASE

Defendant is being prosecuted as an accomplice to a robbery committed by Cohort. The prosecution may not offer evidence that Cohort was convicted of the robbery as proof that the robbery occurred and that Cohort was involved. The prosecution may, however, impeach defense witnesses with their prior convictions pursuant to Rule 609 (the rule governing impeachment with convictions). See § 507.

S. Confrontation Clause [§404]

The Sixth Amendment to the Constitution guarantees a criminal defendant the right "to be **confronted with the witnesses** against him." Among other things, the Confrontation Clause places limits on the prosecution's ability to offer **hearsay against a criminal defendant**. But it is does not erect an absolute bar to its admissibility. The contours of the limits have been the subject of numerous Supreme Court opinions. In some respects, the law is clear; in others, it is in a state of flux.

One situation in which the law is clear is where the hearsay declarant testifies at trial and is subject to cross-examination.

1. No Confrontation Clause Problem If Hearsay Declarant Testifies [§405]

If the hearsay declarant **testifies** at the trial and can be **cross-examined** about his hearsay statements, there is **no Confrontation Clause problem**. This is true even if the declarant has no memory of the underlying event. In *United States v. Owens*, 484 U.S. 554 (1988), the victim of a beating (who suffered severe head injuries) testified that he remembered identifying the defendant as his assailant during his interview with an FBI agent. On cross-examination, however, he admitted that he could not remember seeing his assailant, could not remember any of the numerous hospital visitors he received other than the agent, and could not remember whether any of the other visitors had suggested that defendant was the assailant. The court admitted the victim's out-of-court identification of defendant as a prior statement of identification. The

Supreme Court rejected the defense argument that the victim's lack of memory rendered cross-examination useless and thus violated the Confrontation Clause. The victim's presence on the stand was sufficient to meet the demands of the Confrontation Clause. The Confrontation Clause guarantees the **opportunity for effective cross-examination**, not cross-examination that is effective in whatever way the accused might wish.

2. **If Declarant Does Not Testify: 1980-2004 [§406]**
    Ohio v. Roberts, 448 U.S. 56 (1980), set forth **a two-pronged test** for Confrontation Clause analysis where the declarant did not testify at trial. The two prongs were **unavailability** and **reliability**. The Confrontation Clause demanded first, that if the prosecution did not produce the declarant at trial it must demonstrate that the declarant was unavailable to testify at trial. Second, the hearsay must be reliable. The Court, however, soon began cutting back on the unavailability requirement, see *United States v. Inadi*, 475 U.S. 387 (1986); *White v. Illinois*, 502 U.S. 346 (1992), leaving only the reliability requirement. As long as the hearsay was reliable, therefore, the Confrontation Clause did not bar its admissibility. **Reliability** could be established in either of two ways. First, hearsay was deemed reliable if it fell within a **firmly-rooted hearsay exception**. (Remember, hearsay has to qualify for admission under some hearsay exception before the Confrontation Clause even becomes a problem.) Second, if the hearsay did not fall within a firmly-rooted hearsay exception, the prosecution could show that the statement possessed **particularized guarantees of trustworthiness**.

3. **If Declarant Does Not Testify: Crawford v. Washington (2004) [§407]**
    The Supreme Court dramatically changed its approach to the Confrontation Clause in *Crawford v. Washington*, 541 U.S. 36 (2004). Because the Confrontation Clause guarantees an accused the right to confront "witnesses" against him, and a witness is someone who "bears testimony," the confrontation clause applies only to **"testimonial"** statements. If the prosecution offers hearsay that qualifies as a "testimonial" statement and the declarant does not testify, the Confrontation Clause

demands that the **declarant must be unavailable** and that the accused must have had a **prior opportunity to cross-examine the declarant.**

a. **Possible Definitions of "Testimonial" [§408]**
Crawford offered **three possible definitions** of what would qualify as a "testimonial" statement:

- "*ex parte* **in-court testimony or its functional equivalent**" (i.e., things such as affidavits, custodial examinations, prior testimony that the defendant had been unable to cross-examine, or similar pretrial statements that **declarants** would **reasonably expect** to be used **prosecutorially**);

- "**extrajudicial statements** . . . contained in **formalized testimonial materials**, such as affidavits, depositions, prior testimony, or confessions;" and

- "statements that were made under circumstances which would lead an **objective witness reasonably to believe** that the statement would be **available** for use **at a later trial**."

The Court found that the hearsay statement in the case—a confession made by the accused's wife during a custodial interrogation that implicated the accused—would qualify as "testimonial" under any of the three definitions. Therefore, the Court declined to pick one of these as the definition of "testimonial." The Court merely held that whatever else "testimonial" covers, it applies at a minimum to **prior testimony at** a **preliminary hearing**, before a **grand jury**, or at a **former trial**, and to **police interrogations**.

4. **If Declarant Does Not Testify: *Davis* and *Hammon* (2006) [§409]**
Two years after *Crawford*, the Supreme Court revisited the question of what constitutes a "testimonial" statement in a pair of cases consolidated under the name *Davis v. Washington*, 126 S.Ct. 2266 (2006). Both *Davis* and its

sister case, *Hammon v. Indiana*, involved statements made to law enforcement agents relating to domestic violence incidents. The statements at issue in *Davis* were made by the victim to a 911 operator while the incident was still in progress. The statements in *Hammon* were made to police who came to investigate a report of a domestic disturbance shortly after it ended. The Court held that the statements in *Davis* were **not testimonial**; the statements in *Hammon* were **testimonial**.

a. **Statements to Law Enforcement Agents: Testimonial Defined [§410]**

A statement to a law enforcement agent is **not testimonial** (and thus not subject to the Confrontation Clause) when it is **made in the course of police interrogation** under **circumstances objectively** indicating that the **primary purpose** of the interrogation is to **enable police assistance to meet an ongoing emergency**. Since the statements in *Davis* were made by the victim to a 911 operator while the incident was still in progress, they were not testimonial. A statement to a law enforcement agent is **testimonial** (and thus subject to the Confrontation Clause) when the **circumstances objectively** indicate that there is **no ongoing emergency** and that the **primary purpose** of the interrogation is to **establish or prove past events** potentially relevant to later **criminal prosecution**. Since the statements in *Hammon* were part of an investigation into already-completed criminal conduct, they were testimonial.

Note that in *Davis* and *Hammon* the Court concerned itself **only with statements to law enforcement agents**. Thus, it did not offer a comprehensive definition of "testimonial" to apply in other contexts, such as statements to friends (e.g., a statement implicating the speaker and the defendant), reports by lab technicians (e.g., a lab report concluding that the substance seized from defendant is cocaine), and statements to doctors (e.g., a statement by a child that defendant abused her). Lower courts are grappling with the applicability of the Confrontation Clause to such statements, with mixed results.

V. Witnesses

A. Competency of Witnesses [§411]

In the past, the law deemed numerous categories of witnesses incompetent to testify because of concerns about their trustworthiness. At one time, parties were disqualified from testifying, as were felons, atheists, children, and the insane. The federal rules have dropped almost all such restrictions; common-law jurisdictions have dropped many.

1. FRE General Rule: Everyone is Competent to Testify [§412]

With the exception of judges and jurors, see §§417-418, the federal rules provide that **every person is competent to be a witness**. [FRE 601.] While a witness's youth, infirmity, mental illness, intoxicated state, prison record, etc. may be used to attack the strength of his testimony, these are not grounds for preventing the witness from testifying.

2. Common Law: Ability to Observe, Recall, and Relate Required [§413]

Many common-law jurisdictions hold that a witness is incompetent to testify if she lacks sufficient mental capacity to accurately observe, recall or relate facts. Witnesses are, however, presumed to be competent. Their lack of capacity must be raised through an objection. The judge then has broad discretion in deciding the question of testimonial competence.

a. Age [§414]

Although many jurisdictions used to have minimum age limits for witnesses, this is no longer the case. As long as a child possesses sufficient mental capacity to testify, she will be considered competent.

b. Insane Persons May Testify [§415]

Insane persons may be competent to give meaningful testimony. An adjudication of incompetency to manage one's affairs or insanity is **not conclusive** of a person's incompetency to testify as a witness.

3. Dead Man's Rule [§416]

The federal rules have virtually abandoned what has traditionally been known as the Dead Man's Rule. Therefore, questions on this topic are not likely to arise in an evidence course that focuses on the federal rules. The only time the issue can arise in federal court is when a state law claim is being adjudicated, in which case the federal court uses the state law regarding competency of witnesses as well. Since there is little uniformity among the states on the Dead Man's Rule, it is very difficult to test it without reference to a particular state's rule.

The theory of the Dead Man's Rule is that when one party to a transaction has died, it is unfair to allow the survivor to tell his side of the story because the deceased, of course, is unable to give his version. Typically, therefore, the Dead Man's Rule provides that: (1) in a case brought **by or against the personal representative of a deceased** (i.e., the executor or administrator of the deceased's estate) (2) a **party** (3) may not testify as to a **transaction** (4) with the **deceased**. (But remember, many states no longer have a Dead Man's Rule and in those states that still have one, the details of the rule vary from state to state.)

4. Competency of Judges as Witnesses [§417]

A judge may not testify in a case over which the judge is **presiding**. The reason is obvious: imagine having to cross-examine the judge who is going to be ruling on your later objections. Having the judge testify is considered such bad practice that a party need not object to it in order to preserve the issue for appeal. [FRE 605.]

5. Competency of Jurors as Witnesses [§418]

a. At the Trial [§419]

A juror may not testify as a witness in the trial of a case in which the juror is sitting. The reasoning is much the same as it is for judges. To preserve error, however, objection must be made. The objecting party must be given an opportunity to object outside the presence of the jury. [FRE 606(a).]

b. At Hearing Challenging Validity of Verdict [§420]

After a verdict is reached, lawyers often try to challenge the verdict on the ground that the jurors engaged in misconduct during jury deliberations. FRE 606(b) severely limits this practice by circumscribing the ability of jurors to testify about jury deliberations. The general rule is that a juror may not testify about (a) any **matter or statement** that occurred during the jury's **deliberations**, (b) the **mental process** by which a juror arrived at his or her decision, or (c) **anything that influenced any juror's mental processes** in arriving at a verdict. This rule is based on a desire to protect jurors from harassment and promote the finality of their judgments. The rule also prohibits someone other than a juror from testifying about a juror's statement about such matters.

EXAMPLE

Plaintiff sues Defendant, alleging that Defendant misrepresented the condition of a used car Plaintiff purchased from Defendant. The jury returns a verdict for Plaintiff. In support of his motion for a new trial, Defendant calls Juror to testify, "No one on the jury thought that Defendant had misrepresented the condition of the car. We just felt sorry for Plaintiff and wanted to give him something. We figured Defendant's insurer would pick up the tab." This is inadmissible. A juror ordinarily may not testify as to what happened during jury deliberations.

(1) Exceptions [§421]

There are **three** exceptions to this rule. Jurors may testify as to whether (a) **extraneous prejudicial information** was improperly brought to the jury's attention; (b) **any outside influence** was improperly brought to bear on a juror; and (c) there was a **mistake in entering the verdict** onto the verdict form. The last of these exceptions is designed merely to allow jurors to testify that an error was made in writing down on the verdict form the jury's verdict. The first two exceptions are more frequently invoked, although courts do not always distinguish carefully between the two. **Extraneous prejudicial information** generally refers to **information** about the case that was **not admitted into evidence** (e.g., a newspaper article), and **outside influence** generally refers to a juror's **improper exposure to a third party** (e.g., a threat to a juror's family). Courts interpret these exceptions narrowly. For example, they do not allow a juror to testify that other jurors were using drugs or alcohol. *Tanner v. United States*, 483 U.S. 107 (1987). Moreover, even when one of these two exceptions applies, jurors are still not permitted to testify about how they were affected by the prejudicial information or outside influence.

B. Oath or Affirmation [§422]

Under FRE 603, witnesses are required to declare that they will testify truthfully, by an **oath or affirmation** "administered in a form calculated to awaken the witness' conscience and impress the witness' mind with the duty to do so." No finding is required that the witness understands the obligation to tell the truth. Many common-law jurisdictions require such a finding, but the court has broad discretion. With young children, for example, it may be sufficient for the child to state that she understands "I will be punished if I tell a lie." Some witnesses object on religious grounds to taking either an oath or affirmation. When this happens, courts must attempt to devise an alternative means of impressing upon the witness the duty of testifying truthfully.

C. Personal Knowledge [§423]

With the exception of experts, see §§560-566, witnesses may not testify unless they have **personal knowledge of the matter** about which they are testifying. [FRE 602.] The personal knowledge requirement prevents a witness from speculating about how an event occurred or from offering an opinion based on conjecture rather than the facts. It also precludes a witness who did not observe an event from adopting another person's report of the incident and relating it as the witness's own. Whether or not a witness possesses personal knowledge is a conditional relevancy question to be determined under FRE 104(b). The burden, therefore, is quite low. All that is required is enough evidence so that a reasonable juror could find that the witness has personal knowledge. A witness's testimony that she has personal knowledge is sufficient to establish this.

D. Exclusion of Witnesses: Invoking "The Rule" [§424]

In order to prevent a witness from tailoring his story to match (or contradict) the testimony of another witness, a party is entitled to invoke "The Rule." That is, the party may ask the court to **exclude all witnesses from the courtroom** so that they cannot hear what the other witnesses say. [FRE 615.] In addition, witnesses frequently will be instructed that they may not discuss their testimony with others. No one really knows why this rule is called "The Rule."

1. Four Exceptions [§425]

The federal rule exempts four types of witnesses from being excluded from the trial:

(a) a **party who is a natural person** (i.e., a human being);

(b) an officer or employee of a **non-natural party** (e.g., a corporate party or the state) who is designated as its **representative** by its lawyer;

(c) a person whose presence is shown to be **essential to the presentation** of the party's cause (e.g., an expert whose testimony is going to be based on what other witnesses say); and

(d) a person who is **authorized by statute** to be present. This refers to victims' rights legislation, which, under certain conditions, exempts crime victims from The Rule.

2. Sanctions For Noncompliance [§426]

Courts may impose a variety of sanctions for noncompliance with "The Rule." The more draconian sanctions include refusing to let an offending witness testify, striking testimony that the witness has given, and declaring a mistrial. Less severe sanctions include allowing counsel to cross-examine the witness about the violation, instructing the jury to consider the violation in assessing the witness's credibility, and holding the witness in contempt.

E. Examination of Witnesses: Introduction [§427]

Cross-examination, leading questions, and impeachment often go hand in hand. As a result, they are often spoken of interchangeably. They refer, however, to three different things. Therefore, it is important to keep the following distinctions in mind. **Cross-examination** refers to a stage of questioning; **leading questions**, to the form in which a question is asked; and **impeachment**, to the attempt to attack a witness's credibility. Although it does not happen that often, a witness may be impeached on direct examination through the use of non-leading questions.

1. Stages of Examination [§428]

a. Direct Examination [§429]

Direct examination refers to the initial round of questions put to a witness by the party that called the witness.

b. Cross-Examination [§430]

After the calling party completes its direct examination, the opposing party conducts a cross-examination of the witness.

c. Redirect- and Recross-Examination [§431]

After cross-examination, the calling party may conduct a redirect exam, followed by its opponent's recross-exam.

d. Calling and Questioning Witnesses by the Court [§432]

Under FRE 614, the trial court is authorized to call a witness on its own motion. If it does so, all parties are entitled to cross-examine the witness. In addition, the judge is permitted to interrogate any witness, whether called by the court or by a party.

2. Objections as to Form of Question [§433]

The form in which a question is posed may be objectionable for many reasons.

a. Questions Calling for Narrative [§434]

Open-ended questions that call for an undirected narrative by the witness may be objectionable. If, for example, counsel asks, "What happened that day?" there is a risk that the witness will relate irrelevant or otherwise inadmissible evidence. Opposing counsel is thus denied a fair opportunity to anticipate the answer and thereby make timely and effective objections. The judge has broad discretion to permit or prohibit such questions. [FRE 611(a).]

b. Leading Questions [§435]

A leading question is one that **suggests the answer** the witness is to give. In other words, if an ordinary person would get the impression that the questioner desires one answer rather than another, it is a leading question. Questions that start "Isn't it true that . . ." or "Didn't you then . . ." are examples of leading questions.

c. General Rule: Leading Questions Allowed on Cross, But Not on Direct [§436]

Leading questions are generally **not allowed on direct examination** because it is assumed that a witness will be all too willing to follow the suggestion of the lawyer who called her to testify. But leading questions ordinarily **may be asked on cross-examination** since the witness is not likely to be receptive to opposing counsel's suggestions. [FRE 611(c).]

d. Leading Questions Sometimes Allowed on Direct [§437]

There are a few instances in which leading questions may be asked on direct examination.

(1) Preliminary Matters [§438]

Leading questions may be asked if they relate to preliminary matters not in dispute, such as the name, address, and occupation of the witness. This saves time.

(2) Where Necessary [§439]

Witnesses who are having **difficulty testifying in response to non-leading questions** may be asked leading questions. This includes witnesses with **language** problems, **children**, and **mentally feeble** witnesses. In addition, if a witness is **unable to remember** something, counsel may seek to jog her memory with a leading question (e.g., Q: "Did he say anything else?" A: "No." Q: "You don't remember him making any other statements?" A: "No." Q: "He didn't say anything about a gun?" A: "Oh, yes . . ."). The question should only ask what is necessary to refresh the witness's memory; it should not unduly lead the witness.

(3) Witnesses Unlikely to Follow Lead [§440]
Leading questions may be used on direct examination when the witness is (a) an **adverse party**; (b) a witness **identified with an adverse party** (e.g., the president of the defendant corporation); or (c) **hostile** (i.e., unresponsive to non-leading questions). [FRE 611(c).]

e. Leading Questions Sometimes Disallowed on Cross [§441]
Although leading questions ordinarily are allowed on cross-examination, the court may limit their use. A court is most likely to do this when the **witness is friendly to the cross-examiner** and thus quite willing to follow the cross-examiner's lead. This typically occurs when a party calls an adverse witness to the stand, so that the witness's own lawyer winds up conducting the cross-examination.

f. Argumentative Questions [§442]
Questions that are used by counsel to make or emphasize some point or to argue to the jury rather than to elicit information (e.g., "Do you really expect the jury to believe that?") are objectionable.

g. Questions Assuming Facts Not in Evidence [§443]
A question is improper if it assumes the existence of a fact or facts that have not been proved (e.g., "When did you stop beating your wife?" is improper if no evidence has been introduced that the witness ever beat his wife).

h. Compound Questions [§444]

A question that contains two inquiries but calls for only one answer is improper if the answer would be misleading and unclear (e.g., "Did you see and hear X threaten his wife?"). If, however, the inquiries are so distinct and clearly call for separate answers, the question may be permitted (e.g., "Did you see D on that day and, if so, what time was it?").

i. Ambiguous or Unintelligible Questions [§445]

A question must be clear and intelligible so that the witness and the jury can understand it. The court may, therefore, require counsel to restate, rephrase, or clarify an ambiguous or unintelligible question.

j. Questions Calling for Speculation [§446]

It is improper to ask a witness to speculate or to base an answer on pure conjecture.

k. Repetitive Questions: Asked and Answered [§447]

Objection may be made if the witness already has been asked and has answered a substantially identical question.

l. Non-Responsive Answers to Proper Questions [§448]

A witness must respond only to the question asked and must not go off on tangents. The **questioner** may object to a non-responsive answer. In contrast, most jurisdictions do not allow opposing counsel to object on this ground. Opposing counsel may, however, object on other grounds if the testimony is otherwise inadmissible (e.g., contains hearsay) and request that the court instruct the witness to answer only the questions asked. The non-responsiveness of the answer may also excuse counsel's failure to object more quickly.

3. Refreshing a Witness's Memory [§449]

Sometimes witnesses forget. When this happens, counsel may attempt to jog the witness's memory, to refresh his recollection. Counsel may use **anything** that might help trigger the witness's memory. It may be a writing (**whether or not composed by the witness**), a physical object, a leading question, or the rendition of a Willie Nelson song (by the lawyer, on a CD, or by Willie himself). Typically, of course, a writing is used to refresh recollection.

a. **If the Witness Remembers, No Hearsay Problem [§450]**
    If the witness's memory is successfully refreshed, he can **testify from memory**, and no hearsay problem is presented.

b. **Refreshing Item is Not Evidence [§451]**
    The item used to refresh memory is not evidence; it is only a **device** that is used **to jog the witness's memory** and is **not itself being offered as proof**. Therefore, it need not be authenticated, comply with the Best Evidence Rule, fall within a hearsay exception, or meet any other requirement of admissibility.

c. **But Procedural Safeguards Exist [§452]**
    When a **document** is used to refresh a witness's memory, courts fear that the witness who says his memory is refreshed is really remembering only what he just read in the refreshing document. Therefore, when a document is used to refresh a witness's recollection, some procedural safeguards apply.

    (1) **Memory Refreshed While Witness is Testifying [§453]**
        If a witness's memory is refreshed with a document while he is on the stand, opposing counsel is entitled to **inspect** the document, **cross-examine** the witness about it, and **introduce** into evidence relevant portions of the document. [FRE 612.]

    (2) **Memory Refreshed Before Trial [§454]**
        If the witness reviews a document to refresh his memory **before** he testifies, FRE 612 gives the court **discretion** to order counsel to turn over

the document to his opponent for inspection, cross-examination, and introduction of relevant portions. The common law, however, does not authorize the judge to do this when memory is refreshed prior to trial.

d. Steps in Refreshing Recollection [§455]
The following steps are generally observed in refreshing a witness's recollection.

(1) Counsel establishes that the witness's **memory is exhausted**; that is, that the witness cannot testify fully and accurately from memory.

(2) Counsel shows the item used to refresh recollection to the witness. If counsel uses a document, counsel should hand the witness the document and allow the witness to **read it silently**.

(3) If the witness states that he **can now recall the matter independent** of the document (i.e., that his memory is refreshed), the witness may testify. The court may require the witness to testify without further reference to the document. But that is a matter in the court's discretion, and courts often allow witnesses to refer to the document, particularly if the matter is lengthy and detailed.

(4) If the witness states that he **cannot recall the matter** even after reviewing the document, his testimony is stalled. Counsel can then try to establish that the document meets the requirements of the hearsay exception for past recollection recorded, see §330, or some other hearsay exception.

4. Nature and Scope of Cross-Examination [§456]

a. Form of Questioning [§457]
A cross-examiner ordinarily has broad leeway in using leading questions and in repeating the same question.

However, the trial court is given a great deal of control over such matters, and its rulings are rarely upset on appeal.

b. Scope of Cross-Examination [§458]

FRE 611(b) adopts the majority rule that cross-examination is limited to the **subject matter** of the direct examination and matters affecting the **witness's credibility**. Ordinarily, if a cross-examiner seeks from a witness information unrelated to her direct testimony, the witness must be recalled to the stand when the cross-examiner puts on witnesses. The federal rule does, however, give the trial court **discretion** to permit inquiry during cross-examination into "additional matters as if on direct examination." Note, however, that a **substantial minority** of states allow **"wide-open"** cross-examination (i.e., questioning as to any relevant issue in the case).

EXAMPLE

Plaintiff sues Defendant, claiming that Defendant negligently caused their auto collision and that Plaintiff suffered severe whiplash as a result. Plaintiff calls Witness, who testifies she saw Defendant run a stop sign and crash into Plaintiff's car. On cross-examination, Defendant asks her questions in an effort to show that Witness was standing in a place where she could not have seen what happened. This is permissible. Defendant also seeks to ask Witness about statements Plaintiff allegedly made to Witness that indicate Plaintiff had not suffered any injury from the accident. This goes beyond the scope of the direct examination and so would not ordinarily be allowed under the FRE. Under the minority rule of "wide-open" cross-examination, however, this would be permissible.

c. Redirect and Recross-Examination [§459]

Redirect examination is ordinarily limited to **matters brought out in the preceding cross-examination**. Similarly, recross-examination is ordinarily limited to **matters explored in the preceding redirect exam**. The court, however, has discretion to allow a party to raise issues on redirect that were omitted from the direct examination due to oversight.

5. Right to Confrontation [§460]

Questions under the Confrontation Clause of the Sixth Amendment arise in two settings relevant to the discussion here.

a. Right to Cross-Examine Adverse Witnesses [§461]

The right to cross-examine a witness is considered so important that direct testimony will be stricken if a witness cannot be subjected to full cross-examination due to sickness, death, or a refusal to answer. But reasonable limits may be placed on the method and extent of cross-examination. It is the **opportunity** for effective cross-examination, not effective cross-examination, that is protected. *Delaware v. Fensterer*, 474 U.S. 15 (1985).

b. Right to Face Accuser [§462]

The Confrontation Clause limits the ability of the state to have its witnesses testify outside the presence of the accused. The Supreme Court has sanctioned a procedure that allows a child abuse victim to testify via closed-circuit television (thus physically out of the accused's presence). But this procedure may be employed only if the trial judge first finds that the child would be traumatized by testifying in the presence of the defendant. *Maryland v. Craig*, 497 U.S. 836 (1990).

F. Impeachment in General [§463]

Impeaching a witness involves an attack on the witness's credibility, that is, an attempt to show that the witness is lying, mistaken, or both.

1. Impeaching One's Own Witness [§464]

Ordinarily, a party is going to try to impeach the witnesses called by its opponent. Occasionally, however, a party may want to impeach one of its own witnesses. The common law and FRE disagree as to when a party may impeach its own witness.

a. Common-Law Voucher Rule [§465]

At common law, one who calls a witness is said to vouch for his truthfulness. Therefore, the common law ordinarily forbids a party from impeaching its own witness. An exception is made, however, when the witness unexpectedly testifies in a manner injurious to the calling party. This is known as the **surprise and injury** requirement.

b. Federal Rules: No Voucher Rule [§466]

FRE 607 and many state codes **abandon the voucher rule**, thereby allowing a party to impeach its own witness.

(1) But Party Cannot Call Witness Just to Impeach Him [§467]

Problems arise when a party calls a witness primarily, if not solely, for the purpose of impeaching the witness, and thereby get in front of the jury evidence that would otherwise be inadmissible. This crops up most frequently with attempts to impeach a witness with a prior inconsistent statement. See §479 et seq. Most prior statements of a witness are hearsay if offered for their truth. See §§221, 234. A party is allowed to impeach a witness by showing the witness has made a prior statement that is inconsistent with the witness's trial testimony. But the witness's prior statement is admissible only for impeachment purposes (that is, to show that the witness has told different stories at different times and is therefore not credible). It is not admissible for its truth (that is, as proof that the prior statement is true). The danger arises that a party will call a witness who has, in the past, made a statement favorable to the calling party, but whom the calling party knows will not now give favorable testimony. The calling party might call this witness just so the calling party can impeach the witness with the prior favorable statement (which would otherwise be inadmissible). Courts generally do not permit this practice, stating that a party may not call a witness and impeach him as a subterfuge for

placing otherwise inadmissible evidence before
the jury.

EXAMPLE
Witness told police that she saw Defendant assault
Victim. While being interviewed by the prosecutor a
day before Defendant's trial, Witness says that she did
not see Defendant assault Victim. Despite this,
Prosecutor calls Witness to the stand. When she
testifies that she did not see Defendant assault
Victim, Prosecutor seeks to impeach her by showing
that she had previously told the police that she saw
Defendant assault Victim. Since Prosecutor knew that
Witness was not going to testify adversely to
Defendant, Prosecutor's only reason for calling
Witness to the stand was to get before the jury
Witness's earlier statement to the police. But that
statement is inadmissible hearsay if offered to prove
that Defendant assaulted Victim. Most courts,
therefore, would not allow Prosecutor to impeach
Witness with her prior inconsistent statement.

G. Five Techniques of Impeachment: "BICCC" [§468]
There are five basic ways of attacking a witness's credibility,
each of which has its own set of rules. If you can remember
the brand name of a cheap pen or razor, you can remember
these five techniques: "**BICCC**." **B**ias, **I**nconsistent
Statements, **C**apacity, **C**haracter, **C**ontradiction.

1. Capacity [§469]
Perhaps the most obvious means of impeaching a witness
is by showing defects in the witness's ability to see, hear,
recall, or recount the facts.

a. Physical or Mental Disabilities [§470]
Insanity or other relevant psychological abnormalities
may be used to impeach a witness (e.g., "Don't you
frequently have hallucinations?" "Don't you
sometimes have trouble distinguishing fact from
fantasy?"). A witness may be questioned about her
drug or alcohol use **at the time** she perceived the
event (e.g., "Isn't it true that you had consumed six

margaritas shortly before the events you just described?").

b. Memory [§471]
A cross-examiner may test the memory of a witness by questions concerning the details of events about which the witness has testified (e.g., "What time was that?" "How many people were there?").

c. No Foundation Requirement [§472]
No foundation is needed before asking a witness questions that reveal a lack of capacity. Nor is any foundation required before introducing extrinsic evidence of lack of capacity.

d. Extrinsic Evidence Allowed [§473]
Extrinsic evidence (i.e., evidence other than testimony from the witness) may be offered to prove lack of capacity. The admissibility of such evidence is, of course, subject to **general relevancy rules**. Thus, the trial judge may find in a particular instance that the probative value of the evidence is substantially outweighed by the danger of unfair prejudice, confusion, waste of time, etc.

(1) Expert Opinion [§474]
In a small number of cases, courts have admitted expert testimony regarding a witness's ability to tell the truth (e.g., "In my opinion, Witness is a sociopathic liar."). But courts are generally reluctant to permit so-called experts to give their opinion as to whether a particular witness is telling the truth. In recent years, courts have been more willing to allow witnesses to testify about factors that might affect a witness's ability to tell the truth, particularly with respect to child abuse victims.

2. Bias [§475]
A witness may be impeached by showing that he has some reason, independent of the merits of the case, to give testimony favoring one side or the other. Bias may arise from a variety of sources: a **personal relationship** with a party (e.g., a relative), **animosity** (e.g., a desire for

revenge), a **financial interest** in the outcome (e.g., the witness is the creditor of a party), **intimidation** (e.g., someone has threatened the witness), the **desire to curry favor** with the prosecution (e.g., the witness has criminal charges pending against him), or the witness is being **paid** by a party to testify.

a. Ability to Show Bias Important [§476]

The Supreme Court has held that placing undue limits on an accused's ability to show the bias of a prosecution witness is unconstitutional. *Davis v. Alaska*, 415 U.S. 308 (1974).

b. Foundation Requirement [§477]

Some jurisdictions require that the witness must be **asked about his alleged bias before extrinsic evidence** of acts or statements evidencing the bias may be offered. The **federal rules** contain **no such foundation requirement**. Nevertheless, the court's power to control the order and mode in which evidence is presented includes the authority to require a party, where practicable, to afford the impeached witness the opportunity to admit or deny the facts or statements manifesting the bias.

c. Extrinsic Evidence [§478]

Extrinsic evidence ordinarily may be offered to prove bias. The court must determine the admissibility of such evidence under **general relevancy principles**, balancing the probative value of the evidence against the danger of unfair prejudice, confusion, waste of time, etc. For example, where the witness has admitted to the acts or statements showing bias, the court may exclude the extrinsic evidence on the ground that it is cumulative.

3. Prior Inconsistent Statements "PINS" [§479]

The fact that a witness has previously made statements that are inconsistent with his trial testimony may be used to impeach him.

a. Theory: Why Prior Inconsistent Statements are Not Hearsay When Offered to Impeach [§480]

Suppose Defendant is on trial for murder. The prosecution's key witness is Witness, who testifies that he saw Defendant shoot Victim. On cross-examination, defense counsel seeks to ask Witness about a statement that he made to Buddy the day after the murder in which Witness said Defendant was not the person who shot Victim. Recall from the discussion of hearsay that a witness's own out-of-court statement is hearsay if offered for the truth of the matter asserted. See §§221, 234. Witness's statement to Buddy is **hearsay if offered as substantive evidence** (i.e., to prove that Defendant was not the person who shot Victim). But defense counsel may use Witness's statement to Buddy **to impeach** Witness without running afoul of the hearsay rule. Why? Because the fact that Witness previously made a statement that is inconsistent with his testimony at trial tends to detract from his credibility. It demonstrates that he "blows hot and cold," telling one story one time and another story another time. In theory, defense counsel is **not asking the jury to believe that Witness's statement to Buddy is true**. All defense counsel wants to show (in theory) is that Witness is not a credible witness.

(1) Must Be Witness's Own Prior Statement [§481]

As should be clear from the theory as to why prior inconsistent statements are not hearsay when offered to impeach, this impeachment technique applies only when a witness is being impeached with his or her **own prior statement**. That someone else said something that is inconsistent with the witness's testimony does not tend to show that the witness "blows hot and cold" and is therefore less deserving of belief.

b. Limiting Instruction [§482]

When a party impeaches a witness with his prior inconsistent statement ("PINS"), its opponent is entitled to a limiting instruction. In the above example, the judge would instruct the jury that Witness's statement to Buddy may be considered by them only as evidence of Witness's credibility and not as proof that Defendant was not the person who shot Victim. Quite understandably, the jury will be totally perplexed by this.

c.   **Some Prior Inconsistent Statements are Better Than Others [§483]**

Recall again from the discussion of hearsay that the federal rules define as nonhearsay some prior statements of a witness. See §377. If the witness's PINS was made (a) under **oath,** (b) subject to the **penalty of perjury,** (c) at an earlier **trial, hearing,** or other **proceeding,** or in a **deposition,** FRE 801(d)(1)(a) states that it is not hearsay. This means it can be used for its **truth** as well as to impeach.

EXAMPLE: PINS ADMISSIBLE ONLY TO IMPEACH

Boyfriend is on trial for child abuse. The prosecution's key witness is Mother, who told the police on the day her child was injured that Boyfriend abused Child. However, when the prosecutor calls Mother to testify, Mother surprises the prosecutor and states that Boyfriend did not harm Child. The prosecutor then tries to ask Mother about her statement to the police that Boyfriend abused Child. Mother's statement to the police is a run-of-the-mill prior inconsistent statement. It was not made under oath, subject to the penalty of perjury, at some other legal proceeding. Therefore, it is hearsay if offered as substantive evidence (i.e., as proof that Boyfriend abused Child. It may be used only to impeach Mother's credibility (i.e., to show she told a different story on another occasion and so is less deserving of belief). Note that Prosecutor was surprised that Mother changed her story, and so did not call her to the stand just so he could impeach her with her out-of-court statement.

EXAMPLE: PINS ADMISSIBLE FOR ITS TRUTH AND TO IMPEACH

Suppose that Mother had testified before the grand jury that Boyfriend abused Child. Since this statement was made under oath, subject to the penalty of perjury, at an earlier legal proceeding, it meets the requirements of FRE 801(d)(1)(a). Therefore, it is defined as nonhearsay and the prosecutor may use it as substantive evidence (i.e., as proof that Boyfriend abused Child) as well as to impeach Mother.

d. Degree of Inconsistency Required [§484]

The trial testimony and prior statements need not be directly contradictory. A prior statement will be considered inconsistent, and thus eligible for impeachment, if, taken as a whole, it seems unlikely that someone who believed the truth of his testimony would also have made the earlier statement. The following are examples of types of inconsistencies.

(1) Direct Inconsistency [§485]

The witness's testimony is at variance with her previous statement regarding a material fact.

(2) Prior Silence or Less Detailed Statement [§486]

Sometimes a witness gives testimony that is more detailed than prior statements the witness has made. If the witness would have been expected to provide greater detail in the earlier statement, the earlier statement may be considered inconsistent with the trial testimony. Similarly, if the witness had previously failed to say anything under circumstances where she would have been expected to speak, the silence is inconsistent with the testimony.

EXAMPLE: LESS DETAILED STATEMENT
Girlfriend testifies in Defendant's murder trial that he was with her at the time of the murder, which occurred in the middle of the night. She says she is sure of this because Defendant's snoring woke her up during the night in question and her bedside clock read 2:00 AM. On cross-examination, Prosecution asks her about the statement she made to the police, two days after the murder, in which she said that Defendant was with her but did not mention anything about waking up and seeing it was 2:00 AM.

EXAMPLE: PRIOR SILENCE

Defendant testifies in his murder trial that he acted in self-defense. Prosecution asks him on cross-examination about his failure to mention for two weeks following the killing that he acted in self-defense.

EXAMPLE: PRIOR SILENCE AFTER ARREST

Defendant testifies in his murder trial that he acted in self-defense. Prosecution asks him on cross-examination why, after he was arrested, he remained silent and didn't tell the police he acted in self-defense. Most courts would say this is not proper impeachment. Since most people know that they have a right to remain silent once they are arrested, Defendant's silence occurred under circumstances in which he would not have been expected to speak. In fact, the prosecution is constitutionally forbidden from using an accused's post-*Miranda*-warning silence. *Jenkins v. Anderson*, 447 U.S. 231 (1980). See §258.

(3) Prior Lack of Memory [§487]

A witness may be impeached when she testifies concerning an event about which she previously claimed to have no memory.

(4) Current Claim of Lack of Memory [§488]

A witness who now testifies to having no memory of an event ordinarily may not be impeached with the fact that the witness previously made statements concerning the event. All too often, a witness's memory fades by the time a case comes to trial. Sometimes, however, a court may find that a witness's lack of memory is feigned, and will then allow the witness to be impeached with her prior statement.

(5) Omission of Details Previously Related [§489]

A witness may omit from her trial testimony material details that she has included in previous statements. Whether the previous statement qualifies as a prior inconsistent statement depends on whether the witness has truly forgotten the details or is employing a selective memory. If the latter, impeachment is proper.

e. Foundation Requirement [§490]

The federal rules abandon the traditional foundation requirement of the common law, a requirement that is still followed in many jurisdictions.

(1) Common Law [§491]

The common law requires that a foundation be laid in order to impeach a witness with his PINS. First, the witness must be **asked about the PINS before extrinsic evidence** of the statement may be offered. Second, the witness must be asked about the PINS in a certain way. The question must include (a) the **identity** of the person to whom the statement purportedly was made, (b) the **time** and **place** it was made, and (c) the **substance** of the statement.

EXAMPLE

"Isn't it true that the day after Victim was shot you spoke to Officer Smith at the station house? And didn't you tell her that you saw Defendant shoot Victim?"

(2) Common Law: Written Statements—The Queen's Case [§492]

An old English case, *Queen Caroline's Case*, 129 Eng. Rep. 976 (1820) (often referred to simply as The Queen's Case), held that before a witness could even be asked about a written PINS, the witness had to be shown and given the opportunity to read the writing in which the PINS appeared. Few jurisdictions still adhere to this rule.

(3) Federal Rule [§493]

FRE 613 **abandons the common-law foundation requirement**, as have many states. Under FRE 613, a witness may be asked about a PINS **without** first informing the witness as to the identity, time, place, or contents of the statement.

EXAMPLE
Witness testifies on direct examination that she did not see Defendant shoot Victim. On cross-examination, the first question Lawyer asks is, "Isn't true that you have previously stated that you did see Defendant shoot Victim?" This is proper. But as a practical matter, lawyers rarely use such an abbreviated form of questioning. Most lawyers find it is more effective to interrogate the witness in a manner that conforms to the traditional common-law foundation.

f. **Extrinsic Evidence of Prior Inconsistent Statements [§494]**
Two factors affect whether extrinsic evidence may be presented to prove that the witness made a PINS: (a) procedures (foundation requirement) and (b) whether the PINS relates to a collateral matter.

(1) **Procedure [§495]**
The common law allows extrinsic evidence of a PINS only if the witness first refuses to admit having made the statement. In contrast, FRE 613(b) provides that extrinsic evidence of a PINS is admissible so long as (a) the **witness** is given an **opportunity** to explain or deny the statement and (b) **opposing counsel** is given the chance to **question** the witness about the statement. This opportunity may come, however, after the PINS has been proved. Therefore, extrinsic evidence of a witness's PINS will be permitted if the witness is available to be recalled to the stand. Even this minimal requirement may be waived under FRE 613(b) "in the interests of justice."

(2) **Collateral Matter [§496]**
If the PINS relates to a collateral matter, extrinsic evidence is not permitted. (For an explanation of what is and is not "collateral," see §520 below.)

4. **Character for Truthfulness [§497]**

    A witness may be impeached by showing his poor
    character for truthfulness. Such evidence is offered for
    the inference that the witness is now acting in accordance
    with his character trait, i.e., that he is testifying
    untruthfully. This is the third exception to the general rule
    prohibiting the use of character evidence to show
    conduct. See §164.

5. **Three Ways to Prove Untruthful Character [§498]**

    There are three ways to prove a witness's untruthful
    character: (a) **opinion or reputation** testimony; (b)
    specific acts that did not result in a conviction; and (c)
    convictions. Each method of proof has its own rules.

6. **Opinion or Reputation [§499]**

    To impeach Witness 1, the attacking party may call
    Witness 2 to testify to her opinion of Witness 1's honesty
    (e.g., "In my opinion, Witness 1 is an untruthful
    individual.") or to Witness 1's reputation in the
    community (e.g., "I am familiar with Witness 1's
    reputation in the community for truthfulness, and it is
    terrible."). Witness 2, however, is limited to stating her
    opinion or relating the reputation. She may not cite
    specific instances of dishonest conduct by Witness 1 to
    support the opinion or reputation. [FRE 608(a).] Nor may
    Witness 2 testify that she believes Witness 1 is not telling
    the truth. The testimony is limited to Witness 1's
    character for truthfulness.

    a. **Evidence of Good Character Allowed Only After
        Attack [§500]**

        The proponent of Witness 1 may not offer evidence
        of Witness 1's good character for truthfulness until
        his character has come under attack. At that point,
        the proponent of Witness 1 may call its own
        reputation or opinion witnesses to testify to Witness
        1's good character for truthfulness. [FRE 608(a).]

    b. **But at a Price [§501]**

        Witness 1's opinion or reputation witnesses are
        subject to cross-examination with "Do you know"
        and "Have you heard" questions (e.g., "Do you know
        [Have you heard] that Witness 1 embezzled $1,000

from his daughter's Brownie troop last year?"). The rules here are the same as for other opinion and reputation witnesses: the questions may be asked, but the questioner is bound by the answer. Even if the witness answers in the negative, no extrinsic evidence will be permitted to show that Witness 1 actually embezzled the money. [FRE 608(b).] See §154.

7. **Specific Acts Not Resulting in Conviction [§502]**
   In the discretion of the court, Witness 1 may himself be asked on cross-examination about **specific things** he has done that bear on his **truthful disposition**. [FRE 608(b).] Thus, on cross-examination Witness 1 may be asked, "Isn't it true that you embezzled $1,000 from your daughter's Brownie troop last year?"

   a. **Act Must Relate to Truthfulness [§503]**
      The cited conduct must be probative of untruthful character. Thus, questions relating to acts of dishonesty — acts of deceit, fraud, lying, etc. — are likely to be allowed. Questions about violent conduct are not.

   b. **Good Faith Belief [§504]**
      Counsel must have a good faith belief that the witness actually engaged in the conduct about which she asks.

   c. **Bound By Answer [§505]**
      The questioner is bound by the witness's answer. Extrinsic evidence may not be offered to prove that the witness actually engaged in the specific conduct.

   d. **Minority Rule [§506]**
      Some jurisdictions do not permit a witness to be impeached this way.

8. **Convictions [§507]**
   The fact that a witness has been convicted of certain crimes may be used to prove the witness's untruthful character. The rules governing this method of impeachment differ from state to state (e.g., as to the type of crimes that may be used and the type of balancing test employed).

a. FRE: Crimes Involving Dishonesty or False Statement [§508]

FRE 609 allows a witness to be impeached by showing that he has been convicted of a crime involving dishonesty or false statement. **It does not matter whether the crime was a misdemeanor or felony**. The court **may not balance** the probative value of the conviction against the danger of unfair prejudice. The impeachment must be allowed. [FRE 609(a)(2).]

(1) Dishonesty or False Statement Defined [§509]

Crimes involving dishonesty or false statement include: perjury, false statement, criminal fraud, embezzlement, false pretenses, and other crimes involving some element of deceit, untruthfulness or falsity. Crimes of violence are not considered in this category.

b. FRE: Felonies Not Involving Dishonesty or False Statement [§510]

If a witness has been convicted of a crime that did not involve dishonesty or false statement, he may still be impeached with the crime if it was a **felony**. (A felony is a crime punishable — not necessarily punished — by death or imprisonment for more than a year.) However, under FRE 609(a)(1), the court **must balance** the probative value of the conviction **as it bears on credibility** against the danger of **unfair prejudice**. One balancing test is prescribed for criminal defendants, and another for all other witnesses.

(1) Witness is Criminal Defendant [§511]

If the witness being impeached is the accused, a felony not involving dishonesty or false statement may be used to impeach him only if the court determines that its **probative value outweighs** its prejudicial effect.

EXAMPLE

Defendant, on trial for murder, testifies in his own defense. The prosecution seeks to impeach him by proving that he had previously been convicted of a felony assault. The court should allow this only if it determines that the probative value of the assault **as evidence of Defendant's character for untruthfulness** outweighs the danger of unfair prejudice (i.e., that the jury will use it as evidence of Defendant's violent nature).

(2) Witness is Anyone Else [§512]

Any witness other than the accused ordinarily may be impeached with a felony not involving dishonesty or false statement. The court may, however, exclude the evidence if it determines that its **probative value is substantially outweighed by** the danger of unfair prejudice.

(3) Balancing Factors [§513]

In balancing a conviction's probative value as to credibility against its danger of unfair prejudice, a court may consider (a) the extent to which the crime **relates to veracity**, (b) **how long ago** the crime occurred and the witness's **subsequent history**, (c) the **similarity** between the past crime and the charged crime, (d) the **importance** of the defendant/witness's testimony (i.e., will the defendant be deterred by this type of impeachment from taking the stand), and (e) how **central** the credibility issue is to the case. Factor (c) is the tricky one: **the greater the similarity** between the past crime and the charged crime, the **less likely it can be used** for impeachment. Similarity does not enhance the probative value of the conviction as evidence of the witness's credibility. But if the witness is also the defendant, similarity between the past crime and the charged crime increases the danger of unfair prejudice.

c. Special Balancing Test For Remote Convictions [§514]

If a conviction is old ("remote"), it may be used to impeach a witness only if the court specifically finds that its probative value **substantially outweighs** its prejudicial effect. A conviction is remote if **ten years** have elapsed since the witness was released from confinement for that conviction. If the witness never served any time, the ten years runs from the date of conviction. The special balancing test applies even if the remote conviction was for a crime involving dishonesty or false statement. [FRE 609(b).]

d. Rehabilitation or Pardon [§515]
A conviction may not be used for impeachment if it has been the subject of (a) a pardon, annulment, or certificate of rehabilitation, based on a finding of rehabilitation, and the witness has not subsequently been convicted of a felony, or (b) a pardon or annulment based on a finding of innocence.

e. Proof of Convictions [§516]
A witness's prior conviction typically is proved either by **asking the witness** about the impeaching conviction or by means of a **public record**. It is improper to refer to any aggravating facts or details of the crime (e.g., "Isn't it true you were convicted of beating your wife and son with a baseball bat?").

f. Defendant Must Testify to Preserve Objection [§517]
Criminal defendants with prior convictions often ask the trial judge to issue an in limine ruling barring the prosecution from using prior convictions to impeach the defendant. If the judge refuses to issue such an order, the defendant must testify to preserve for appeal a challenge to the judge's ruling. A defendant who chooses not to testify waives this issue on appeal. *Luce v. United States*, 469 U.S. 38 (1984).

9. WARNING: These Rules Apply Only to Attacks on the Witness's Character for Truthfulness [§518]
Watch out for situations where evidence of a specific act that did not result in a conviction (or a conviction that would not qualify under the above rules) is used to impeach by a theory other than showing the witness's poor character for truthfulness.

EXAMPLE

Suppose Defendant Company seeks to impeach one of Plaintiff's witnesses by asking him, "Isn't it true you threatened to kill all the officers of Defendant Company last year?" Although such a question could not be asked to prove the witness's untruthful character (threats of violence don't go to truthfulness), it may be used to demonstrate that the witness is **biased** against Defendant Company. Since the theory of impeachment is bias, the question may be asked and, if the witness denies that he made the threat, extrinsic evidence may be offered to prove that he did. Moral — Always ask: What is the Evidence Being Offered to Prove.

10. Contradiction [§519]

A routine method of attacking a witness's credibility is to try to get the witness to retract or contradict something to which she had earlier testified. There is no problem in doing that. The only issue that arises in connection with this last technique of impeachment is: when will the impeaching party be allowed to offer **extrinsic evidence** for the purpose of contradicting some aspect of the witness's testimony?

a. The Collateral Matter Rule [§520]

The collateral matter rule is easily stated (but less easily understood). If the extrinsic evidence is relevant solely because it tends to discredit the witness, it is said to relate to a collateral matter and is therefore inadmissible. If, however, the evidence is also relevant to prove or disprove a substantive fact in dispute, it is not collateral, and extrinsic evidence may be offered.

EXAMPLE: COLLATERAL MATTER.

Defendant is on trial for committing a bank robbery in Boston on October 1. To support his alibi defense, he calls Alex, the owner of a sporting goods store in Washington. Alex testifies that Defendant worked in his sporting goods store all day long on October 1. On cross-examination, Prosecutor asks Alex, "Would you say that Defendant had worked in your store every day for the preceding month?" Alex answers, "Yes." During its rebuttal case, Prosecutor then calls Fred to testify that he was with Defendant on a camping trip on September 4 through 6. This would contradict Alex's testimony that Defendant had worked in the store every day for the preceding month. Fred's testimony, however, goes to a collateral issue and is inadmissible. It is not relevant to any substantive fact: no one cares where Defendant was in early September. The only point in eliciting Fred's testimony would be to discredit Alex by showing that one of his answers (albeit to an inconsequential question) is wrong.

EXAMPLE: NOT COLLATERAL.
Same case. During its rebuttal case, Prosecutor calls Jerry to testify that he works in Alex's sporting goods store, and that Defendant did not work there on October 1, the day of the bank robbery. This testimony is admissible. It contradicts Alex's testimony and discredits him, but it is also directly relevant to a substantive issue in the case: Where was Defendant the day of the crime?

b. **Really a Matter of Balancing [§521]**
The federal rules and most state rules say nothing about the collateral matter test. In fact, the reason for excluding extrinsic evidence on collateral matters is that the probative value of such evidence is rarely worth the time and the risk of diverting the jury's attention from the real issues in the case. Therefore, courts exclude this evidence on the basis of a FRE 403 balancing.

c. **Apply This Rule With Prior Inconsistent Statements ("PINS") Also [§522]**
Even if the procedural prerequisites have been met, **extrinsic evidence** of a PINS may be offered only if the statement is relevant to a substantive issue in the case. If a witness gives testimony that is inconsistent with a previous statement only as to an inconsequential detail (e.g., the witness testifies at trial that he was wearing a blue sweater that day and had earlier said he was wearing a green sweater), extrinsic evidence of that PINS will not be allowed.

11. Supporting a Witness's Credibility [§523]

The process of impeachment is aimed at destroying a witness's credibility. Bolstering and rehabilitation seek to build up the credibility of a witness.

a. Bolstering [§524]

Bolstering refers to efforts to build up the credibility of a witness **before** it is attacked. Many courts and texts state that, as a general matter, bolstering is not permitted because witnesses are presumed to be credible until they are attacked. This is not quite accurate. The FRE (and most state rules) contain no general rule prohibiting bolstering. In fact, courts routinely allow some degree of bolstering. For example, **background facts** about a witness (e.g., family, employment, address, how long she has lived in the community) may be elicited from the witness in an effort to allow the jury to gauge her standing and assess her credibility. An eyewitness will be allowed to testify to her powers of **perception** (e.g., that she has 20/20 vision) or her **lack of bias** (e.g., she does not know the defendant and has no reason to accuse him). The rules against bolstering really are directed toward preventing evidence of (a) a witness's **good character for truthfulness** and (b) a witness's **prior consistent statement**s.

(1) Witness's Truthful Character [§525]

As discussed above (see §500), evidence of a witness's truthful character may be offered **only after an attack** has been leveled at the witness's character for truthfulness. This traditional rule is codified in FRE 608(a).

(2) Witness's Prior Consistent Statements [§526]

The rule limiting the use of a witness's prior consistent statements to enhance the witness's credibility in the absence of an attack on the witness's credibility flows from the view that a witness's own out-of-court statements are hearsay if offered for their truth. Allowing a party to elicit a witness's out-of-court statements on direct examination in the guise of enhancing the witness's credibility would allow the party effectively to circumvent the hearsay rule. A witness's prior consistent statements may, however, be used if (a) they are **independently admissible** under a hearsay exception or exemption (e.g., the witness's statement qualifies as an excited utterance or is a prior statement of identification); or (b) to **rehabilitate** the witness in certain circumstances. See §529.

b. **Rehabilitation [§527]**

Once a witness's **credibility has been attacked**, her proponent may, like "all the king's horses and all the king's men," try to put her back together again. This is the process of rehabilitation. The general rule here is simple. The rehabilitation technique must **match the impeachment technique**. If the witness has been attacked by showing bias, try to show lack of bias (e.g., "Yeah, I was mad at Plaintiff for a long time, but I forgave him years ago"); if the attack is lack of capacity, show capacity (e.g., "No, I wasn't wearing my glasses, [pause] but I was wearing my contact lenses.").

(1) **Truthful Character [§528]**

A witness whose character for truthfulness has been attacked may be rehabilitated with reputation or opinion evidence of her truthful character, in accordance with the rules stated above.

(2) **Prior Consistent Statements: Recent Fabrication, Yes; "PINS," No [§529]**

Although it may seem odd, a witness who has been impeached with her prior inconsistent statement may **not** be rehabilitated by showing that she previously made statements consistent with her trial testimony. The justification for this rule is that a witness whose credibility has been attacked by showing that she tells Story A one time and Story B another time is not made more credible by a showing that she told Story A twice and Story B only once.

Prior consistent statements may, however, be used to **rebut a charge** that the witness **changed** her story or recently **fabricated** her testimony if the prior statements were made **before the motive to change the story or fabricate** the testimony arose. In *United States v. Tome*, 515 U.S. 150 (1995), the defendant was charged with sexually abusing his daughter. He claimed that Daughter concocted the story so that she could stay with her mother rather than with him. Daughter, who was six years old at the time of trial, became quite reticent during cross-examination. The prosecution then called several witnesses to testify to Daughter's prior statements that the defendant had abused her. The prosecution offered these to rebut the defendant's charge that Daughter had fabricated her story. The defendant argued that the statements were inadmissible because they were all made after Daughter's motive to fabricate arose. The Supreme Court agreed, holding that only "pre-motive" prior consistent statements were admissible to rebut a charge of recent fabrication or improper influence or motive.

Recall that when such prior consistent statements are admissible, they qualify as nonhearsay and thus can be used as substantive evidence as well as to rehabilitate. See §380.

VI. Opinion and Expert Testimony

A. Opinion Testimony in General [§530]
A body of law governs when a witness may give testimony in the form of an opinion, draw an inference from the facts, or state a conclusion. There is one set of rules for "expert" witnesses and another for non-expert ("lay") witnesses.

B. Lay Witness Opinions [§531]
A lay witness is a witness who is not testifying as an expert. An "expert" may testify as a lay witness when she testifies about something outside the field of her expertise. For example, a doctor who witnessed a car collision would be

testifying as a lay witness when she relates that she saw the defendant go through the red light.

1. **Common-Law Rule [§532]**
    The oft-stated common-law rule was that lay witnesses were **not allowed to testify in the form of an opinion.** Because lay witnesses were no more skilled than jurors at drawing inferences or conclusions from the facts, they were limited to relating the facts and leaving it to the jury to draw its own conclusions.

    a. **Illusory Distinction Between Fact and Opinion [§533]**
        The common-law rule was based on the notion that facts could be distinguished from opinions. But such a distinction is often difficult to draw. For example, if a witness testified that it was windy or that two people were married, objection could be made that the witness was giving an opinion and should be forced to relate the facts that led the witness to reach such a conclusion.

    b. **Numerous Exceptions [§534]**
        As a result, numerous exceptions were made to the common-law rule. Courts allowed witnesses to testify to what were referred as **"short-hand renditions of fact"** or **"collective facts."** Witnesses thus were allowed to testify that someone was drunk (or not), to matters of identification (handwriting, voice, visual), mental competency, vehicular speed, colors, smells, intoxication, or emotions, and to opinions about themselves (e.g., value of their own property or services, physical condition, personal history), to give but a few examples.

2. **Modern Approach [§535]**
    The federal rules and many states have abandoned the common-law prohibition on lay witness opinions. Now, lay witnesses may testify in the form of an opinion or inference if **two requirements** are met. First, the opinion must be **rationally based on the witness's perception.** Second, it must be **helpful** to a clear understanding of the witness's testimony or the determination of a fact in issue. [FRE 701.] This approach eliminates the need to draw

meaningless distinctions between fact and opinion and allows witnesses who would be tongue-tied by a rigid application of the no-opinion rule to testify in a manner that will be helpful to the factfinder.

a. **Perception of the Witness [§536]**
    The witness must have **personal knowledge** of the events from which he is drawing his opinion. For example, a witness may not testify that the defendant was "speeding" without having actually seen the defendant driving. In contrast, experts may testify as to opinions without having personal knowledge of the underlying facts.

b. **Rationally Derived [§537]**
    In addition, a lay witness's opinion must be rationally derived from his personal knowledge. This requirement prevents a lay witness from testifying to an opinion that is irrational or requires specialized knowledge, such as that someone appeared to have a ruptured spleen.

c. **Helpfulness [§538]**
    Lay opinion testimony must also be helpful to a clear understanding of the witness's testimony or to a determination of a fact in issue. Witnesses, especially inarticulate ones, may find themselves unable to communicate effectively if they are allowed to relate only the most concrete of facts.

d. **Comparison With Common Law [§539]**
    Since the common-law rule was riddled with exceptions, the more liberal-sounding modern approach does not change the law that much. Nevertheless, courts are somewhat more receptive to lay opinions now than under the common law. For example, courts are more likely to allow a witness to testify to her opinion concerning the meaning of another's conduct, such as that someone "nodded yes," "indicated agreement," or "started" or "provoked" a fight.

e. Foundation [§540]

A question may sometimes arise as to whether a lay witness has personal knowledge of the facts upon which she is basing her opinion. The burden is on the witness's proponent to make this showing. For example, a lay witness who testifies that smoke smelled like marijuana may first be required to establish her familiarity with the smell of marijuana.

f. Preference for Facts [§541]

The more central the matter is to the issue in dispute, the more likely a court will require a witness to relate the facts within her knowledge rather than to merely state her opinion. For example, although courts routinely allow witnesses to state that someone was "married," if the marital status of a party is at the center of a dispute (e.g., a bigamy prosecution) the court is more likely to require the witness to give specifics.

g. No Experts [§542]

The federal rules of civil and criminal procedure contain provisions requiring parties to make certain disclosures regarding expert testimony they intend to offer. Courts often sanction a failure to comply with these provisions by not permitting the expert to testify. To avoid such a sanction, some litigants have argued that their expert is testifying only as a lay witness and is therefore not subject to the disclosure rules. FRE 701 now includes a proviso designed to prevent parties from trying to circumvent the disclosure provisions. It provides that **lay testimony may not be based** on scientific, technical or other specialized knowledge that forms the basis of expert testimony.

C. Expert Testimony [§543]

Unlike lay opinion testimony, courts have long valued and admitted the opinions of experts. Courts have recognized that experts are able to draw inferences that jurors are not competent to draw. In fact, in some cases, a party cannot prevail as a matter of law without presenting expert testimony. Several requirements must be met before expert testimony is admissible: the witness must **qualify** as an expert; the **subject**

matter of the testimony must be appropriate for expert testimony; the testimony must be **helpful** to the factfinder; and the expert's opinion must be sufficiently **reliable**. Several other issues commonly arise concerning expert testimony. These include the proper **basis** for an expert's opinion; how expert testimony may be **presented**; and opinions relating to **ultimate issues**.

1. **Qualifications [§544]**

    The proponent of an expert witness bears the burden of establishing the witness's expertise. That is, the proponent must show that the witness possesses sufficient scientific, technical or other specialized knowledge to render the proffered opinion. The witness's qualifications must be measured with respect to the opinion the witness seeks to offer. For example, a pediatric cardiologist may be qualified to testify about heart murmurs in children, but not about Alzheimer's disease.

    a. **How Expertise is Gained [§545]**

        No magic formula exists for how the requisite knowledge may be obtained. It may come through **formal education**, as evidenced by degrees and certificates, or it may come through **informal study**, **self-study**, or **experience**. The only question is whether the witness possesses the specialized knowledge.

    b. **Voir Dire [§546]**

        The proponent usually proves an expert's qualifications by offering testimony about the witness's education, experience, etc. Before the court accepts her as an expert, the opposing party ordinarily has the right to "take the witness on voir dire" to cross-examine her about her qualifications.

    c. **Preliminary Question [§547]**

        The admissibility of expert testimony is a preliminary question for the judge to decide. The judge's ruling will be reversed only for an abuse of discretion.

2. **Subject Matter [§548]**

    The federal rules and many modern codes allow expert testimony regarding **scientific, technical,** or **other specialized knowledge** if it will assist the factfinder to understand the evidence or to determine a fact in issue. [FRE 702.] This is a broad standard. So long as the testimony concerns some type of "specialized knowledge" and will be helpful to the jury, it is a proper subject for expert testimony.

    a. **Beyond Common Understanding [§549]**

        At common law, some courts allowed expert testimony only if it related to a matter beyond the common knowledge and experience of the factfinder. The federal rules and many states no longer adhere rigidly to this standard. Expert testimony is sometimes allowed even if it concerns a matter within the jury's experience. For example, expert testimony about the reliability of eyewitness identifications is sometimes allowed. The key issue is whether the testimony will **assist the jury**. Not surprisingly, courts are less likely to conclude that expert testimony meets this "assist the jury" standard when the testimony concerns matters within the jury's knowledge and experience.

    b. **Types of Expert Testimony [§550]**

        It would be both impossible and pointless to compile an exhaustive list of the various fields in which experts have been permitted to testify. The topics include medical practice, earning capacity, peanut farming, accident reconstruction, meaning of slang terms in the drug trade, engineering, design, handwriting, etc.

3. **Reliability of Expert Testimony [§551]**

    For years, many courts employed a special threshold test when a party offered expert testimony concerning some **novel scientific** test, theory or principle. This test, which became widely known as the *Frye* **test**, is still used in some jurisdictions. But the federal and many state courts have rejected it. In its place, they have substituted a more flexible "reliability" standard and have extended the new threshold reliability standard to all expert testimony. FRE

702 was amended in 2000 to codify the reliability standard. The use of a special threshold test for expert testimony is justified on the ground that jurors tend to **overvalue** expert testimony and are **ill-equipped** to detect and discount unreliable expert opinions. The danger that experts will present unreliable opinions is enhanced by the practice of allowing parties to **hire** and **compensate** their own experts.

a. **The *Frye* Test [§552]**
    Derived from a 1923 court of appeals case (*Frye v. United States*, 293 F. 1013 (D.C. Cir. 1923)), the *Frye* test states that the proponent of novel scientific evidence must demonstrate that the proffered test, theory, or principle has gained **general acceptance** in the relevant scientific community.

b. ***Frye* Rejected—The *Daubert* Case [§553]**
    The federal rules and most state codes make no mention of the *Frye* standard. In 1993, the Supreme Court held in *Daubert v. Merrell Dow Pharmaceuticals, Inc.*, 509 U.S. 579 (1993), that the federal rules did not incorporate *Frye's* general acceptance test. But the Court did not totally abandon a special admissibility standard for scientific expert testimony. The Court stated that trial judges must act as **"gatekeepers"** and must admit scientific opinions only if the opinions are **reliable** and **relevant**. The Court equated reliability with **scientific validity** and listed several **factors** for trial judges to consider in determining the reliability of a scientific opinion. *Daubert* emphasized the non-exclusive nature of its list of factors, and other cases have added additional factors. These are discussed in §556 below.

c. **Daubert Extended to Nonscientific Testimony [§554]**
    Six years after *Daubert*, the Supreme Court extended the reliability threshold test to nonscientific expert testimony (i.e., testimony involving **technical or other specialized** forms of knowledge). In *Kumho Tire Co. v. Carmichael*, 526 U.S. 137 (1999), the Court held that trial judges must determine whether the

expert's opinion has "a reliable basis in the knowledge and experience of [the relevant] discipline." It emphasized that the factors listed in *Daubert* were not exclusive and, indeed, might not even be pertinent to evaluating the reliability of certain types of expert testimony.

d. **Federal Rules Codify Reliability Standard For Expert Testimony [§555]**
An amendment to FRE 702 codified the basic holdings of *Daubert* and *Kumho Tire*. Now, under FRE 702 **three components** comprise the threshold reliability test. First, the expert must base her opinion upon **sufficient facts or data**. Second, the expert's opinion must be grounded in **reliable principles and methods**. Third, the expert must **apply** those principles and methods to the facts of the case in a reliable manner.

e. **Reliability Factors [§556]**
The three reliability components listed in FRE 702 are fairly broad. Courts have developed a number of more specific factors that can be helpful in assessing the reliability of an expert's opinion. *Daubert* listed four such factors:

- whether the theory or technique in question can be and has been **tested**;
- whether the theory or technique has been subjected to **peer review** and publication;
- the known or potential **rate of error** of the particular theory or technique and whether means exist for controlling its operation; and
- the extent to which the theory or technique has been **generally accepted**.

Subsequent courts added other factors to this list:
- whether the expert has adequately accounted for obvious **alternative explanations**;
- whether the expert has employed the **same care** in reaching the litigation-related opinions as the expert employs in performing his or her regular professional work;

- whether there is **"too great an analytical gap"** between the data and the opinion (i.e., the underlying facts don't support the expert's conclusion);
- whether the expert testimony is based on research the expert conducted independent of the litigation.

Because courts must determine the reliability of expert opinions access a wide range of subject matters, any given factor may be more or less weighty in a particular case.

f.   Establishing Reliability [§557]

The proponent of expert testimony bears the burden of establishing its reliability. Reliability determinations are sometimes done before trial, after a hearing involving testimony (often referred to as a *"Daubert* hearing"). Alternatively, a court may choose to base its decision on the written record after the parties have submitted documents such as deposition transcripts, affidavits, and publications. Often, reliability determinations are not made until the expert is called at trial. Then, the court has the option of either conducting a hearing outside the jury's presence or having the expert testify and then striking the testimony if the court decides it lacks the requisite degree of reliability. Once a test, theory, or principle has become sufficiently well established, a court may take judicial notice of its validity. For example, courts no longer require proof of the principles underlying the use of radar guns.

g.   Proper Application of Established Principles [§558]

Even when the principles underlying an expert's opinion have been widely accepted, the proponent must still show that the expert applied them properly. For example, although no proof is required regarding the principles underlying the use of radar guns, the prosecution will still have to establish that the radar gun the officer used to clock the defendant at 77 mph was in good working order and that the officer knew how to use it properly.

h. Relevance [§559]

Courts must determine that expert testimony is relevant as well as reliable. The expert's opinion must have a valid connection to the issues in the case.

4. Basis of Expert Opinions [§560]

Unlike lay witnesses, **experts need not base their opinions on personal knowledge**.

a. Common Law [§561]

Under common-law rules, an expert may base an opinion on (1) **personal knowledge**, (2) **facts** in the **record**, or (3) a **combination** of the two.

(1) Hypothetical Question [§562]

When an expert bases an opinion (in whole or in part) on facts not within his personal knowledge, the facts are typically provided to him through a hypothetical question. Under this procedure, the lawyer recites a series of facts, asks the expert to assume the truth of these facts, and then asks the expert to give his opinion. All facts contained in the hypothetical question must be **in evidence by the close of the case**.

EXAMPLE

"Doctor, assuming Plaintiff had a high fever, was allergic to sulfa drugs, and had a history of rheumatic fever, what, if anything, would a reasonable doctor in Dallas prescribe if Plaintiff complained of violent chest pains?"

(2) Hypothetical Question: Variant—Expert Observes Testimony [§563]

A variant of the hypothetical question may be used when the expert observes the testimony of other witnesses. The lawyer may then ask the expert to assume the truth of the other witnesses' testimony (or parts of it) and render an opinion.

EXAMPLE

"Doctor, assuming the truth of the testimony Plaintiff gave about his symptoms and medical history and that Nurse gave about her observations of Plaintiff, what, if anything, would a reasonable doctor in Dallas prescribe in response to Plaintiff's complaints of violent chest pains?"

b. Modern Approach [§564]

The federal rules and the rules of many jurisdictions liberalize the proper basis for expert testimony. Under Federal Rule 703, an expert may base his opinion on facts **"perceived by or made known to the expert at or before the hearing."**

(1) Includes Common-Law Methods [§565]

This includes all the methods permitted at common law.

(2) Goes Beyond Common Law [§566]

This liberalizes the common law by allowing an expert to base an opinion **solely** on facts **outside his personal knowledge** and **not in the record**. Indeed, the facts upon which an expert may base an opinion **need not even be admissible** in evidence. That is, an expert may base an opinion upon hearsay statements that themselves would not be admissible in evidence. But an expert may do this only if such facts or data are **of a type reasonably relied upon** by experts in the same field. [FRE 703.]

EXAMPLE

A doctor may base an opinion on medical records he has reviewed, conversations with other medical personnel about the patient, and interviews with the patient's family, even if none of these has been introduced into evidence, so long as the court decides that these are the types of things that other doctors in the field reasonably rely upon in making diagnoses.

(3) Opinion is Admissible; Underlying Facts May Not Be [§567]

FRE 703 allows an expert to **base** an opinion upon facts or data that are not admitted (or that may be inadmissible) in evidence. Whether the expert may **relate** to the jury the otherwise inadmissible underlying data is a separate question. FRE 703 provides that the trial judge should allow the expert to disclose such data only when the probative value of disclosure **substantially outweighs** its prejudicial effect. The probative value is measured in terms of the extent to which disclosure would assist the jury in evaluating the expert's opinion. Unfair prejudice is measured in terms of the danger that the jury will misuse the evidence for substantive purposes.

(4) Hypothetical Question Not Required [§568]

Experts who lack personal knowledge about the underlying facts may give their opinions without being asked a hypothetical question. Federal Rule 705 authorizes an expert to state his opinion **without prior disclosure** of the underlying facts, leaving it to the cross-examiner to probe the basis of the opinion. The rule, however, empowers the court to require the expert to first disclose the underlying facts. Note that Rule 705 **does not abolish** the use of hypothetical questions. It merely makes their use **optional**.

5. Examination of Expert Witnesses [§569]

In addition to being subject on cross-examination to the kinds of questions asked of other witnesses, an expert may be questioned as to: (a) his **qualifications**; (b) the **bases** of his opinions; (c) the **compensation** he is receiving for testifying; and (d) **discrepancies** between opinions expressed by the expert and statements contained in treatises and articles.

a. Treatises and Articles: Common Law [§570]

Under the common-law rule, a cross-examiner is permitted to impeach an expert by pointing out discrepancies between the expert's testimony and statements made in a treatise or article if the witness has acknowledged the **authoritative nature** of the treatise or article or that he **relied upon it** in forming his opinion.

b. **Treatises and Articles: Federal Rule [§571]**

An expert may be impeached as under the common law. In addition, the federal rules create a **hearsay exception** for statements in treatises, periodicals, or pamphlets that have been established as reliable authority by expert testimony or judicial notice. [FRE 803(18).] See §326. Statements in such works may be read to the jury to the extent that they are **called to the attention** of an expert on **cross-examination** or **relied upon** by an expert witness on **direct examination**.

c. **Court-Appointed Experts [§572]**

The court may, on its own motion, appoint and call an expert witness. [FRE 706.]

6. **Opinions on Ultimate Issues [§573]**

Common-law courts frequently excluded opinions embracing the ultimate issue in the case on the ground that such opinions "invade the province of the jury." The federal rules and most states **reject this as a valid objection**. [FRE 704(a).] Nevertheless, an opinion — lay or expert — is admissible only if the expert is qualified and the opinion meets the helpfulness test. Therefore, courts still frequently exclude opinions as to **mixed questions of law and fact**, especially when the danger exists that the witness is not familiar with the proper legal standard.

EXAMPLE

Testimony that a testator "lacked testamentary capacity" is likely to be excluded unless it is first shown that the witness understands how the law defines "testamentary capacity." In contrast, testimony that the testator "had the capacity to know the nature and extent of his property and the natural objects of his bounty and to formulate a rational scheme of distribution" is likely to be admitted.

a. Hinckley Rule [§574]

After John Hinckley was acquitted by reason of insanity in the shooting of President Reagan, Congress amended FRE 704 to prohibit **experts** from testifying as to whether a **criminal defendant** "did or did not have the **mental state or condition** constituting an **element** of the crime charged or of a **defense** thereto."

EXAMPLE

Defendant pleads not guilty by reason of insanity. He may not call a psychiatrists to testify, "In my opinion, Defendant was insane at the time of shooting." But the psychiatrist may testify as to the nature and ramifications of any mental illness afflicting Defendant.

VII. Authentication

A. Overview [§575]

Before a writing may be introduced into evidence, it must be "authenticated;" that is, its proponent must establish that **it is what it purports to be**. Under the federal rules, the authentication requirement applies not only to writings, but to other forms of physical evidence (e.g., the murder weapon) and to less tangible things, such as voices. [FRE 901.]

1. Conditional Relevance Standard [§576]

The authentication requirement is really a means of establishing the relevance of the proffered item. The standard for authentication is the low one associated with conditional relevance. See §40. The proponent of the evidence need only introduce **enough evidence for a reasonable juror to find that the item is what it purports to be**. [FRE 901(a).] Even if the court does not believe that an item is what it purports to be, it is still authenticated if a reasonable juror could find that it is.

EXAMPLE

Plaintiff wants to introduce a letter allegedly written by Defendant that contains admissions damaging to Defendant's case. Plaintiff must first authenticate the letter by showing that the letter is what it purports to be. As long as Plaintiff introduces sufficient evidence for a reasonable juror to find that it is a letter written by Defendant, Plaintiff has authenticated it. This holds true even if the court does not itself believe that Defendant wrote the letter. Ultimately, the jury will decide whether it is or is not Defendant's letter.

2. Real and Demonstrative Evidence [§577]

The term **real evidence** refers to tangible items that actually **played a role** in the matter in dispute (e.g., the murder weapon, the contract in issue). **Demonstrative evidence** refers to tangible items that did not actually play a role in the matter in dispute, but are used for **illustrative purposes** (e.g., a map, photograph, skeleton). The proponent of a piece of demonstrative evidence must establish that the evidence is a **fair and accurate representation** of what it purports to depict.

B. Authentication of Writings [§578]

There are several ways in which a writing may be authenticated.

1. Personal Knowledge [§579]

A writing may be authenticated by a person who has personal knowledge that the writing is what it is claimed to be. [FRE 901(b)(1).] For example, a witness may testify that she authored the document or saw the purported author execute the document.

2. Authentication by Circumstantial Evidence [§580]

A writing may be authenticated by circumstantial evidence. There are innumerable ways in which this might be done. Some standard techniques of authentication by circumstantial evidence have evolved over the years.

a. Handwriting [§581]

A document may be authenticated through the author's handwriting.

b. Handwriting: Lay Witness [§582]

A lay witness who has **personal knowledge** of a person's handwriting may give an opinion that a specific writing was or was not made by that person. Under the federal rules, however, a lay witness's familiarity with the handwriting must not have been acquired for purposes of the litigation. [FRE 901(b)(2).]

c. **Handwriting: Expert Witness [§583]**
    An expert witness may compare a genuine sample of the purported author's handwriting (i.e., an "exemplar") with the writing in question, and give an opinion as to authorship. [FRE 901(b)(3).]

d. **Handwriting: Comparison by the Trier of Fact [§584]**
    A genuine exemplar of the purported author's handwriting and the contested writing may be submitted directly to the factfinder for comparison. [FRE 901(b)(3).]

    (1) **Genuineness of Exemplar [§585]**
        The exemplar itself must be established as genuine before it can be used for comparison purposes. At common law, the court had to be satisfied that it was genuine. Under FRE 901(b)(3), an exemplar may be used if its proponent introduces **sufficient evidence to support a finding** that it is genuine.

e. **Reply-Message Doctrine [§586]**
    If (a) the contents of a writing indicate that it is in reply to a previous communication addressed to the purported author and (b) it is unlikely that anyone other than the purported author would have sent the response, the writing will be authenticated. [FRE 901(b)(4).]

EXAMPLE
Defendant testifies that she sent Plaintiff a fax the morning of March 1, asking for assurance that Plaintiff would ship Defendant's order within one week. Defendant offers a fax that she received later that morning, which is on Plaintiff's letterhead. It states, "In response to your fax this morning, please be assured that your order will be shipped no later than three days from now." This is sufficient to authenticate the fax as having come from Plaintiff.

f. Ancient Documents [§587]

A writing may be authenticated if it (a) is in such a condition as to create **no suspicion** as to its authenticity; (b) was found where it would have **likely been kept**; and (c) is at least **20** years old. [FRE 901(b)(8).] At common law, a document had to be at least 30 years old to invoke the ancient documents doctrine.

g. Public Records or Reports [§588]

Evidence that a public record or report has been recorded or filed in a public office (e.g., a deed) suffices for authentication. [FRE 901(b)(7).]

h. Content [§589]

A writing may be authenticated if its contents include information likely to be known only by its purported author. [FRE 901(b)(4).]

C. Authentication of Objects [§590]

All tangible objects must be authenticated before being admitted into evidence. As was the case with writings, authentication may be done in innumerable ways. The objective is to show that the item is what it purports to be.

1. Personal Knowledge [§591]

A witness may testify that he recognizes the object based on its unique markings, properly affixed labels, or any other reasonable basis. [FRE 901(b)(1).]

2. Authentication by Circumstantial Evidence [§592]

An object may be authenticated by circumstantial evidence. There are many ways this may be done.

a. Distinctive Characteristics [§593]

An object's distinctive characteristics, appearance, contents, or internal patterns may be used to show that it is what it purports to be. [FRE 901(b)(4).]

EXAMPLE

Defendant is charged with the criminal extortion of Victim. Victim testifies that he received an unsigned, handwritten note threatening him. Defendant objects that it has not been authenticated. The prosecutor presents evidence that the note was written on very unusual paper of the type that Defendant regularly used and with an unusual ink of the kind that Defendant regularly used. This is sufficient evidence to authenticate that Defendant wrote the note.

b. Chain of Custody [§594]

An object may be authenticated by proving an unbroken chain of custody from the time it came into its proponent's possession until its submission into evidence. The proponent should be able to account for its whereabouts at all times in order to negate the possibility of tampering with the object. However, courts often admit objects even when the proponent is unable to establish every link in the custody or chain.

3. Photos, Maps, Models [§595]

Photographs, maps, and models are often used as demonstrative evidence and thus are admissible so long as the witness testifies from personal knowledge that the exhibit is a **fair representation** of what it purports to be. The **photographer** or person who prepared the exhibit **need not** testify.

4. X-Rays, MRI'S, Cat Scans, Etc. [§596]

No one can testify from personal knowledge that an x-ray, MRI, CAT scan, or other such depiction of internal organs is a fair and accurate representation of the object depicted. Instead, authentication here requires testimony that the process used is accurate (the court may take judicial notice of this) and that the machine used was in good working order.

5. Computer Recreations and Simulations [§597]

A computer recreation or simulation demonstrating how an event occurred may be used if a proper foundation is laid. If it simply depicts a witness's account of how the accident occurred (e.g., a depiction of a car collision at an intersection based on eyewitness testimony), the only foundation required is the eyewitness's testimony that the recreation is a fair and accurate portrayal of what he witnessed.

Sometimes, however, computers are used to simulate how an accident might have occurred where there are no eyewitnesses (e.g., an airline crash). In such instances, authentication typically will entail a showing that (a) the data used as a basis for the simulation are accurate (e.g., using data obtained from the "black box"), (b) the data were correctly entered, and (c) the software used to produce the simulation can accurately produce the relevant images. This may require testimony from several witnesses. The qualifications of the person or persons who produced the simulation will also have to be established.

D. Authentication of Voices [§598]
The use of telephones and audio recordings requires means of establishing in court that a voice heard or recorded belonged to a particular person.

1. Personal Knowledge [§599]
A voice may be identified (whether heard firsthand or on an audio recording) by any person who testifies that he recognizes the voice based upon having heard it under circumstances connecting it with the alleged speaker. [FRE 901(b)(5).]

2. Authentication by Circumstantial Evidence [§600]
Voices may be authenticated through any one of a number of techniques involving circumstantial evidence.

a. Contents [§601]
As is the case with writings, the identity of a speaker may be shown if the contents of the statement include information likely to be known only by the purported speaker. The reply-message doctrine (see §586) also applies to spoken communications. [FRE 901(b)(4).]

b. **Distinctive Characteristics [§602]**
    The identity of a speaker may also be shown by the
    distinctive characteristics of the speaker, such as a
    strange accent or idiosyncratic use of language. [FRE
    901(b)(4).]

c. **Special Rules for Telephone Communications
    [§603]**
    Merely producing evidence that a caller identified
    herself as "Sue Snow" is not sufficient to establish
    that the speaker was in fact Sue Snow. In addition to
    the methods of authentication listed above, there are
    special rules that have been developed for telephone
    communications.

    (1) Personal Identity [§604]
        An individual may be identified as the speaker if a
        witness testifies that (a) he **properly dialed** the
        number (b) **listed** in the telephone directory and
        (c) circumstances, including **self-identification**,
        show the person answering to be the one listed
        and called. [FRE 901(b)(6).]

    EXAMPLE
    Witness testifies that she looked up Sue Snow's
    number in the phone book, dialed it, and that the
    person who answered said, "This is Sue Snow." This
    is sufficient to identify the speaker as Sue Snow.

    (2) Business [§605]
        A witness may establish that she spoke to a
        representative of a business if she testifies that
        she (a) **properly dialed** the number (b) **listed** in
        the telephone directory and (c) the conversation
        related to the type of business commonly
        transacted over the telephone. [FRE 901(b)(6).]

    (3) Caller ID [§606]
        Although the FRE do not include a special
        provision dealing with caller ID, testimony that
        caller ID revealed a phone call to come from a
        particular person or phone number is evidence
        that can be considered in establishing the source
        of the call.

E. Self-Authentication [§607]

With some items, the likelihood of forgery or tampering is deemed to be so small that they are "self-authenticating." That is, the proponent of such an item is **not required to present any evidence** to establish that the item is what it purports to be. All the proponent needs to do is present the item at trial. To remember which items are self-authenticating, use the mnemonic **"CONTAC"**: **C**ommercial paper; **O**fficial publications; **T**rade inscriptions; **N**ewspapers and periodicals; **A**cknowledged documents; **C**ertain public records. [FRE 902.] In addition, the federal rules list under the self-authentication rule a method of authentication for business records that falls short of true self-authentication. [FRE 902(11), (12).]

1. Commercial Paper [§608]

To the extent provided by general commercial law, commercial paper, signatures on commercial paper, and related documents are self-authenticating. [FRE 902(9).]

2. Official Publications [§609]

Publications purporting to be issued by public authority, such as the reports of a government agency, are self-authenticating. [FRE 902(5).]

3. Newspapers and Periodicals [§610]

Newspapers and periodicals are self-authenticating.

EXAMPLE

In a libel action against the New York Times, the plaintiff has only to bring in a copy of the offending paper. He need not present further evidence that it really is a copy of the New York Times. [FRE 902(6).]

4. Trade Inscriptions and the Like [§611]

Under the federal rules, ownership, control, or origin may be established by an inscription, sign, tag, or label that (a) purports to have been affixed in the course of the business and (b) indicates ownership, control, or origin. [FRE 902(7).]

EXAMPLE
Plaintiff offers into evidence a can bearing the label "Red Tomato Co., Inc." in which she claims to have found a dead mouse. This is sufficient to authenticate the can as a product of the defendant Red Tomato Company.

5. **Acknowledged Documents [§612]**
    A document that has already been acknowledged before a notary public or other officer authorized by law to take acknowledgements is self-authenticating. [FRE 902(8).]

6. **Certain Public Records [§613]**
    Public records may be self-authenticating. The requirements vary, depending on whether the document is foreign or domestic, under seal or not, and whether it is certified as correct or not. It is not worth memorizing the particulars unless your teacher indicates that he or she thinks it is important. [FRE 902(1)-(4).]

7. **Business Records [§614]**
    FRE 902 provides a means for "self-authenticating" domestic business records and, in civil cases, foreign business records. The records must be accompanied by the **written declaration** of someone who is qualified to testify that the records meet the **requirements of the business records exception**. A party must provide its adversaries **notice** of its intention to use this method of introducing the records and make the records **available for inspection**. Note that this is not really self-authentication. Rather, it is a means by which a party may use otherwise inadmissible hearsay—the written declaration—both to prove the authenticity of the record and to establish that it meets the requirements of the business record exception to the hearsay rule.

VIII.   Best Evidence Rule

A. **Best Evidence Rule ("BER") [§615]**
    The Best Evidence Rule is one of the most confusing rules in the law of evidence. Despite its name, the Best Evidence Rule **does not** require a party to offer **the best evidence** available. Instead, it requires only that when a party seeks to **prove the contents** of a writing, recording, or photograph, the party must use the **original** writing, recording, or photograph. In

fact, the phrase "Best Evidence Rule" is so misleading that the federal rules have dropped it. The section of the FRE dealing with the BER is called "Contents of Writings, Recordings, and Photographs." Despite this, it is still widely referred to as the Best Evidence Rule.

1. Rationale [§616]

The BER is a product of the days when documents were hand-copied by monks and the Bob Crachits of the world. The risk of error in transcription was significant, and so the law developed a preference for the original of a writing. Technological advances such as the photocopying machines reduce this danger, and the law of evidence thus created exceptions to the BER. Today, the BER can best be justified on efficiency grounds. By preferring production of a writing over testimony about the writing, it eliminates disputes about what the writing says. More recently, digitization has created the problem that it is increasingly easy to alter documents without detection.

B. Analysis of a BER Problem [§617]

The BER provides that when a party seeks to prove the contents of a writing, recording, or photograph, the party must use the original writing, recording, or photograph unless an exception applies. **Four questions**, therefore, immediately arise. First, what do we mean by **"proving the contents"** of a writing, recording, or photograph? Second, what qualifies as a **"writing, recording, or photograph"**? Third, what qualifies as an **"original"**? Fourth, what are the **exceptions** to the BER?

C. Proving the Contents of a Writing [§618]

The most difficult part of BER analysis relates to the threshold question of whether the offered evidence is used to prove the contents of a writing, recording, or photograph. This element of the rule is satisfied if the evidence falls into one of the following three categories. If it does not, the BER is inapplicable.

1. Category 1: Writings with Independent Legal Significance [§619]

Where the fundamental issue in a case relates to rights or obligations arising **directly** from a writing, etc., the precise words (i.e., the contents) of the writing possess **independent legal significance**. In such cases, even slight variations in the words can significantly and directly affect the legal relationships, and because of the fear of fraud or mistake, the original writing is required.

a.   Types of Actions [§620]
This category applies whenever the litigation directly involves a writing such as a contract, lease, will, libel, photograph, or book (e.g., a copyright action). It does not apply where the writing is only "evidence" of a fact (e.g., receipts, minutes, transcripts). The writing itself must have a **direct legal impact**.

EXAMPLE
Plaintiff sues Defendant for breach of a written contract. In his testimony, Plaintiff states what he believes to be an essential provision of the agreement. Defendant's BER objection would be sustained because the terms (contents) of the writing are themselves in issue.

EXAMPLE
Defendant is on trial for selling obscene magazines. A member of the vice squad seeks to describe the photos he saw in magazines in Defendant's store. Defendant's BER objection would be sustained because the witness is attempting to testify to the contents of the photos.

b.   No Hearsay Problems [§621]
Although writings are out-of-court statements, the types of writings that fall under Category 1 BER analysis are not hearsay because they are operative facts (i.e., words of independent legal significance).

2.   Category 2: Writing Offered in Evidence [§622]
If a party physically **offers a writing** in evidence, she thereby puts the terms of the writing in issue (by asking the trier of fact to rely on it). Thus, if Defendant seeks to prove that she paid Plaintiff $100 by offering a receipt from the transaction, she must offer the original unless one of the exceptions to the BER applies. But Defendant may also prove payment by testifying, "I remember paying Plaintiff $100." In the latter instance, she is not

proving the fact through a writing, and so the BER does not apply.

3. **Category 3: Testimony Relying Upon a Writing [§623]**

The most elusive context in which the BER applies involves testimony in which the **witness relies** totally upon a writing. If the witness is telling the trier of fact what the writing says, the writing, not the witness, is the basis of the information. Consequently, the witness has put the writing into issue and must produce the original unless one of the exceptions to the BER applies.

EXAMPLE: WRITING OFFERED IN EVIDENCE

Defendant seeks to prove that she paid Plaintiff $500 on March 1 by using a business record that contains that information. This implicates the BER. She must introduce the original of the record unless one of the exceptions to the BER applies.

EXAMPLE: TESTIMONY RELYING UPON A WRITING

Defendant seeks to prove that she paid Plaintiff $500 on March 1 by testifying, "my records show that I paid Plaintiff $500 on March 1." The BER applies because she is seeking to prove the contents of those records.

EXAMPLE: BER NOT APPLICABLE

Defendant seeks to prove that she paid Plaintiff $500 on March 1 by testifying, "I remember paying Plaintiff $500 on March 1." There is no BER problem because she is testifying as to her independent knowledge of an event. The fact that the event has been memorialized in a business record does not matter.

4. **Hearsay Problems [§624]**

Both **Category 2** and **Category 3** of the BER analysis may raise hearsay problems as well. For example, when Defendant attempts to use her business records to prove that she paid Plaintiff, Plaintiff can raise both hearsay and BER objections. Defendant can meet the hearsay objection by showing that the record qualifies under the business record exception and the BER objection by producing the original.

D. Writing, Recording, Photograph Defined [§625]

These terms are **defined broadly** so as to include every tangible process of recording words, pictures or sounds. Thus a **"writing"** includes not only printed material but material recorded electronically on a computer disk. [FRE 1001(1).] **"Photographs"** include movies, video tapes and X-rays. [FRE 1001(2).] Although photographs are usually used in trial for illustrative purposes, occasionally a party tries to prove the contents of a photograph.

EXAMPLE: BER NOT APPLICABLE
Plaintiff seeks to offer a photograph of the intersection where the auto accident occurred. Plaintiff authenticates the photo by testifying that it is a fair and accurate representation of the what the intersection looked like at the time of the accident. The BER is not applicable, as the photo is merely being used to illustrate Plaintiff's knowledge of the intersection.

EXAMPLE: BER APPLICABLE
Defendant is charged with bank robbery. No eyewitnesses testify. To prove it was Defendant who robbed the bank, the prosecution offers a bank surveillance photo. The BER applies. The photo is being offered for its contents, i.e., to identify Defendant as the robber.

E. Original Defined [§626]

The original typically is the writing or recording itself. [FRE 1001(3).] But other things count as "originals" for BER purposes.

1. Counterparts [§627]

If the person executing or issuing the writing intends a counterpart to have the same effect, the counterpart will be considered an original. [FRE 1001(3).] For example, if parties to a contract make and sign two copies of the contract, each will be considered an "original." These are sometimes referred to as "duplicate originals."

2. Photographs [§628]

An original of a photograph includes the negative or any print made from the negative. [FRE 1001(2).] This definition predates digital photography. Digital photographs are treated like other digital forms of information. See §629.

3. Computers and Similar Devices [§629]

The original includes not only the original data (on the hard drive or other storage unit), but also any printout or other output readable by sight, shown to reflect the data accurately. [FRE 1001(3).]

F. Exceptions [§630]

There are several exceptions to the BER. Some of the exceptions allow a **particular kind** of evidence to be used **in lieu of** the original. Some of the exceptions dispense with the BER entirely, and allow **any kind of proof** (oral or written) of the contents of the writing.

1. Duplicate [§631]

Unless a genuine question is raised about the authenticity of the original, a duplicate may be used **in lieu of** the original. [FRE 1003.]

a. Duplicate Defined [§632]

A duplicate is a counterpart produced by the **same impression** as the original (e.g., a carbon copy), from the **same matrix** (e.g., from the same printing plate), by means of **photography** (e.g., a picture of a document), or by **mechanical or electronic re-recording** or by **chemical reproduction** or other **equivalent techniques**. [FRE 1001(4).] In other words, a duplicate is a copy that is produced by a mechanical technique that accurately reproduces the original.

2. Public Records [§633]

A **certified** copy of a public record may be used **in lieu of** the original. Alternatively, a copy that is **testified to be correct** by a witness who has compared it with the original may be used. [FRE 1005.]

3. Summaries [§634]

If the original is **voluminous**, its contents may be presented in the form of a **chart, summary,** or **calculation**. Opposing parties, however, must have been afforded reasonable opportunity to inspect and copy the original. [FRE 1006.]

4. Unavailability of Original [§635]

If the original is unavailable through **no fault** of the proponent, **any evidence** (oral or written) may be used.

a. Lost or Destroyed [§636]

If the original is lost or destroyed, the BER is inapplicable, unless the proponent lost or destroyed the original in bad faith. [FRE 1004(1).]

b. Original Not Obtainable [§637]

If the original cannot be obtained by judicial process or procedure (e.g., because it is outside the court's subpoena jurisdiction), the BER is inapplicable. [FRE 1004(2).]

c. Original in Opponent's Possession [§638]

If the opponent has control of the original, has been put on notice that its contents would be the subject of proof at trial, and does not produce it, the BER is inapplicable. [FRE 1004(3).]

5. Collateral Matters [§639]

If the contents of the writing, recording, or photograph do not closely relate to a controlling issue in the case, the BER is inapplicable. [FRE 1004(4).]

6. Chattels [§640]

If the writing appears on something that is impracticable to produce in court (e.g., a tombstone), the court will find that the object is a chattel rather than a writing and declare the BER inapplicable.

G. Expert Testimony [§641]

Where an expert testifies and bases an opinion on a writing, recording, or photograph, there is no BER problem. An expert may base an opinion on facts that are not admissible in evidence if they are the kinds of facts that such experts reasonably rely upon. [FRE 703.] For example, a doctor may base an opinion on an X-ray she has reviewed without running afoul of the BER.

IX. Privileges

A. Privileges in General [§642]

The existence of privileges demonstrates that the law of evidence is not solely concerned with achieving accurate factfinding. Privileges result in the exclusion from evidence of information that may be quite probative. The law recognizes privileges because it has determined that the cost incurred by the loss of reliable evidence is outweighed by the social benefits that accrue from having privileges. Because the cost is high, however, courts often state that privileges are to be construed narrowly.

1. Two Kinds of Privileges [§643]

Privileges may be divided into (a) a group that protects confidential communications and (b) a group of miscellaneous privileges.

2. Federal Rules: No Enumerated Privilege Rules [§644]

The proposed federal rules contained privilege rules that proved to be quite controversial. Many critics thought the proposed privilege for state secrets was too broad. Others complained the proposed privileges were not broad enough. They lacked, for example, a doctor-patient privilege. Rather than resolving the controversy itself, Congress left the issue to the courts. FRE 501, the only privilege rule in the FRE, simply provides that privileges are to be "governed by the **principles of the common law**" as interpreted by the courts "**in light of reason and experience.**" However, in diversity cases and other cases in which state **substantive law governs**, the federal courts must apply **state privilege** law.

3. Variation Among States [§645]

Less uniformity exists among jurisdictions regarding privileges than in any other area of the law of evidence. Therefore, if you are being tested about a particular jurisdiction's privilege rules, it is important to learn that jurisdiction's rules. Nevertheless, there are certain basics that are common to most jurisdictions.

B. Confidential Communication Privileges: Overview [§646]
The generally accepted confidential communication privileges
are: the **attorney-client** privilege; the **physician-patient**
privilege; the **psychotherapist-patient** privilege; the
husband-wife privilege; and the privilege for
communications with a member of the **clergy**. In addition,
some jurisdictions recognize privileges for communications
between: accountant and client; parent and child; and social
worker and client; and spousal abuse counselor and victim.

1. **Rationale [§647]**
Each of the confidential communication privileges is
based on the view that guaranteeing **confidentiality is
necessary to foster** what society deems to be an
important relationship. The benefits gained from
fostering the relationship outweigh the harm caused by
shielding the communication from disclosure.

2. **Scope of Privilege [§648]**
A confidential communication privilege allows the holder
of the privilege (a) to **refuse to disclose** and (b) to
prevent others from disclosing the protected
communication.

3. **Communications are Privileged; Information is Not
[§649]**
It is crucial to understand that communication privileges
protect **communications**, but **not the underlying
information**. Thus, when Plaintiff deposes Defendant,
Plaintiff will not be able to ask Defendant, "Did you tell
your lawyer that you ran the stop sign?" But Plaintiff will
be allowed to ask Defendant, "Did you run the stop
sign?" A party is not allowed to insulate relevant
information from disclosure simply by relating it to his
lawyer.

4. **Approach to Privilege Issues [§650]**
You can easily detect and answer most privilege questions
if you ask yourself the following six questions whenever
you suspect a confidential communication privilege may
be lurking.
   1. **Relationship.** Is there a privileged relationship?
   2. **Communication.** Was there a germane
   communication?

3. **Confidentiality**. Was the communication confidential?

4. **Holder**. Is the holder asserting the privilege?

5. **Waiver**. Did the holder waive the privilege?

6. **Exceptions**. Is there an exception to the privilege?

C. Attorney-Client Privilege [§651]

Every state recognizes the attorney-client privilege, either by rule, statute or common law. The privilege allows (a) a client (b) to refuse to disclose and to prevent others from disclosing (c) confidential (d) communications (e) made between the attorney and client or their representatives (f) for the purpose of facilitating the rendition of legal services.

1. Only Attorney-Client Communications [§652]

Traditional definitions of the attorney-client privilege state that the privilege protects communications by a client to a lawyer. But the privilege also protects communications by a lawyer to a client, at least to the extent that revealing the lawyer-client communication would tend to reveal what the client told the lawyer. More modern formulations of the privilege are broader in scope.

Many jurisdictions now provide that the attorney-client privilege protects communications **between or among the lawyer and client, and their representatives.** Thus, the privilege covers communications between the lawyer (or the lawyer's representative) and client (or the client's representative); the client and the client's representatives; the lawyer and the lawyer's representatives; and representatives of the client. The attorney-client privilege ordinarily does not protect communications between the lawyer or client and a third party.

a. "Joint Defense" Communications [§653]

In one instance, the attorney-client privilege protects communications to persons outside the lawyer-client relationship. Sometimes multiple parties, each with its own lawyer, share a common interest in a legal matter and choose to share information or mount a joint defense. In such instances, the attorney-client privilege will cover communications between the lawyers representing the different parties or between one of the parties and a lawyer representing one of the other parties. This is sometimes referred to as **"joint defense"** or **"pooled information"** privilege, but is really just an extension of the attorney-client privilege.

EXAMPLE
Defendant 1 and Defendant 2 are accused of committing an armed robbery together. Each has his own lawyer (Lawyer 1 and Lawyer 2, respectively.) Communications between Lawyer 1 and Lawyer 2 or between Defendant 1 and Lawyer 2 concerning the defendants' joint defense are privileged.

2. **Lawyer [§654]**
A lawyer is someone who is licensed to practice law. In the past, communications made to someone whom the "client" mistakenly believed to be a lawyer were held to fall outside the privilege. Now, however, most jurisdictions hold that the attorney-client privilege covers communications made to someone whom the "client" reasonably believed to be a lawyer.

3. **Client [§655]**
A client may be an individual or an entity such as a corporation. One who consults a lawyer with the **idea of obtaining legal services** is considered a client. Thus, an attorney-client relationship will be recognized even if the client and lawyer had no prior relationship, the lawyer is not formally retained by the client, the lawyer is not paid, or the lawyer eventually declines to represent the client.

4. **Representatives of Lawyers and Clients [§656]**
Both lawyers and clients may communicate through representatives.

a. **Representative of Lawyer [§657]**
Someone employed by the lawyer to assist in the rendition of legal services (such as a clerk, paralegal, or even an expert whom the lawyer consults) is a representative of the lawyer. Thus, confidential statements made by a client to an accountant whom the lawyer has employed to assist in rendering legal advice will be protected.

b. Representative of a Client—Individual [§658]
Someone who has the authority (a) to obtain legal services for the client, or (b) to act on advice rendered by counsel on behalf of the client qualifies as the client's representative. Thus, the attorney-client privilege covers communications between a lawyer representing a child and the child's parent or guardian.

c. Representative of a Client—Entity [§659]
When a client is an entity, such as a corporation, the question arises: "Who speaks for the entity?" For example, suppose an explosion occurs at a company plant. In preparing for litigation, the company's lawyer interviews corporate officials and employees. Which if any of these conversations will be protected by the attorney-client privilege? Several tests have been advanced.

(1) Control Group Test [§660]
Only members of the control group of an entity (e.g., officers and directors) are representatives of the client whose communications to the entity's lawyer are privileged.

(2) Subject Matter Test [§661]
In *Diversified Industries, Inc. v. Meredith*, 572 F.2d 596 (8th Cir. 1978), the Eighth Circuit held that the attorney-client privilege protects a communication made by an employee who is outside the control group if (a) the employee made the communication at the **behest of his superior**; (b) the superior made the request so the entity **could secure legal advice**; and the communication (c) was made for the **purpose of securing legal advice**, (d) concerned a matter within the **scope of the employee's duties**, and (e) was **not disseminated** beyond those persons who needed to know its contents.

(3) Supreme Court Rejects Control Group Test [§662]

In *Upjohn Co. v. United States*, 449 U.S. 383 (1981), the Court rejected the control group test. Although it declined to set forth a comprehensive test for courts to follow, the Court cited factors consistent with the subject matter test set forth in the *Diversified Industries* case. Some states, however, still favor the control group test.

5. Communication [§663]

The privilege applies only to communications that are made for the purpose of **facilitating the rendition of professional legal services**.

a. Facilitating Rendition of Legal Services [§664]

The privilege protects only those communications that are intended to relate to the lawyer's provision of **legal** services to the client. The privilege does not apply to communications that are made to a lawyer who is acting in a non-legal capacity. Thus, communications made to a lawyer who is serving as a business advisor or tax preparer, rather than providing legal advice, are not privileged.

b. Communication [§665]

Communications generally are verbal, either oral or written. Non-verbal statements intended to communicate information (such as nodding or pointing) are also communications.

(1) Observations [§666]

Observations made by the lawyer during the relationship are generally not considered communications. For example, a lawyer may be required to testify that her client was bleeding or screaming inappropriately during a consultation.

(2) Writings [§667]

A writing by a client that did not originate as a communication to his lawyer is not privileged, even if he subsequently turns it over to the lawyer. For example, the privilege does not cover pre-existing business files or personal letters that a client hands over to his lawyer. In contrast, if a client writes down **for his lawyer** the history of a dispute, the privilege will apply.

6. Confidentiality [§668]

To be privileged, a communication must have been made in confidence.

a. Presence of Third Persons [§669]

Confidentiality is destroyed by the presence of someone other than the lawyer, client, their representatives, or a person **reasonably necessary** for the transmission of information (e.g., an interpreter). Thus, the presence of a secretary, clerk, interpreter, or consultant does not destroy confidentiality; the presence of a friend whose attendance is unnecessary does.

b. Intent to Maintain Confidentiality Decisive [§670]

Most courts now hold that a communication is confidential if the client intended that it would be disclosed only to (a) the lawyer and (b) anyone else to whom disclosure is necessary to help provide legal services or communicate the information.

(1) Eavesdroppers [§671]

Under this standard, a lawyer-client conversation that is overheard by an eavesdropper retains its confidentiality so long as it was the client's **intent that it remain confidential**. Some jurisdictions, however, still adhere to the common-law view that an eavesdropper (or someone who uncovers a written communication) is permitted to testify as to the communication.

(2) Communication Made With Intent to Disclose [§672]

A communication is not privileged if the client tells the lawyer something with the intent that the lawyer disclose it to a third person.

7. **Client is Holder [§673]**
The client is the holder of the privilege and is thus entitled to assert it or waive it. The lawyer may assert it **on the client's behalf.** The privilege **survives the client's death** and may be asserted by the client's successor or personal representative. *Swidler & Berlin v. United States,* 524 U.S. 399 (1998).

8. **Privilege May Be Waived [§674]**
A communication loses its privileged status if the client (a) **fails to assert** the privilege in a timely fashion or (b) **voluntarily reveals** a significant part of the communication. If someone other than the client makes an unauthorized disclosure, the privilege is not lost.

   a. **Privileged Disclosure [§675]**
   If a client discloses a privileged communication to someone else with whom the client has a privileged relationship, no waiver occurs.

   EXAMPLE
   After consulting with his lawyer, a client tells his wife what his lawyer told him. The privilege still applies, as the client's confidential communications with his wife are themselves privileged by the husband-wife privilege.

9. **Exceptions [§676]**
There are several exceptions to the attorney-client privilege.

   a. **Crime or Fraud [§677]**
   The privilege does not attach to a communication made by a client who is seeking the lawyer's advice to enable the client to commit what he knew or should have known was a crime or fraud.

      (1) **Distinguish Between Past and Future Crimes/Frauds [§678]**
      This exception applies only to communications **concerning ongoing or future** crimes or frauds. A client may legitimately seek legal advice for crimes or frauds that have already been committed.

EXAMPLE

Defendant deliberately burned down his house and is charged with arson. He retains Lawyer to defend him. Their communications are privileged. Defendant is seeking legal services regarding a completed crime.

EXAMPLE

Defendant deliberately burned down his house. He goes to Lawyer and asks Lawyer questions in a effort to figure out how he can best file an insurance claim and fraudulently collect on his home owner's policy. He is subsequently charged with attempted fraud. His communications with Lawyer are not privileged. Defendant sought Lawyer's advice to enable him to commit what he knew or should have known was a crime or fraud It doesn't matter whether Lawyer was aware of Defendant's nefarious plan.

(2) Burden of Proof [§679]

The party seeking to take advantage of the crime-fraud exception bears the burden of establishing its applicability. It must make out a **prima facie case** sufficient to satisfy the court that the client was engaged in an ongoing crime or fraud or was seeking to commit a crime or fraud at the time the communication was made.

(3) In Camera Review [§680]

May a trial judge conduct an in camera review of allegedly privileged communications to determine whether the crime-fraud exception applies? Many jurisdictions have not answered that question. But the Supreme Court requires a threshold test to be met before such a review can occur. The threshold is fairly low. The party seeking the in camera review must show, through non-privileged materials, that there exists a **factual basis** to support a **reasonable belief** that an in camera review "may reveal evidence to establish the claim that the crime-fraud exception applies." *United States v. Zolin*, 491 U.S. 554 (1989).

b. Breach of Duty [§681]

Communications relevant to an issue of breach of duty between the lawyer and client (e.g., failure to pay fees, malpractice) are not privileged.

c. Joint Clients [§682]

When two or more clients who jointly consult a lawyer on a matter of common interest later find themselves in a dispute, relevant communications made by either of them to the lawyer are not privileged **as against the other** joint client or clients. This exception does not apply to a third party's attempt to use such communications.

d. Document Attested By Lawyer [§683]

Communications relevant to an issue concerning a document to which the lawyer was an attesting witness are not privileged.

e. Claimants Through Deceased Client [§684]

If two or more parties are claiming through the same deceased client, communications relevant to their dispute are not privileged. Thus, if a will is ambiguous as to which of the client's two nieces was supposed to take under her will, relevant communications to the lawyer who drafted the will may be revealed.

10. Privilege v. Work Product v. Obligation to Maintain Confidentiality [§685]

These three doctrines are related, but distinct. The attorney-client **privilege** empowers the client to refuse to reveal, and to prevent someone else from revealing, attorney-client communications. The **work-product** doctrine shields from discovery certain information created or obtained by the lawyer in anticipation of litigation or preparation for trial. This includes information obtained from third parties and therefore not covered by the attorney-client privilege. The **professional obligation** to maintain confidentiality is imposed by professional rules of ethics (e.g., the Code of Professional Responsibility or Rules of Professional Conduct). This obligation forbids lawyers from voluntarily disclosing information about their clients, including information not protected by the privilege.

D. Physician-Patient Privilege [§686]

Although most states recognize a physician-patient privilege, its status in the federal courts is less certain. Several courts of appeals have declined to recognize such a privilege. Even in those jurisdictions where the privilege is recognized, it is **riddled with exceptions** and is virtually useless as a means of encouraging patients to confide in their physicians. Consequently, proponents of the physician-patient privilege often emphasize its role in protecting patients' **privacy** interests, even if it has little or no effect on an individual's decision to seek medical advice or to confide in the physician.

1. Physician-Patient Relationship [§687]

The patient must consult the doctor for purposes of diagnosis or treatment. The physician must be licensed to practice medicine. If the patient consults someone whom she mistakenly but reasonably believes to be a doctor, the privilege applies.

2. Communications [§688]

The privilege protects communications between a physician (and other representatives of a physician, such as a nurse) and a patient that are made for the purpose of diagnosing or treating the patient's medical condition. In addition, many physician-patient privileges also protect the **identity** of a patient, a patient's medical **records**, and **observations** made by the physician through physical examinations and tests. For example, the results of a blood-alcohol test performed on a patient are privileged.

3. Confidentiality [§689]

The privilege protects only confidential communications. The presence of **necessary third parties** (nurses, attendants, consultants, and the like) does not destroy confidentiality. In addition, the privilege applies when a patient communicates with her physician through an intermediary (e.g., a family member).

4. Patient is Holder [§690]

The patient is the holder of the privilege. The physician may assert the privilege **on behalf of** the patient. If the patient is incompetent, her guardian may assert it on her behalf. The privilege does not die with the patient; it may

be asserted by her personal representative, and in some
states, by her successor.

5. **Waiver [§691]**
    Waiver is accomplished in the same way as the attorney-
    client privilege: by the holder's **failure to assert** it in a
    timely manner or by **voluntary disclosure** of a significant
    part of the privileged communication.

6. **Exceptions [§692]**
    Different states have different exceptions. The following
    are the most common and most important.

    a. **Criminal Proceedings [§693]**
        In many states the privilege does not apply in criminal
        proceedings.

    b. **Patient-Litigant [§694]**
        If the patient (or the patient's representative if the
        patient is incompetent or dead) puts her physical or
        mental condition into issue, the privilege may not be
        asserted to prevent the disclosure and introduction of
        relevant medical evidence. Thus, if a plaintiff claims
        that her ailment resulted from using the defendant's
        product, she would not be able to assert the privilege
        to prevent the defendant from discovering and
        introducing her medical records to rebut her claim.

    c. **Breach of Duty [§695]**
        The privilege does not protect relevant material in fee
        disputes or malpractice actions between the physician
        and patient.

    d. **Court-Appointed Physician [§696]**
        No privilege attaches when a patient is examined by a
        court-appointed physician.

E. **Psychotherapist-Patient Privilege [§697]**
    Every state has a psychotherapist-patient privilege of some
    kind, and the Supreme Court has recognized a
    psychotherapist-patient privilege under FRE 501. *Jaffee v.
    Redmond*, 581 U.S. 1 (1996). The basics of the
    psychotherapist-patient privilege are similar to those discussed
    above for the physician-patient privilege. Some additional

points regarding the psychotherapist-patient privilege should be noted.

1. **Definition of Psychotherapist [§698]**
   States vary as to how they define psychotherapist (e.g., whether therapists other than psychiatrists and psychologists are included). In *Jaffee v. Redmond,* the Supreme Court held that the privilege extended to communications made to licensed social workers in the course of psychotherapy.

2. **Exceptions [§699]**
   As is the case with the physician-patient privilege, the exceptions vary from state to state. Those applicable to the physician-patient privilege under state law are often applicable to the psychotherapist-patient privilege as well. In *Jaffee,* the Supreme Court noted that exceptions to the privilege will undoubtedly have to be recognized under federal law. The Court declined, however, to enumerate what those exceptions might be.

F. **Communications with Members of the Clergy [§700]**
   Most states recognize a privilege for communications made with a member of the clergy. Some are narrow in scope and apply only to confessions made to a priest. Others are much broader and apply to any confidential communication made to and by a minister, priest, rabbi, or other similar functionary of a religious organization **in his or her capacity as a spiritual adviser.** This may include, for example, communications made in the course of marriage counseling with a minister. There are no generally accepted exceptions to this privilege.

G. **Accountant-Client Privilege [§701]**
   Most states do not recognize an accountant-client privilege. A limited federal privilege has been statutorily created for communications to federally-authorized tax practitioners.

H. **Marital Communication Privilege [§702]**
   There are **two privileges** involving spouses. One is for confidential **communications** made **during the marriage**; the other privilege (the **testimonial** privilege) permits a person to **refuse to testify** against his or her spouse in a criminal case. We deal here with the **communication**

privilege, which is founded on the rather dubious notion that spouses will be deterred from confiding in one another unless the law gives them the right to prevent the disclosure of their confidences during the course of a trial.

1. **Marital Relationship [§703]**
    The parties to the communication must be legally married **at the time the communication is made**. A common-law marriage qualifies if the couple's jurisdiction of residence recognizes common-law marriages. An erroneous belief that a marriage exists, however, is not sufficient.

    a. **Effect of Divorce [§704]**
        The privilege survives divorce but relates only to communications made during the marriage. Remember, this privilege is designed to protect communications made in the bosom of the marital relationship.

        EXAMPLE: PRIVILEGED
        Defendant is on trial for fraud. The plaintiff calls Defendant's ex-wife to testify about statements Defendant made to her while they were still married. Defendant may assert the marital communication privilege.

        EXAMPLE: NOT PRIVILEGED
        Defendant is on trial for fraud. The plaintiff calls Defendant's wife to testify about statements Defendant made to her before they married. Defendant may not assert the marital communication privilege.

    b. **Married But Separated [§705]**
        Federal courts are increasingly willing to hold that a communication made between a husband and wife whose marriage is **no longer viable** (although still legally intact) is not protected by the privilege.

2. **Communication [§706]**
    Courts are split over what constitutes a "communication." Some courts hold that only verbal statements and non-verbal acts intended to be communicative (e.g., nodding, pointing) are protected. A minority of courts favor a

broader interpretation, embracing private observations made during the marriage if it appears that one spouse, relying upon the confidential nature of the marital relationship, allowed the other spouse to observe.

EXAMPLE
Husband comes home one night with a sack full of money. He makes no attempt to hide it from his wife. When she asks him what it is, he tells her it is money he has just stolen from a convenience store. While his comment to her clearly qualifies as a communication, courts disagree as to whether her observation of the sack of money is a protected communication. Most would hold that it is not privileged.

3. **Confidentiality [§707]**
The communication must be made privately. The presence of even the couple's child (other, perhaps, than a young child) is enough to destroy confidentiality. Moreover, the communicating spouse must intend the communication to be confidential.

4. **Both Spouses Are Holders [§708]**
Most courts hold that both spouses are holders of the privilege and either one may assert it. Thus, if Husband wants to testify as to a communication and Wife invokes the privilege, Husband will not be permitted to testify. Some states, however, vest the privilege only in the **communicating** spouse.

5. **Waiver [§709]**
The privilege is waived the same way as other communication privileges: by **failure to assert** it in a timely manner or by **voluntary disclosure** of a significant part of the privileged communication.

6. **Exceptions [§710]**
Recognized exceptions to the marital communications privilege vary from jurisdiction to jurisdiction. The following are the most common.

   a. **Actions Between Spouses [§711]**
   The privilege may not be asserted in an action between the spouses, such as a divorce proceeding.

b. Crime or Fraud [§712]
The privilege does not apply to communications made by a spouse in furtherance of a crime or fraud in which both spouses participated.

c. Crime Against Family Member [§713]
An exception is made in many jurisdictions when the spouse is charged with a crime against a family member (e.g., wife beating, child abuse).

I. Parent-Child [§714]
By analogy to the marital communication privilege, numerous commentators and litigants have argued for recognition of a privilege for parent-child communications. Both the federal courts and the overwhelming majority of state courts **reject** such a privilege.

J. Miscellaneous Privileges [§715]
A number of privileges have been created for matters other than confidential communications. These include the **spousal testimonial** privilege; the **voter's** privilege; the **trade secrets** privilege; the **informer's identity** privilege; the **state secrets** privilege; and the **journalist's** privilege. In addition, the constitution provides a basis for the **executive** privilege as well as the privilege against **self-incrimination**.

K. Spousal Testimonial Privilege [§716]
This is the second of the two husband-wife privileges. Unlike the privilege for marital communications, the testimonial privilege applies in **criminal cases** only.

1. Common-Law Rule [§717]
The common-law rule gives a criminal defendant the right to prevent his spouse from testifying against him. The privilege is **held by the accused**, not the testifying spouse. This rule is still followed in a number of states.

2. Modern Trend [§718]
The modern trend is to give a spouse the right to refuse to testify against a criminal defendant spouse. This vests the privilege in the **witness spouse**, not the defendant spouse. If the witness spouse chooses to testify, she may do so. The Supreme Court has followed the modern trend. *Trammel v. United States*, 445 U.S. 40 (1980).

3. **Rationale [§719]**

    The spousal testimonial privilege is usually justified on the ground that forcing a spouse to give testimony that could result in her spouse's conviction places the testifying spouse in an untenable position. She must either testify adversely to her spouse, commit perjury, or face contempt for refusing to testify. This is deemed too destructive of the marital relationship. In short, the theory is: It's not nice to force a wife to testify against her husband (or vice-versa) in a criminal case. This rationale does not carry over to civil cases; the testimonial privilege applies only in criminal cases.

4. **End of Marriage, End of Privilege [§720]**

    Although it may not be nice to force a wife to testify against her criminal defendant husband, the law has no qualms about compelling an ex-wife to testify against her ex-husband. The right of a spouse to refuse to testify against a spouse **terminates with the end of the marriage**.

5. **Even if Spouse Testifies, Communication Privilege Still Exists [§721]**

    The marital communication and spousal testimonial privileges **are two independent privileges**. Therefore, even in a jurisdiction that allows the wife to choose to testify against her husband, the husband may prevent her from revealing confidential communications made to her during the marriage.

EXAMPLE: DURING MARRIAGE

Husband is on trial in federal court for bank robbery. The prosecutor calls Wife to testify that (a) the night of the robbery she saw Husband come into the house carrying a satchel marked "First State Bank" and (b) Husband told her that night that he had committed the bank robbery. Wife may assert her spousal testimonial privilege and refuse to testify. Even if she chooses to testify, however, Husband may prevent her from relating what he told her. That is a confidential communication. But her observation of Husband carrying the satchel is not considered a confidential communication (in most jurisdictions), and Husband cannot prevent Wife from testifying about it.

EXAMPLE: AFTER DIVORCE
Husband is on trial in federal court for bank robbery. The prosecutor calls Ex-Wife to testify that (a) the night of the robbery (at which time they were still married) she saw Husband come into the house carrying a satchel marked "First State Bank" and (b) Husband told her that night that he had committed the bank robbery. Ex-Wife asserts her testimonial privilege and refuses to testify against him. She cannot do this. Since she is an ex-wife, she may be forced to testify against her former spouse. Husband may, however, prevent her from testifying as to what he told her. That is a confidential communication.

6. **Exceptions [§722]**
   Certain exceptions have been recognized to the testimonial privilege.

   a. **Crime Against Family Member [§723]**
      An exception is made in many jurisdictions when the spouse is charged with a crime against a family member (e.g., wife beating, child abuse). In such cases, therefore, the spouse can be compelled to testify.

   b. **Marrying the Eyewitness [§724]**
      In some jurisdictions, the testimonial privilege does not apply to events that occurred before the marriage. This is to prevent an accused from marrying an important witness against him and keeping her off the stand.

7. **Marital Communication Privilege Distinguished From Spousal Testimonial Privilege [§725]**
   The marital **communication** privilege protects (a) confidential communications (b) made during the marriage. If a communication was made during marriage, it remains privileged even if the marriage subsequently ends. The communication privilege applies in both civil and criminal cases. The spousal **testimonial** privilege (a) applies only in criminal cases and (b) allows a spouse to refuse to testify against her criminal defendant spouse

about anything. The right to refuse to testify disappears
with the end of the marriage.

L. Political Vote [§726]
A person may refuse to reveal how he voted in a secret ballot
unless he voted illegally.

M. Trade Secrets [§727]
The trade secrets privilege allows a person to refuse to
disclose (and prevent others from disclosing) a trade secret
owned by him. This is a qualified privilege, however, and the
court may order disclosure pursuant to a protective order.

N. Identity of Informer [§728]
The government may refuse to disclose the identity of a
person who has furnished information to law enforcement
officials regarding illegal conduct. However, if the court finds
it is probable that the informer can give testimony necessary
to a fair trial and the government still refuses to disclose the
informer's identity, the court must dismiss the relevant
charges against the defendant.

O. State Secrets [§729]
A privilege for matters such as military secrets and other
classified information has traditionally been recognized. *United
States v. Reynolds*, 345 U.S. 1 (1953). Case law is limited,
however, and Congress has enacted special legislation to deal
with this problem.

P. Executive Privilege [§730]
The executive privilege protects the confidential
communications between the president and his immediate
advisers. The privilege is only a qualified one, however, and
does not protect communications if there exists a
demonstrated, specific need for the information in a criminal
trial. *United States v. Nixon*, 418 U.S. 683 (1974).

Q. Journalist's Privilege [§731]
The Supreme Court has held that the First Amendment does
not create a privilege that allows journalists to refuse to
divulge information about the sources of their stories.
Branzburg v. Hayes, 408 U.S. 665 (1972). Many states have
enacted statutory privileges with varying coverage and

exceptions. Even in states with broad statutory privileges, however, the privilege may have to yield to a defendant's right to compulsory process.

R. Privilege Against Self-Incrimination [§732]

The Fifth Amendment privilege against self-incrimination has **two components**. First, it protects an individual from being (a) compelled to engage (b) in testimonial conduct (c) that would tend to incriminate himself. Second, it gives a criminal defendant the right not to take the stand, and thus precludes the prosecution from calling the accused as a witness.

1. Activity Must Be Compelled [§733]

The privilege against self-incrimination only protects an individual from being **compelled** to engage in **testimonial activity**. Thus the contents of voluntarily-created written materials (e.g., a diary) are not privileged. In addition, the privilege is personal: a defendant may not prevent someone else (e.g., a co-defendant) from testifying in an incriminating manner.

2. Activity Must Be Testimonial [§734]

The privilege protects against compelled testimonial activity. If the compelled activity is non-testimonial in nature, the privilege is inapplicable.

a. Testimonial Activity Defined [§735]

Compelled activity is testimonial in nature if the individual is being forced to reveal, directly or indirectly, his **knowledge of facts or his belief about a matter**.

b. Examples of Non-Testimonial Activity [§736]

An individual may be compelled to provide a blood sample, participate in a line-up, read a transcript, give a handwriting exemplar, submit to a breathalyzer test, and sign a consent directive authorizing a bank to disclose records of any account over which the individual may happen to have a right of withdrawal.

c. Implicit Testimonial Activity [§737]

An individual may refuse to comply with a subpoena directing him to produce enumerated documents. Although the **contents of the documents** are not themselves protected (because they were voluntarily created), the **act of production** may involve **implicit testimonial activity**. That is, when an individual hands over the requested materials, he is implicitly admitting that the materials exist, that they are in his possession, and that they are the requested materials. *United States v. Doe.*, 465 U.S. 605 (1984).

3. Must Tend to Incriminate [§738]

The privilege protects against compelled testimonial activity only if it would tend to incriminate the individual. Information tends to incriminate an individual if it would constitute a **link in a chain** of evidence that might lead to his conviction.

a. Civil Liability Not Incriminatory [§739]

The fact that an answer might result in civil, rather than criminal, liability is not sufficient to invoke the privilege. But if a penalty that is nominally civil is really criminal in nature, the privilege may be invoked. *In re Gault*, 387 U.S. 1 (1967), for example, held that the privilege against self-incrimination applies in juvenile delinquency proceedings, even though they are designated as civil proceedings.

b. Privilege May Be Invoked in Civil Proceedings [§740]

Whether an answer tends to incriminate is determined by the **consequences** that may befall the witness, **not the type of proceeding** in which the answer is compelled. For example, a witness in a civil fraud action may invoke the privilege and refuse to discuss his role in the fraud — not because the answers might result in civil liability, but because the answers might be used to convict him of criminal fraud.

c. Immunity [§741]

The **danger of incrimination may be removed** by granting the witness immunity. State or federal prosecutors may grant a person immunity which, at the least, guarantees that the testimony the person gives (and the fruits of such testimony) cannot be used against him in subsequent criminal proceedings.

Having been given such **use immunity**, the witness can no longer contend that his answers would tend to incriminate him. Therefore, he can be compelled to testify. A broader form of immunity is **transactional immunity**, under which the witness may not be prosecuted at all for the criminal transactions discussed in his testimony.

4. **Right Not to Testify [§742]**
A criminal defendant has a right not to testify. The prosecution may not call the defendant and force him to assert this privilege. Further, the prosecutor may not comment upon the defendant's failure to take the stand and argue that the jury should draw a negative inference therefrom. *Griffin v. California*, 380 U.S. 609 (1965).

a. **Comment in Civil Cases [§743]**
In contrast to criminal cases, some courts allow civil litigants to comment up on their opponent's invocation of the privilege against self-incrimination and permit the court to instruct the jury that it may draw a negative inference therefrom. Some federal courts go still further, and allow a negative inference to be drawn from a **non-party witness's** invocation of the privilege against self-incrimination.

EXAMPLE
Plaintiff sues Defendant Corporation. When Plaintiff calls Defendant Corporation's former president to testify, he asserts his privilege against self-incrimination and refuses to answer any questions about alleged fraudulent actions he took when he was Defendant Corporation's president. The jury may draw a negative inference from his invocation of the privilege (i.e., it may infer that had he answered the questions he would have revealed that he engaged in fraudulent actions).

5. **Waiver [§744]**
If a party, including the defendant in a criminal case, voluntarily testifies, he waives the right to refuse to answer questions on cross-examination that are related to the testimony. However, a party who has testified in one proceeding may change his mind and invoke the privilege

against self-incrimination in a later proceeding and refuse to testify.

X. Judicial Notice

A. Judicial Notice [§745]
Judicial notice is an **evidentiary shortcut**. It allows trial and appellate courts to accept certain facts or propositions of law as true without requiring formal proof.

1. Rationale [§746]
Judicial notice is designed to (1) **save time and expense** in proving facts that are not subject to reasonable dispute and (2) **avoid the disrespect** for the court system that would result if trials resulted in factual findings that everyone knows to be false.

B. Three Types of Judicial Notice: "L.A. Law." [§747]
Courts may take judicial notice of (1) **legislative facts**, (2) **adjudicative facts**, and (3) **law**. (**Mnemonic** device: L.A. Law.) The Federal Rules of Evidence contain provisions governing judicial notice only of **adjudicative facts**. [FRE 201.]

C. Adjudicative Facts [§748]
Adjudicative facts are facts that relate to the **immediate parties or event**. For example, was the defendant intoxicated? Had the sun set by the time of the accident? Judicial notice may be taken of an adjudicative fact if it is **indisputable**. There are two situations in which this occurs.

1. Commonly-Known Facts [§749]
Courts may take judicial notice of facts that **well-informed persons** in the community **generally know and accept**.

a. Well-Informed Persons [§750]
Not everyone in the community must know the fact for it to be judicially noticed. The standard is whether well-informed persons in the community in which the court is sitting know it. [FRE 201(b)(1).]

EXAMPLE

A court sitting in Chicago may judicially notice that the Chicago Cubs play in Wrigley Field and that for many years the Cubs played home games only during the daytime.

b. Judge's Own Knowledge [§751]

Private knowledge of certain facts by the judge is not sufficient for judicial notice. Thus, a judge familiar with a particular intersection cannot take judicial notice of its unique characteristics unless the party seeking judicial notice can show that those facts are generally known in the community.

2. Readily-Verifiable Facts [§752]

Certain facts are not generally known, but can be **easily verified** by resort to sources whose **accuracy cannot reasonably be questioned**. [FRE 201(b)(2).]

a. Sources of Verification [§753]

The verification must come from a reputable and reasonably accessible source that establishes the truth of the fact beyond reasonable dispute.

EXAMPLE

Courts may take judicial notice of natural phenomena (e.g., time of sunrise or sunset), chronology (e.g., December 30, 1988 was a Friday), history (e.g., President Kennedy was assassinated on November 22, 1963), geography (e.g., the tallest mountain in the U.S. is in Alaska), demography (e.g., the population of a city), and scientific theories, facts, and conclusions (e.g., that heated oxygen will combine with lead to form lead oxide). This last category includes the scientific basis for various tests (e.g., radar, ballistics, breathalyzer, DNA).

3. Effect of Judicial Notice [§754]

The effect of judicially noticing a fact depends on whether it is a civil or criminal case.

a. Civil [§755]

If a court takes judicial notice of a fact in a civil case, it will instruct the jury to **accept the truth of that**

fact. Once the fact is noticed, evidence to disprove its truth is **inadmissible**. [FRE 201(g).]

b. Criminal [§756]

Under the federal rules and in many jurisdictions, the court in a criminal case is permitted only to instruct the jury that it **may, but is not required to**, accept the truth of a judicially-noticed fact. [FRE 201(g).]

D. Legislative Facts [§757]

Legislative facts are those facts that a court considers in making policy decisions in the course of **interpreting various common-law doctrines, statutes, and the constitution**. In this context, the court is operating as a quasi law-making body and its determinations are based on certain social, political, and economic assumptions that are not amenable to indisputable proof. For example, in determining whether the witness spouse or defendant spouse should be the holder of the spousal testimonial privilege, the court's decision is informed by certain assumptions about marital relationships.

1. Not Codified [§758]

Neither the federal rules nor most state evidence rules contain provisions governing judicial notice of legislative facts. Courts may notice legislative facts without regard to whether they are indisputable and may consider reports, books, articles, studies, etc., without following any particular procedure.

E. Judicial Notice of Law [§759]

With a few exceptions, judges may take judicial notice of the law. That is, judges may do their own research to determine what the relevant law is; they are not restricted to considering only the law that the parties present. The **two exceptions** to this general rule are **foreign law and municipal ordinances**. Jurisdictions vary as to whether foreign law and municipal ordinances must be proved or whether courts may take notice of them. For example, the Federal Rules of Civil Procedure provide for judicial notice of foreign law. [Rule 44.1.] Municipal ordinances are usually singled out for special treatment (and must be proved) because they are less accessible than state laws or regulations.

F. Procedures [§760]

A court **may** take judicial notice of adjudicative facts on its **own motion**. **Upon request** by a party, a court **must** take judicial notice if supplied with the necessary information by the party.

1. Hearing [§761]

A party may request a hearing regarding the **propriety** of taking judicial notice (i.e., whether this is a fact that is generally known) and the **tenor** of the matter noticed (i.e., although the fact is generally known, whether the court got it right).

G. When Notice May Be Taken [§762]

Judicial notice may be taken at **any time**. Even an appellate court may take judicial notice of facts not presented to the trial court.

XI. Burdens of Proof and Presumptions

A. Burdens of Proof [§763]

The term "burden of proof" is employed to mean two different things. It is sometimes used to refer to the **burden of production** (also known as the burden of going forward with the evidence). At other times it is used to refer to the **burden of persuasion** (also known as the risk of non-persuasion). The party that bears the burden of production and fails to meet it loses **without getting to the jury**. The party that bears the burden of persuasion may get to the jury but will lose if it fails to meet this burden.

1. Who Bears the Burden of Persuasion [§764]

The substantive law determines which party bears the burden of persuasion as to an issue.

a. Civil Cases [§765]

Generally, the plaintiff has the burden of persuasion as to the elements of its claim, while the defendant bears the burden of persuasion as to any affirmative defenses raised.

EXAMPLE

Plaintiff sues Defendant for defamation. Plaintiff has the burden of proving that a defamatory statement was made by Defendant. If Defendant seeks to assert truth as a defense, Defendant has the burden of establishing that the statement was true.

b. Criminal Cases [§766]

The prosecution has the burden of persuasion as to every element of the crime charged. This is mandated by the Due Process Clause. *In re Winship*, 397 U.S. 358 (1970). The Supreme Court has held that the burden of persuasion as to an affirmative defense (such as self-defense or insanity) may, however, be placed on the accused. *Leland v. Oregon*, 343 U.S. 790 (1952) (insanity); *Martin v. Ohio*, 480 U.S. 228 (1987) (self-defense). Thus, states may choose to place the burden of persuasion as to a particular affirmative defense on either the prosecution or the accused.

2. How Heavy is The Burden of Persuasion [§767]

The weight of the burden of persuasion varies with the type of case.

a. Preponderance of the Evidence [§768]

Ordinarily, the party with the burden of persuasion in a **civil** case must prove its case by a preponderance of the evidence. This means that it must satisfy the factfinder that it is **more likely than not** that the facts that establish its claim exist. This is the 50-50 standard. In a typical civil case, the plaintiff must convince the jury that the odds are better than 50-50 that its version of the facts is true.

b. Clear and Convincing Evidence [§769]

In some instances (e.g., some kinds of fraud) the jury must be convinced of the relevant facts by "clear and convincing evidence." This is a higher standard of proof, although courts make no effort to quantify it.

c. Beyond a Reasonable Doubt [§770]

This is the familiar standard of proof for **criminal** cases. The prosecution must meet its burden of persuasion as to each element of the crime by presenting proof that satisfies the jury "beyond a reasonable doubt." *In re Winship*, 397 U.S. 358 (1970).

3. **Burden of Production [§771]**

The burden of production (the burden of going forward with the evidence) is a means of allocating decision-making between the judge and jury. A party that fails to meet its burden of production will lose **without getting to the jury**; that is, the judge will grant a directed verdict against the party.

a. **Meeting the Burden of Production [§772]**

A party meets its burden of production if it produces **enough evidence so that a reasonable juror could find** for the party. A party with the burden of production as to a particular fact need not persuade the judge that the fact exists; it is sufficient that the judge believes that a reasonable juror could believe that it exists.

4. **Traffic Light Explanation of Burdens [§773]**

Imagine that Plaintiff sues Defendant for damages arising out of an auto accident. The only issue is whether Defendant drove negligently. The amount of damages is stipulated. This is a typical civil case: Plaintiff has the burden of persuasion.

a. **Red Light [§774]**

Suppose the only evidence Plaintiff introduces is that Plaintiff's and Defendant's cars collided. No evidence indicating Defendant was at fault is introduced. Defendant would be entitled to a directed verdict because no reasonable juror could find that Defendant was negligent. Thus, the judge would (figuratively) hold up a red light, stopping Plaintiff from getting his case to the jury. Plaintiff has not only failed to meet his burden of persuasion, he has failed to meet his burden of production.

b. **Yellow Light [§775]**

Suppose Plaintiff introduces some evidence (not particularly strong, however) indicating that Defendant was at fault. Defendant's motion for a directed verdict would now fail. A reasonable juror could find for Plaintiff; but he could also reasonably find for Defendant. Thus, the judge would hold up a yellow light, allowing the case to go to the jury.

Plaintiff has met his burden of production. Whether he has met his burden of persuasion is up to the jury.

c. **Green Light [§776]**
Suppose Plaintiff introduces a great deal of unchallenged evidence establishing Defendant's negligence. At this point, if Defendant fails to produce some counter-evidence, the judge would have to grant Plaintiff's motion for a directed verdict. In other words, absent some evidence from Defendant, the judge would have to conclude that no reasonable juror could rule for Defendant. At this point, the judge would hold up a red light **to Defendant**, preventing Defendant from getting to the jury (hence the green light for Plaintiff). The **burden of production** has, therefore, **shifted** from Plaintiff to Defendant.

d. **Yellow Light Again [§777]**
Suppose Defendant now introduces some counter-evidence. At this point, the judge would conclude that a reasonable juror could find either for Plaintiff or Defendant and let the case go to the jury. Defendant would have met her burden of production.

e. **Although Burden of Production May Shift, Burden of Persuasion Does Not [§778]**
Note that in the above example, the burden of production shifted to Defendant when the evidence was overwhelmingly against her. However, the burden of persuasion never shifted; it remained with Plaintiff throughout.

B. **Presumptions in Civil Cases [§779]**
Normally, the jury has discretion in deciding what inferences should be drawn from the evidence. A presumption, however, is a procedural device that **requires** the jury to draw a **particular conclusion from certain proved facts**.

1. **Basic and Presumed Facts [§780]**
The proved fact that triggers the finding of a prescribed conclusion is called the **basic fact**. The prescribed conclusion is called the **presumed fact**.

EXAMPLE

The law presumes that a letter that was properly addressed and mailed will be received in due course by the addressee. Note that even without this presumption, the jury could permissibly infer receipt of a letter from evidence of proper mailing. The presumption, however, **requires** the jury to find that the letter was received if it believes the letter was properly addressed and mailed. (This presumption may be rebutted. More on that later.) The facts of "proper addressing" and "proper mailing" are the **basic facts** that must be proved; "receipt of the letter" is the **presumed fact** that must be inferred if the basic facts are proved.

2. **How Presumptions Work in General [§781]**

    In dealing with presumptions, it is important to distinguish between the treatment of basic facts and presumed facts.

    a. **Basic Facts [§782]**

    Presumptions come into play **only if the proponent proves the basic facts**. If there is no dispute about the basic facts, the presumption is triggered. If there is a dispute about the basic facts, the presumption comes into play only if the jury finds that the basic facts exist. **The opponent of a presumption may always try to show that the basic facts don't exist**.

    b. **Effect of Triggering the Presumption [§783]**

    If the basic facts are found to exist, the presumption is triggered. The effect of the presumption differs, however, depending on whether it is an **irrebuttable** (or conclusive) presumption or a **rebuttable** presumption. If an **irrebuttable** (conclusive) presumption is triggered, its opponent **may not attempt to disprove the presumed fact**. With a **rebuttable** presumption, the opponent **may try to disprove the presumed fact** as well as the basic facts.

3. **Irrebuttable (Conclusive) Presumptions [§784]**

    With an irrebuttable presumption, if the basic facts are shown to exist, the presumed fact is **conclusively established**. No evidence contrary to the presumed fact will be received.

EXAMPLE

Suppose a jurisdiction has a conclusive presumption that a child born to a married woman is presumed to be legitimate if the woman was cohabiting with her husband at the time of conception. If the basic facts required to trigger the presumption are established (that the mother was married and cohabiting with her husband at the time of conception), the presumed fact (that the child is legitimate) is conclusively established. Evidence that might prove the husband is not the biological father (e.g., DNA testing) will not be received.

    a.   **Really a Substantive Rule of Law In Disguise [§785]**

A conclusive presumption is really a substantive rule of law masquerading as a rule of evidence. In the above example, the presumption effectively states that, under certain circumstances, biological and legal paternity are two different things.

    b.   **Basic Facts May Be Challenged [§786]**

Remember, even a conclusive presumption operates only if the factfinder is convinced of the existence of the basic facts. Therefore, the party opposing an irrebuttable presumption may always challenge the existence of the **basic facts**. In the above example, for instance, evidence might be offered that husband and wife were not cohabiting at the time of conception.

4.   Rebuttable Presumptions [§787]

Most presumptions are rebuttable. If the basic facts of a rebuttable presumption are proved, the jury is required to find the presumed fact unless the opponent of the presumption rebuts it. How much evidence the opponent must produce to negate the effect of the presumption depends on the jurisdiction's approach to rebuttable presumptions. There are **two basic approaches** to rebuttable presumptions.

    a.   **Presumption Shifts Burden of Persuasion [§788]**

One view of rebuttable presumptions (often referred to as the **Morgan-McCormick** approach, in honor of two famous Evidence scholars) is that they **shift**

the burden of persuasion. If the proponent triggers the presumption by establishing the basic facts, the jury must find that the presumed fact exists **unless the opponent persuades it that the presumed fact does not exist**. That is, the effect of this type of presumption is to place on the opponent the burden of persuading the jury that the presumed fact does not exist.

EXAMPLE

Plaintiff is trying to prove that Defendant received a particular letter. Plaintiff testifies that she properly addressed and mailed the letter to Defendant. Defendant cross-examines plaintiff about her testimony. Later, Defendant testifies that he never received the letter. The judge should instruct the jury that if they find that Plaintiff properly addressed and mailed the letter to Defendant, they must find that Defendant received it unless Defendant convinces them by a preponderance of the evidence that he did not receive it.

(1) Designed to Further Public Policy [§789]

By shifting the burden of persuasion to the opponent of the presumed fact, the Morgan-McCormick presumption makes it more likely that the presumed fact will be found. This reflects a view that presumptions should be used to promote public policy by increasing the likelihood that juries will reach certain outcomes.

b. Presumption Shifts Burden of Production: The Bursting-Bubble Approach [§790]

Under this approach (sometimes referred to as the **Thayer-Wigmore** approach, also in honor of two famous Evidence scholars), the presumption acts merely to **shift the burden of production** to the opponent. In other words, the opponent of the presumption may negate its effect **by producing evidence that would allow a juror to find that the presumed fact does not exist**. If the opponent does this, the presumption **disappears** from the case (the bubble bursts). Thus, this type of presumption has a practical effect only if the opponent of the presumption fails to produce evidence to rebut the presumed fact.

EXAMPLE

Plaintiff is trying to prove that Defendant received a particular letter. Plaintiff testifies that she properly addressed and mailed the letter to Defendant. Defendant cross-examines Plaintiff about her testimony. Later, Defendant testifies that he never received the letter. **Under the bursting bubble approach, the judge should not give the jury an instruction**. By testifying that he did not receive the letter, Defendant has produced sufficient evidence for the jury to find that the presumed fact (receipt of the letter) does not exist. Thus he has met his production burden and eliminated the presumption from the case. Remember, Defendant does not have to persuade the judge or jury that he did not receive the letter in order to negate the presumption; he need only produce evidence of non-receipt.

(1) Presumption is Gone, But Logical Inference Remains [§791]

Although the procedural effect of the presumption may be overcome, any logical inference that flows from the basic facts remains. Thus, in the example above, if the jury believes that the letter was properly addressed and mailed, it may still infer that Defendant received it.

(2) Presumption Only a Procedural Convenience [§792]

The bursting bubble approach to presumptions reflects a view that presumptions are merely procedural conveniences designed to expedite litigation and (sometimes) to force the party with greater access to the evidence to come forward with it. Under this view, therefore, they should be given little weight.

c. Determining Which View to Apply [§793]

FRE 301 adopts the weaker form of presumption, shifting only the **burden of production** and not the burden of persuasion to the opponent of the presumption. (In diversity and other cases in which state law governs, the federal rules defer to the state law of presumptions.) If an exam question is not based on the federal rules, it will probably indicate how the relevant jurisdiction treats presumptions. If it does not, and it is an essay question, discuss both views. Keep in mind that the bursting bubble (FRE) approach views presumptions merely as a procedural convenience, whereas the Morgan-McCormick approach views presumptions as a means of advancing public policy.

d. Jury Not Told Directly About Presumption [§794]

A jury is not told directly about the existence of a presumption. The judge simply instructs the jury as to the consequence of finding the basic facts. That is, without ever mentioning the word "presumption," the judge will instruct the jury, "If you find [the basic facts], then . . ." Of course, what the consequence will be of finding the basic facts depends on the type of presumption.

5. Summary of Presumptions in Civil Cases [§795]

In dealing with presumptions, it is important to focus on three things: (a) the **type** of presumption involved; (b) whether the **basic facts** have been contested; and (c) whether evidence has been introduced that disputes the existence of the **presumed facts**. The following are examples of instructions that would be given the jury depending on these three factors. In each example, the basic facts are abbreviated as "BF" and the presumed fact as "PF".

a. Instructions for Conclusive Presumptions [§796]

Remember, if the basic facts are established, the opponent will not be allowed to disprove the presumed fact.

(1) Basic Facts Uncontroverted [§797]

"You must find PF."

(2) Basic Facts Disputed [§798]

"If you find BF, you must find PF."

b. Instructions for Morgan-McCormick Presumptions [§799]

Remember, this type of presumption shifts the burden of persuasion to the opponent of the presumption.

(1) BF Uncontroverted, No Evidence on PF [§800]

"You must find PF."

(2) BF Disputed, No Evidence on PF [§801]

"If you find BF, you must find PF."

(3) BF Uncontroverted, Evidence Disputing PF [§802]

"You must find PF unless Opponent persuades you by a preponderance of the evidence that PF does not exist."

(4) BF Disputed, Evidence Disputing PF [§803]

"If you find BF, you must find PF unless Opponent persuades you by a preponderance of the evidence that PF does not exist."

c. Instructions For Bursting Bubble Presumptions [§804]

Recall again that this type of presumption merely shifts the production burden to the opponent of the presumption.

(1) BF Uncontroverted, No Evidence on PF [§805]

"You must find PF."

(2) BF Disputed, No Evidence on PF [§806]

"If you find BF, you must find PF."

(3) BF Uncontroverted, Evidence Disputing PF [§807]

No instruction. Remember: once the opponent introduces evidence from which a juror could find that the presumed fact does not exist, the **presumption disappears** from the case. The jury may still infer the presumed fact from the basic fact, but this is as a matter of logic and not because of the presumption.

(4) BF Disputed, Evidence Disputing PF [§808]
No instruction.

Summary of Presumptions in Civil Cases

IRREBUTTABLE PRESUMPTIONS

	PF Not Controverted	**PF Controverted**
BF Not Controverted	You must find PF (or dircted verdict on issue)	You must find PF (or directed verdict on issue) [Opponent may not controvert PF]
BF Controverted	If you find BF, you must find PF	If you find BF, you must find PF [Opponent may not controvert PF]

REBUTTABLE PRESUMPTIONS
MORGAN-MCCORMICK (Shifting burden of persuasion)

	PF Not Controverted	PF Controverted
BF Not Controverted	You must find PF (or directed verdict on issue)	You must find PF unless opponent persuades you that PF does not exist
BF Controverted	If you find BF, you must find PF	If you find BF, you must find PF unless opponent persuades you that PF does not exist

REBUTTABLE PRESUMPTIONS
THAYER-WIGMORE (Shifting burden of production)

	PF Not Controverted	PF Controverted
BF Not Controverted	You must find PF (or directed verdict on issue)	Presumption gone (though inference may be drawn)
BF Controverted	If you find BF, you must find PF	Presumption gone (though inference may be drawn)

6. **Battle of the Presumptions: Conflicting Presumptions [§809]**
   Suppose two presumptions are relevant to the same case and the basic facts of Presumption 1 create a presumption that Presumed Fact A exists, while the basic facts of

Presumption 2 create a presumption that Presumed Fact A does not exist. If both are bursting bubble presumptions, this presents no problem. When the basic facts of Presumption 1 are established, there is sufficient evidence of Presumed Fact A to knock Presumption 2 out of the case, and vice versa. If they are not both bursting bubble presumptions, courts tend to apply the presumption that is based on stronger considerations of logic and policy.

C. Presumptions in Criminal Cases [§810]

Recall that the constitution requires the state to prove each element of the crime beyond a reasonable doubt. This limits the ability of the state to use a presumption to prove an element of a crime.

1. Conclusive Presumptions [§811]

Attempts to use conclusive presumptions are rarely, if ever, found in criminal cases. The use of a conclusive presumption would effectively relieve the prosecution of its duty to prove an element of the crime. In *Sandstrom v. Montana*, 442 U.S. 510 (1979), the Supreme Court considered a jury instruction that the law "presumes that a person intends the ordinary consequences of his voluntary acts." Since the jurors might have understood this as requiring them to find intent, it was unconstitutional.

2. Rebuttable Presumptions [§812]

To the extent they are used, presumptions in criminal cases ordinarily are rebuttable. But what are sometimes referred to in criminal cases as presumptions are not really presumptions. Instead, some criminal "presumptions" have no burden-shifting effect whatsoever. These are what the Supreme Court refers to as **"permissive inferences."** Others have a burden-shifting effect (although it is often unclear whether the presumption is shifting the burden of production or burden of persuasion). The Supreme Court refers to these as **"mandatory inferences."**

a. Permissive Inferences [§813]

A "permissive" inference is one in which the court tells the jury that it **may infer** the "presumed" fact from proof of the basic fact. The jury is free to accept or reject the inference and is still told that it must find that the prosecution has proved all elements of the crime beyond a reasonable doubt. A permissive inference is constitutional if (a) under the facts of the case, the **connection** between the basic fact and the presumed fact is **rational** and (b) the presumed fact **more likely than not flows** from the basic fact.

b. **Mandatory Inferences [§814]**

A "mandatory" inference is one in which the court tells the jury that if it finds the basic fact, it **must find the presumed fact unless** the defendant comes forward with evidence to rebut the presumed fact. The jury is not free to disregard the presumption unless the defendant comes forward with counter-evidence. The Supreme Court has stated that a mandatory inference is permissible only if the court finds, independent of the facts of the particular case, that the proof of the basic facts establishes the existence of the presumed fact **beyond a reasonable doubt**. *Francis v. Franklin,* 471 U.S. 307 (1985); *County Court of Ulster County v. Allen*, 442 U.S. 140 (1979).

References are to section numbers

A

ACCOUNTANT-CLIENT PRIVILEGE, 646; 701
ADMISSION BY PARTY OPPONENT
    Generally, 245-251
    Adoptive admission, 255
    Limited admissibility, 248
    Non-hearsay, 238; 246
    Personal knowledge, 249; 263
    Preliminary question, 268
    Privity, 269
    Rationale, 247
    Vicarious admission, 259
        Employee or agent, 260
        Co-conspirator, 264
ANCIENT DOCUMENTS
    Authentication, 587
    Hearsay exception, 395
ATTORNEY-CLIENT PRIVILEGE
    Generally, 651
    Client, 655
    Representative of client, 658-662
    Communication defined, 665
    Confidentiality, 668
    Control group test, 660
    Corporate client, 658-659
    Diversified Industries test, 661
    Eavesdropper, 671
    Exceptions, 676
    Germane communication, 664
    Holder of privilege, 673
    Joint defense, 653
    Lawyer, 654
        In non-lawyer capacity, 664
        Representative of lawyer, 657
    Obligation to maintain confidentiality distinguished, 685
    Waiver, 674
    Work-product distinguished, 685
AUTHENTICATION
    Generally, 575
    Ancient documents, 587
    Business records, 614
    Chain of custody, 594

Computer simulations, 597
Conditional relevance standard, 579
Demonstrative evidence, 577
Distinctive characteristics, 593; 602
Handwriting, 581
Maps, 595
Models, 595
Photographs, 595
Objects, 590
Real evidence, 577
Reply-message doctrine, 586
Self-authentication, 607
Telephone communications, 603
Voices, 598
X-rays, 596
Writings, 578

B

BEST EVIDENCE RULE
Generally, 615
Chattels, 640
Collateral matters, 639
Definitions, 625
Exceptions, 630
Expert testimony, 641
Proving contents of writing, 618
Rationale, 616
Summaries, 634
BOLSTERING, 524
BURDEN OF PROOF
Generally, 763
Civil cases, 765; 768-769
Criminal cases, 766; 770
Going forward, burden of, 763; 771-778
Non-persuasion, risk of, 763-770; 778
Persuasion, burden of, 763-770; 778
Production, burden of, 763; 771-778
BUSINESS CUSTOM, 189
BUSINESS RECORD
Generally, 300
Absence of record, 314
Authentication, 614
Business defined, 312
Contemplation of litigation, 310

Foundation, 313
Lack of trustworthiness, 309
Personal knowledge requirement, 303
Rationale, 302

C

CATCH-ALL EXCEPTION, 338-343
CHAIN OF CUSTODY, 594
CHARACTER
   Generally, 121
   Character of accused, 146; 178-181
   Character of victim, 157; 165
   Character of witness, 164; 497
      See IMPEACHMENT
   Child molestation, 178-181
   Civil cases, 163; 178-181
   Cross-examination of character witness, 151
   "Do you know" questions, 152
   Element of claim or defense, 124
   Habit distinguished, 183
   "Have you heard" questions, 152
   Opinion, 125; 142; 148; 150
   Other crimes evidence, 190-205
      See OTHER CRIMES EVIDENCE
   Reputation, 125; 134; 137; 148; 150; 166
   Sexual assault; 165; 167-181
   Sexual behavior, 165
   Specific acts, 125; 144; 151; 171; 178-181
   To prove conduct, 126-181
CHILD MOLESTATION, 178-181
CIRCUMSTANTIAL EVIDENCE, 36
CLERGY, COMMUNICATIONS TO, 700
COLLATERAL MATTERS
   Generally, 520
   Best evidence rule, 639
   Impeachment, 520-522
COMPETENCY
   Generally, 411
   Age, 414
   Dead man's statute, 416
   Insanity, 415
   Judge, 417
   Juror, 418

COMPROMISES AND OFFERS TO COMPROMISE
  Generally, 95
  Criminal Cases, 101
  Dispute, 98
  Elements, 96
  Rationale, 97
  Statements made during negotiations, 100
  When admissible, 102
COMPUTER SIMULATIONS, 597
CONDITIONAL RELEVANCY
  Generally, 40
  Authentication, 576
  Jury decides, 29
CONFRONTATION CLAUSE
  Generally, 404; 460
  Child abuse cases, 462
  Face-to-face confrontation, 462
  Hearsay, relationship to, 404
  Right to cross-examine witnesses, 461
  Testimonial statements, 408-410
CROSS-EXAMINATION
  Character witnesses, 151; 501
  Confrontation Clause, 461
  Defined, 430
  Impeachment distinguished, 427
  Leading questions, use of, 436; 457
  Re-cross examination, 459
  Scope of examination, 458

D

DEAD MAN'S STATUTE, 416
DECLARATION AGAINST INTEREST
  Generally, 355
  Admission by party opponent distinguished, 366
DEMONSTRATIVE EVIDENCE, 577
DEMONSTRATIONS, 72
DIRECT EVIDENCE, 36
DOCUMENTS AFFECTING PROPERTY INTERESTS, 396
DYING DECLARATION, 349

E

EXCITED UTTERANCE, 272
EXCLUSION OF WITNESSES, 424
EXECUTIVE PRIVILEGE, 730

EXPERIMENTS, 72
EXPERT WITNESS
    Generally, 543
    Basis of testimony, 560
    Best evidence rule, 639
    Court-appointed, 572
    Daubert, 553
    Examination, 569
    Frye test, 552
    Hypothetical question, 562
    Personal knowledge, 423; 564
    Qualification, 544
    Reliability, 551
    Scientific evidence, 551
    Subject matter, 548
    Ultimate issue, 573
    Voir dire, 546

F

FAMILY RECORDS, 392
FEDERAL RULES OF EVIDENCE, 7
FORMER TESTIMONY, 367
FRYE TEST, 552

H

HABIT, 182
HEARSAY
    See also INDIVIDUAL HEARSAY EXCEPTIONS
    Generally, 207-242
    Animals, 222
    "Basic" hearsay, 210-222
    Common law rule, 223; 229
    Confrontation clause, 404
    Declarant defined, 221
    Definition, 208
    Exceptions
        Generally, 243
        Admission by party opponent, 238; 245
        Adoptive admission, 255
        Ancient documents, 395
        Business record, 300
        Catch-all, 338
        Co-conspirator admission, 264
        Declaration against interest, 355

Documents affecting property interests, 396; 402

Dying declaration, 349

Equivalency, 338

Excited utterance, 272

Family records, 392

Forfeiture, 375

Former testimony, 367

Judgment of previous conviction, 403

Judgments, 394; 400

Learned treatise, 326

Market reports, 401

Marriage, baptismal certificates, 391

Past recollection recorded, 330

Property interest, 396

Present sense impression, 279

Public record, 315

Records of religious organizations, 390

Reputation, 393; 399; 402

Residual, 338

State of mind, 285

Statement for medical diagnosis or treatment, 293

Statement of personal or family history, 376; 385

Vital statistics, 389

Explicit verbal assertions, 224

Federal rule, 223; 230

Impeachment not hearsay, 219; 480

Independent legal significance, 218

Legally operative facts, 218

Limited admissibility, 23; 241

Limiting instruction, 23; 241

Machines, 222

"More sophisticated" hearsay, 223

Multiple hearsay, 239

Non-assertive verbal conduct, 227

Non-hearsay, statements defined as

Admission by party opponent, 238; 245

Prior consistent statement, 236; 380; 526; 529

Prior identification, 237; 381

Prior inconsistent statement, 235; 379; 483

Non-verbal conduct

Intended as assertion, 213; 225

Not intended as assertion, 226

Rationale, 209

Silence, 242

Statement defined, 211
Unavailability
    Defined, 345
    When required, 344
    Verbal acts, 218
    Verbal assertions used inferentially, 228
Written statements, 213
HOSTILE WITNESS, 440
HYPOTHETICAL QUESTION, 562-568

I

IMPEACHMENT
    Generally, 463
    Bias, 475
    Capacity, 469
    Character for trustworthiness
      See also CHARACTER
      Generally, 497
      Convictions, 507
      Evidence of good character, 499; 528
      Extrinsic evidence, 505; 516
      Opinion, 499
      Reputation, 499
      Specific acts not resulting in conviction, 502
    Contradiction, 519
    Defined, 427; 463
    Extrinsic evidence, use of, 473; 478; 483; 505; 516; 520; 522
    Impeaching own witness, 464
    Prior inconsistent statement, 479
      See also PRIOR INCONSISTENT STATEMENT
    Rehabilitation, 527
    Surprise and injury requirement, 465
    Techniques of impeachment, 468
    Voucher rule, 465
IN LIMINE, MOTION, 16
INFORMER'S IDENTITY PRIVILEGE, 728
INSURANCE
    Generally, 115
    Rationale, 116
    When admissible, 117-119

J

JOURNALIST'S PRIVILEGE, 731
JUDGMENT OF PREVIOUS CONVICTION, 403

JUDGMENTS, 394; 400
JUDICIAL NOTICE
   Generally, 745
   Adjudicative facts, 748
   Effect of judicial notice, 754
   Law, 759
   Legislative facts, 757
   Procedure, 760
   Rationale, 746
JURY VIEWS, 78

L

LEADING QUESTIONS
   Generally, 435
   Defined, 435
   Use on direct examination, 437
LEARNED TREATISES, 326
LIMITED ADMISSIBILITY
   Character witness, 155
   Hearsay, 23; 241
   Prior inconsistent statement, 482
LIMITING INSTRUCTIONS
   Character witness, 155
   Hearsay, 23; 241
   Prior inconsistent statement, 482

M

MARITAL PRIVILEGES
   Generally, 702; 716
   Communication privilege
     Generally, 702
        Communication defined, 706
        Effect of divorce, 704
        Exceptions, 710
        Holder, 708
        Rationale, 702
        Separated spouses, 705
   Testimonial privilege
     Generally, 716
        Common law rule, 717
        Exceptions, 722
        Modern trend, 718
        Rationale, 719
        Relationship to communication privilege, 721; 725

Termination of privilege, 720
Two privileges, 702; 725
MARKET REPORTS, 401
MARRIAGE CERTIFICATES, 391
MOTION IN LIMINE, 16

N

NOVEL SCIENTIFIC EVIDENCE, 552

O

OATH OR AFFIRMATION, 422
OBJECTIONS
Form of question, 433
Necessity of, 11-23
OFFERS TO COMPROMISE, 95
See COMPROMISES AND OFFERS TO COMPROMISE
OFFERS TO PAY MEDICAL EXPENSES, 107
OPINION TESTIMONY
Generally, 523
Expert witness
See EXPERT WITNESS
Lay witness
Common law rule, 532
Modern approach, 535
Ultimate issue, 573
OTHER CRIMES EVIDENCE
Generally, 190
Acquittal, effect of, 206
Procedural considerations, 201
When admissible, 192-200

P

PARENT-CHILD PRIVILEGE, 714
PAST RECOLLECTION RECORDED
Generally, 330
Present recollection refreshed distinguished, 337
PAST SEXUAL BEHAVIOR, 165
PAYMENT OF MEDICAL EXPENSES, 107
PERSONAL KNOWLEDGE
Generally, 423
Admissions by party opponent, 249; 263
Expert witness, 423; 560
PHOTOGRAPHS, 590
PHYSICIAN-PATIENT PRIVILEGE, 686
PLEAS

Guilty, 108
Nolo contendere
Conviction based upon, 403
Plea, 108
Offers to plead, 108
Statements made during plea process, 109
POLITICAL VOTE PRIVILEGE, 726
PREJUDICE, UNFAIR, 50
PRELIMINARY QUESTION OF FACT
Generally, 24-25
Decided by jury, 26
PRESENT RECOLLECTION REFRESHED
Generally, 449
Past recollection recorded distinguished, 337
Procedural safeguards, 452
Recollection refreshed before trial, 454
PRESENT SENSE IMPRESSION, 279
PRESERVING ERROR, 11-23
PRESUMPTIONS
Generally, 779; 810
Basic facts defined, 780
Civil cases, 779
Conclusive presumptions, 784; 811
Conflicting presumptions, 809
Criminal cases, 810
Irrebuttable presumptions, 784; 811
Jury instruction, 794; 795
Mandatory inference, 814
Permissive inference, 813
Presumed facts defined, 780
Rebuttable presumptions
Generally, 787; 812
Bursting bubbles, 790; 804
Morgan-McCormick approach, 788; 799
Thayer-Wigmore approach, 790; 804
Summary, 795
PRIOR CONSISTENT STATEMENTS, 236; 380; 526; 529
PRIOR IDENTIFICATION, 237; 381
PRIOR INCONSISTENT STATEMENTS
Generally, 235; 379; 479
Degree of inconsistency, 484
Extrinsic evidence, 494; 522
Foundation requirement, 490
Limiting instruction, 482

Non-hearsay, some defined as, 235; 483
Queen Caroline's Case, 492
Theory, why not hearsay, 480
PRIVILEGES
  Generally, 642
  Accountant-client, 701
  Attorney-client, 651
    See ATTORNEY-CLIENT PRIVILEGE
  Clergy, communications to, 700
  Confidential communication privileges, 646
  Executive privilege, 730
  Federal rules, 644
  Informer's identity, 728
  Journalist's privilege, 731
  Marital communication, 702; 725
    See MARITAL PRIVILEGES
  Parent-child, 714
  Physician-patient, 686
  Political vote, 726
  Psychotherapist-patient, 697
  Self-incrimination, 732
    See SELF-INCRIMINATION, PRIVILEGE AGAINST
  Spousal testimonial, 716
    See MARITAL PRIVILEGES
  State secrets, 729
  Trade secrets, 727
PSYCHOTHERAPIST-PATIENT PRIVILEGE, 697
PUBLIC RECORD, 315
  Factual findings, 321
  Criminal case, 318-320

Q
QUEEN CAROLINE'S CASE, 492

R
RAPE SHIELD LAWS, 165
REAL EVIDENCE, 577
RECORDS OF RELIGIOUS ORGANIZATIONS, 390
REENACTMENTS, 72
REHABILITATION, 527
RELEVANCY
  Conditional relevancy, 40
  Definition, 32
  Demonstrations, 72

Discretionary exclusion, 44; 46-79
Experiments, 72
Industry standard, 73
Jury views, 78
Legal relevancy, 45
Logical relevancy, 45
Materiality, 33
Photographs, 77
Probative value, 47
Reasons for exclusion, 41
Reenactments, 72
Similar happenings, 55
Statistical evidence, 76
Sufficiency compared, 34
REPLY-MESSAGE DOCTRINE, 586
REPUTATION
As evidence of character, 125; 134; 137; 148; 150; 166
Hearsay exception, 393; 399; 402
RESIDUAL EXCEPTION, 338

S
SELF-AUTHENTICATION, 607
SELF-INCRIMINATION, PRIVILEGE AGAINST
Generally, 732
Civil cases, 739; 740; 743
Compulsion, 733
Right not to testify, 742
Tendency to incriminate, 738
Testimonial activity, 734
Waiver, 744
SETTLEMENTS, 95
See COMPROMISES AND OFFERS TO COMPROMISE
SEXUAL ASSAULT, 178
SEXUAL BEHAVIOR, 165
SEXUAL DISPOSITION, 165
SIMILAR HAPPENINGS
Generally, 55
Business custom, 70
Causation, 69
Non-occurrences, 60
Other contracts or dealings, 58-59
Previous claims or lawsuits, 66
Prior or subsequent accidents, 57
Sales of similar property, 64

SPONTANEOUS STATEMENTS, 271
  See EXCITED UTTERANCE AND PRESENT SENSE IMPRESSION
SPOUSAL PRIVILEGES, 702; 716
  See MARITAL PRIVILEGES
STATE OF MIND
  Distinguished from non-hearsay state of mind, 292
  Hillmon case, 288
  Improper use of state of mind exception, 289
  Intent to do something in future, 288; 291
  Medical diagnosis or treatment, 293
  Rationale, 286
  Statements relating to will, 290
STATE SECRETS PRIVILEGE, 729
STATEMENTS FOR MEDICAL DIAGNOSIS OR TREATMENT, 293
STATEMENTS OF PERSONAL OR FAMILY HISTORY, 376; 385
STATISTICAL EVIDENCE, 76
SUBSEQUENT REMEDIAL MEASURES
  Generally, 81
  Defined, 84-85
  Product liability cases, 87
  Rationale, 83
  Third-party, 93
  When admissible, 89-94

T
  "THE RULE", 424
  TRADE SECRETS PRIVILEGE, 727

U
  UNAVAILABILITY
    Defined, 345
    When required, 344

V
  VITAL STATISTICS, 389
  VOIR DIRE, 583

W
  WITNESSES
    Generally, 411-574
    "The Rule", 424
    Bolstering, 523-524
    Competency, 411
      See COMPETENCY OF WITNESSES

Court, calling and questioning witness, 432
Cross-examination, 430; 457-459; 461
  See CROSS-EXAMINATION
Exclusion of witnesses, 424
Form of question, 433
Impeachment, 463-522
  See IMPEACHMENT
Leading question, 435
  See LEADING QUESTIONS
Oath or affirmation, 422
Personal knowledge, 423; 560
Present recollection refreshed, 449
  See PRESENT RECOLLECTION REFRESHED
Rehabilitation, 527